Praise for *Fragile Power*

Dr. Paul reminds us that happiness is an inside job—even for billionaires. This smart and timely book reveals the cultural and economic issues that divide us. Polarization leads us to believe that if we can get past the velvet rope and achieve social identity through wealth and power, it will heal us. Dr. Paul's core idea is that social cohesion follows from self-awareness, empathy, and connection. No one's power can buy their way out of that hard work. Important commentary for all.

—**RICHARD SOCARIDES,** human rights advocate, communications strategist, attorney, CNN political commentator, and writer for *The New Yorker*

Paul Hokemeyer pulls the curtain back, exposing the internal battles of upscale and privileged individuals in our culture. *Fragile Power* is filled with anecdotal examples where he lays bare the unique types of loneliness, despair, and fragility within the addictive climate of "celebrity," while exploring the challenges these people face in seeking help and counsel. Hokemeyer reveals the pain behind lavish lifestyles and seemingly enviable situations. A must-read.

—**SUSAN WEITZMAN, PhD, LCSW,** author of *"Not to People Like Us"*

Fragile Power explores the under-studied and often misunderstood world of the wealthy and powerful. This book reads like a novel with eloquent descriptions of the author's personal experiences and raw vulnerability that allow him to connect with this subject both intimately and professionally. This is a must-read for health care professionals and an eye-opener for the general public. While those with extreme wealth are often envied and worshiped in many ways, Dr. Paul uncovers the

silent suffering and void that many experience. He brilliantly makes connections between mental health and addictive and relational issues that—when combined with financial and power status—often create the perfect storm. Dr. Paul subtly educates the reader about psychological and treatment topics that relate to this population—which you will come to see as a cultural minority that deserves specialized care and compassion.

—SARAH ALLEN BENTON, MS, LMHC, LPC,
author of *Understanding the High-Functioning Alcoholic*

A wonderful reminder that irrespective of status, elevated or otherwise, we all experience suffering and we all deserve respect. . . . Certain types of people are drawn to certain professions. . . . Those who were most neglected might seek fame, those who were rejected or neglected as a child might paint themselves into the isolated immunity of extreme success, and someone whose childhood climate was fear might be driven to succeed, yet often all at a devastating cost. In his book, Dr. Paul acknowledges that cost—the price paid by the privileged—while compassionately teaching us to identify as people and challenge the "them and us" paradigm, to stand back and reconsider our own projections and . . . to never give up on yourself if you want help—no matter who (or what) you are.

—MANDY SALIGARI, MSc, MBACP, NCAC, SMMGP,
author of *Proactive Parenting*

Fragile Power is an important contribution to our understanding of the human being who embodies the paradox of power and powerlessness, of control and vulnerability, of worth and worthlessness—and how when untreated and unresolved, can destroy a life.

—KATHLEEN O'HARA, MA, LPC, author of *A Grief Like No Other*

I adore this book! Dr. Paul delicately takes the reader on an explorative journey on every page of *Fragile Power*. Offering an authentic blend of Paul's own personal journey . . . with resources and teachings, each chapter weaves an experience with such insightful depth that, as a professional, I felt compelled to keep turning the page. It is a book I will come back to for years to come.

—SAMANTHA H. QUINLAN, influencer and cofounder of iCAAD.COM

I highly recommend you pick up this book and read it! Thank you, Dr. Paul, for giving us a peek into your magic world of "fragile power"—a world so few understand. This is a must-read for anyone in the recovery field, and the way it's written is exactly who Paul is: funny, witty, and compassionate!

—JANIQUE SVEDBERG, author, recovery coach, and interventionist

Wealth. Power. Melancholia? With empathy and insight, Dr. Hokemeyer examines the worlds of successful people—those we admire and emulate—only to find deeply troubled souls at their core. This book provides essential insight into the challenges that face those who, on the surface, embody the perfect human being. Truly a must-read.

—JOHNNY LOPS, DO, author of *Reinvent Yourself*

In his eloquent and refreshingly revolutionary *Fragile Power*, Dr. Paul Hokemeyer compassionately critiques the intoxicating allure of celebrity privilege and worship. Drawn from the author's decades of research and experiences as a world-renowned psychotherapist and media specialist, *Fragile Power* posits an optimistic, yet highly plausible, way forward in which we collectively overthrow traditional, divisive notions of status and identity in favor of a new paradigm of authentic community. I cannot recommend this book highly enough as an invaluable asset to those both inside and outside of the profession!

—HEATHER R. HAYES, MEd, LPC, BRI II,
consultant, therapist, and interventionist

At last, the illusion of great wealth, world fame, and stunning beauty being the panacea to a perfect life is shattered by Dr. Paul's engaging book. He goes beyond the velvet rope of elite power . . . and creates an essential read for professionals and a fascinating read for the general public.

—DAVID CHARKHAM, addiction recovery coach, speaker, and actor

For decades, our culture has been pretending that the upper echelon in the world is too wealthy or powerful to succumb to illness or disease. Dr. Hokemeyer brilliantly addresses this misconception in *Fragile Power* by sharing his clinical prowess and expertise and presenting successful strategies for behavioral health clinicians worldwide to absorb.

—DENISE BERTIN-EPP, RN, MSA,
international health care consultant and CEO

Dr. Hokemeyer expertly weaves complicated clinical concepts into easily relatable stories. In doing so, he humanizes a subgroup of people whose money, connections, and influence don't shield them from the need for genuine connection. We would do well to remember that our tolerance for difference must extend to those who seem to breathe rarefied air.

—DARCI CRAMER, PhD, LMFT, therapist

Dr. Hokemeyer's book approaches clinical populations—the wealthy, the powerful, the celebrated, the beautiful—with a self-reflective, approachable, and informed narrative. Unafraid to explore his own vulnerability and fallibility, he does a masterful job of mounting the argument for a clinically informed and compassionate approach to aspects of identity that have heretofore gone unaddressed and unacknowledged due to the misguided premise that those who have what others want have no right to their own challenges, losses, and suffering. It is a tour de force of humanity and humor relying on and seamlessly integrating psychological science, popular psychology, the lessons of recovery, and the author's hard-won experience and insight. Where many psychological works are a trudge through jargon, impenetrable prose, and arcane references, this is a work that is accessible to the lay reader or the professional with the courage to struggle with issues of power, privilege, beauty, envy, and their own unsatisfied desires. I am a better clinician for having read Dr. Hokemeyer's seminal work.

—STEPHEN C. PHILLIPS, JD, PsyD, therapist

FRAGILE POWER

FRAGILE POWER

$$$

Why Having Everything Is Never Enough

DR. PAUL L. HOKEMEYER

Hazelden
Publishing

Hazelden Publishing
Center City, Minnesota 55012
hazelden.org/bookstore

ISBN: 978-1-61649-764-4

Library of Congress Cataloging-in-Publication Data is on file
with the Library of Congress.

Editor's note
Clients' names and circumstances have been changed to protect privacy; any simi-
larities are unintentional and unintended.

This publication is not intended as a substitute for the advice of health care
professionals.

Readers should be aware that websites listed in this work may have changed or
disappeared between when this work was written and when it is read.

Alcoholics Anonymous, AA, and the Big Book are registered trademarks of
Alcoholics Anonymous World Services, Inc.

Epigraph from "Whitney on the Record," *Newsweek*, November 23, 1998, 76.

23 22 21 20 19   1 2 3 4 5 6

Cover design: Theresa Jaeger Gedig
Art director: Terri Kinne
Acquisitions and development editor: Vanessa Torrado
Editorial project manager: April Ebb

I'd like to dedicate this book to my parents, Bill and Teresa Hokemeyer, who passed a few months before this manuscript was completed. Thank you for instilling in me a solid middle-class work ethic and the importance of higher education. I miss you every single day. I'd also like to dedicate this book to my husband, Jim Johnson. Thank you for providing me a secure base of love to explore the world and find my place in it. I'm eternally grateful to have you as my soul mate and fellow explorer. To be continued.

"I was talking to [another celebrity] the other night . . .
and we were talking about being a regular person
years ago and how we wanted the fame and fortune.
But then we got it—we lost our lives. He wondered
if we'd made the right choice. . . . It's been more than
I bargained for . . ."

—*Whitney Houston*

Contents

A Note from Dr. Paul

During the editing of this book, I turned on my phone one soggy June morning and was assaulted by a news cycle that got to the heart of the research and therapeutic approach I've developed during the past fifteen years of treating the fragility of patients who live in the world in positions of power, celebrity, and wealth. Playing out on the news that morning were the dynamics that I treat in my clinical practice and that I'll be addressing in this book. It was not the first time since starting my journey as a clinician treating the world's elite that the themes I'm submerged in were suddenly mirrored back to me through current events, but for some reason this particular storyline and the response to it felt different—pivotal, deep, and redefining. It pinched me with an urgency that I'd not felt so intensely before.

What was it that morning that caught my attention and the attention of so many others? With so much going on in the world, the news focused on Demi Lovato—one of the entertainment world's brightest lights, who had reportedly relapsed back into drug use after a period of well-publicized sobriety. Perhaps because Lovato had shared with her adoring public the details of her challenges with self-harm, substance use, anorexia, bulimia, and bipolar disorder (MacMillen 2015), it was widely assumed these issues were behind her—something the power inherent in her celebrity had allowed her to bury in her past. As a result, the public was shocked when it was reported she'd been hospitalized for a possible overdose.

Even before asking myself why and how this story felt different, I got the sense that we were at a social and cultural tipping point. The public was sick and tired of losing its brightest lights to the ravages of mental health issues and wanted answers. We were angry and frustrated but for too long had misdirected our anger toward the fragile human beings we demand exist in the world as objects, vested with superhuman powers simply by virtue of features of their being—their wealth, their surname, their titles, their beauty and talent—in short, whatever gave them an elevated position of power and "celebrity" in our culture.

Socially, we've been uneducated for too long in the fact that fault lies not with the celebrities who suffer, but in the professionals in the mental health field. These men and women, some of them well-intentioned, but many not, have failed to address the distinct cultural markers of celebrity patients in a clinically effective frame. Yes, they're willing to spend time, money, and intellectual capital to develop sophisticated marketing campaigns to "capture" these patients in their practices, but they've done precious little to understand what it's like to live in their skin.

As a clinician, the pinch I felt that morning carried with it an urgency to find a wider audience for the empirical data and clinical skill set I've developed in effectively treating celebrity patients. My professional focus has been researching the lived experience of elite patient populations, treating them in my private practice and using the knowledge I've gained to train clinicians around the world on effective clinical formulations that transcend the veneers of these human beings' power in order to connect with their fragility while artfully moving them in a reparative direction.

While the news for much of that day focused on one celebrity, the reality is the narrative being told wasn't just about Demi Lovato. Nor was it just about *celebrity*, per se—as fame is just one element that gives a person a distinguished type of power in our world. What was *really* being debated in the news that morning was a set of questions that have been around for a long time but up until the publishing of this book haven't been properly answered. The real questions being asked were these:

- When people seem to have "everything"—professional success, an elite education, aristocratic breeding, fame, power, freedom, beauty, and financial security—why are they still unable to "rise above" their problems and get the help they need?

- Why are so many successful, wealthy, famous, powerful people unable to find lasting help and recovery from their substance abuse and behavioral health issues?

- Why do so many people who "have it all" seem to become even more fragile with greater success?

- Why is it that we seem to prioritize this impossible-to-attain goal of "having it all," and why is it that the small percentage of people who manage to "have everything" never seem to feel they have enough?

- And the most terrifying question of all: If a celebrity, a person whom we see as having *everything*, could succumb to the deathly and seductive pull of substance use and mental health issues, what chance do the rest of us have in transcending our challenges?

As I waded through the media bog surrounding Ms. Lovato's plight, I discovered a range of public responses. There was voyeuristic fascination. There was pity. There was anger and even outrage. Many felt schadenfreude over Lovato's pain. In the days following the news about Lovato's hospitalization, I came upon a heartbreaking comment that had been posted in one of the leading entertainment websites:

> Demi Grow up and put your self together. I don't feel sorry for you, bc you have the resources and the money to get help, but you chose not too . . . Demons will be greeting you with open arms. Hells gates are wide open. [sic] (Khatchatourian 2018)

Even though I've read this comment many times, my stomach still lurches every time I revisit it. In four sentences, it manages to capture the lack of empathy and the hostility the general public has toward people like Lovato, people who have reached elevated positions of power and success, but who struggle with the fragility inherent in their humanness.

I've had the privilege of working as a licensed marriage and family therapist specializing in addictive and relational disorders with individuals, couples, and families who manifest their identities in the world through the labels of celebrity that I listed above—and a number of others that I'll discuss in this book. Through this work and in my research on elite identity constructs, I've discovered that while we've been acculturated to believe otherwise, celebrity identities and the power inherent in them are not enough to protect the human beings who live underneath them from the problems all human beings face. In fact, the power, property, and prestige that come with these identities actually complicate and cause different forms of pathology. We think power and fame are the keys that provide liberation from life's challenges, but my experience and research show they do not. Yes, at the edges of life they can provide physical protection and comfort, but at the core of existence, a place we call the self, they can create a fragility that causes destruction and despair.

Admittedly, this concept is difficult for many people to accept, and my work is frequently met with overt and covert hostility. During a week of celebrity deaths that included the loss of Kate Spade and Anthony Bourdain by reported suicides, I was asked by several media outlets to comment on why people who have so much take their own lives. In response to my assertion that celebrity patients need specialized care, I received the following email from a colleague:

> I couldn't disagree with you more. We hear about celebrity suicides because they are public figures. . . . But "ordinary" people don't have a team of agents, publicists, staff, etc. to help and who are actually paid to help. Nor do they have the struggle to find and pay for a therapist or medication. **It is the people without resources that are of most concern.** (email exchange with author, 2018) (emphasis added)

This email captures the essence of the challenges of my work in transcending the didactics of a more deserving/less deserving, better than/less than paradigm we've internalized from our families, our religions, and the zeitgeist in which we live about the virtues of the poor and the sins of the rich. It also highlights the top three conscious and unconscious prejudices laypeople and the majority of treating professionals hold against powerful patients. The first of these prejudgments is that these patients are possessed of an abundance of resources that enable them to transcend the challenges inherent in life. The second is that they're less deserving of care than "less fortunate" human beings, and the third is that because they're stereotypically seen as "mean, entitled, and narcissistic," humiliation and punishment need to be part of their treatment.

My work—and this book, as an extension of it—has had a driving purpose: *To acknowledge that everyone, regardless of their place on the power and economic spectrum, deserves to be valued for the fullness of their humanness rather than deified or demonized as an object.*

I've worked with powerful and celebrity patients to transcend the labels of *other* that have been assigned to them. They've internalized these labels to connect with their pain; I help them move in a reparative direction. Through this process, I've developed a paradigm of treatment to repair the damage we've all—regardless of our economic position—sustained to our individual and relational psyches through the destructive step of splitting off of *us* from *them*. My goal is to bridge the gulf that exists between human beings based on external labels—such as *rich, famous, poor,* or *uneducated*—so that we can finally transcend the narrative of betrayal that has caused pain to our souls, the souls of our families, and the soul of our world.

Surprisingly, it's a bigger task than one would think.

Throughout my career, I've met hostility and even exploitation when I explain the focus of my work. From the celebrated existential psychotherapist who rejected serving on my dissertation committee asking, "Why would you waste your time studying rich people?" to treatment centers that sought to use my work to "upsell" patients to their higher-profit-margin programs, to being criticized for treating my patients as "special," my journey has been an onerous one.

But it's a journey that's been intellectually illuminating, personally healing, and professionally rewarding to travel.

Unless you live in a cave, off the grid of our hyper-connected modern world, you can't escape the fact that we're living in a profoundly divided world. The gulf between the "haves" and the "have-nots" is extraordinarily wide and grows wider each and every day. Division defines politics. At the time of this book's writing, a disenfranchised and frustrated constituency elected a self-proclaimed billionaire to the highest, most esteemed, and most powerful position in the world. For this group, the American dream has turned into a nightmare of chronic unemployment, erosion of family values, and destruction of communities and families through drug addiction and gun violence. Cheap foreign labor and artificial intelligence have gutted America's working and middle classes, and the prospects for their future are grim. For the first time since the end of World War II, parents can no longer hope that their children's financial future will be better than their own. Capital is held in fewer and fewer hands and is being used to destroy our planet.

My work sounds political, because it is. In building a new paradigm of treatment, I looked to the contributions of the first- and second-wave feminists, thought leaders, and clinicians who taught us that the personal is political and that unequal power dynamics have a pernicious impact on our individual and social well-being. It's also rooted in basic principles of social psychology—a discipline that maintains personal health is a function of our social well-being and the contemporary zeitgeist in which human interactions occur.

But unlike other researchers, clinicians, and thought leaders who focus on minorities of powerlessness, my work focuses on human beings who willingly or unwillingly hold enormous power. It's intended to be an exploration of the fundamental pain and fragility inherent in the marginalization that occurs from living in the world as any minority, and the individual, relational, and social healing that occurs when that person is finally seen and heard in the fullness of their being.

My intention is not to elevate one social class or group above another, but rather to level the playing field by finding the common thread of humanness shared between them. It's also my intention to defend my view that all of my patients, regardless of their place on the socioeconomic spectrum, are *special*. These patients have included transgender sex workers whom I treated at a free clinic in Los Angeles and who live in states of acute oppression and powerlessness, as well as some of the world's most celebrated and powerful individuals, couples, and families through my private practices in Manhattan and Telluride, Colorado.

For the patients I've had the privilege of treating throughout my career, please know that you hold an esteemed place in my heart. You trusted me with your psyche and allowed me to walk with you on your reparative journey. It's a gift that I cherish and one that I've taken extreme measures to protect in this book.

For the layperson reading this book, I hope it provides you with greater compassion toward yourself, someone you love, someone you've aspired to become, or someone you've resented or envied. For clinicians and professionals who work—or desire to work—with elite patients or clients, I hope it provides you with greater personal insights and a new paradigm of treatment to provide clinically excellent and culturally competent care to human beings who manifest their identities as a distinct minority group defined by their power. If you're a person who lives within an elite identity, I hope it provides you with a road map for navigating the fragility inherent in your power to avoid self- and relational destruction while finding reparative connections.

Division destroys. Understanding and compassion heal. I hope this book unites human beings divided by polarizing labels by illuminating our shared fragility and reacquaints us with the healing power of compassion.

With warm regards and deep appreciation,
Dr. Paul

Introduction

Existence precedes essence.
—JEAN-PAUL SARTRE

Several months ago, I received a handwritten note on an exquisite piece of letterpress stationery. Its message, like the paper it was written on, was simple and elegant: "Thank you for being you." The sender, a current patient named Sally, was a former supermodel who entered into therapy with me three years prior to address a "passionless marriage." At that time, she was approaching sixty and struggling not only with the malaise of her marriage, but also with her physical transformation from bombshell to doyenne. Although she discounted the milestone birthday as insignificant, claiming she "became invisible and irrelevant twenty years ago," her body radiated terror when I broached the topic of her age.

Since she sought to avoid the issue, I knew it needed to be clinically addressed, but I struggled to do so artfully.

"So what does sixty mean to you?" I asked in the middle of our third session.

Without missing a beat, she snapped back with disdain: "Oh lord, you're a cliché. What it means is you're deaf. I've repeatedly told you turning sixty is a nonevent. I've already accepted my age. The real question is why am I wasting my time and money seeing you?"

Her response stung, but it injected therapeutic tension into our relationship. For the first time, I felt Sally's vulnerability instead of scratching as an outsider on her beautifully polished veneer. I also appreciated her honesty. Her concerns were real and deserved to be addressed directly.

I've spent the last decade and a half mapping out the coordinates of the psychotherapeutic frame and creating a specialized process to work in it with Sally and people like her. Anchoring this frame is my fundamental premise that every human being deserves to be treated with respect and an appreciation for his or her distinct cultural markers. In my journey as a therapist, I've had the privilege of working with patients who exist in the margins of society in positions of extreme powerlessness and extreme power. I began my career working with the former at a free clinic in Los Angeles, California, and then when I developed my practice I shifted my focus to the latter, working with human beings who exist in positions of elite power by virtue of a feature of their being— their wealth, their talent, their surname, or their beauty.

Some of you will have a hostile reaction to the approach I've created for treating these human beings. But I encourage you to keep an open mind. I also encourage your dissent. The purpose of this book is to expand the construct of cultural competency— in all aspects of our lives, personally and professionally—rather than limit it. In my work and life, I define *cultural competency* as the willingness and capacity to understand what it means to exist in the world as an "othered" human being whose objective features eclipse their subjective being.

I don't need your approval, but I welcome your respectful consideration, reactions, and thoughts.

Some of you will think I'm advocating for special treatment for a class of people whom you feel don't deserve it. If that's the case, know that I admit to being guilty as charged, for *every human being, every couple, every family who comes into my office for treatment is special and deserves clinically excellent and culturally competent care.*

Some of you will make fun of this work. It may even become fodder for critics who want to roast me for my fundamental premise that we need to develop empathy and compassion for "the rich and famous." There are precedents. When two of my colleagues, Stephen Golbart and Joan DiFuria, were promoting their construct of "sudden wealth syndrome," it led to a sardonic interview in 2012 on *The Daily Show with Jon Stewart,* wherein he asked people to consider "walking a mile in a rich person's Ferragamos . . . [to] learn the paralyzing anxiety of sudden wealth" (Golbart and DiFuria 2012). The irony of a rich and famous man assailing a clinical construct intended to heal others in his social class speaks to the covert and overt hostility human beings who exist in positions of elite power face every minute of their lives—hostility that drives them deeper and deeper into their self- and relational destruction.

•

One of the things we'll unpack in this book is that although our world creates a privileging of celebrity, wealth, and power, we don't appreciate the degree to which those features isolate the human beings who live within that identity. It's much easier to see the isolation of people who exist in positions of powerlessness in our society than to see it in human beings we've been trained by our families, our communities, our capitalistic marketing machine, and even our religions to adore and aspire to become—or to resent, envy, and disdain.

Through my academic and clinical work, however, I've studied the thread of humanity that unites the binary labels of "rich" and "poor." As a clinician, I've had the privilege to work with individuals, couples, and families on both extremes of the economic and power bell curve. In chapter 6, you'll meet Willow, a woman who tried escaping her legacy of abuse, poverty, racism, and misogyny by moving to Hollywood to try her luck amid the garish lights and searing stars of Tinseltown. As a resident of Telluride, Colorado, I work with men and women who, in a town of ever-growing power and privilege, are invisible, struggling to survive as the "have-nots." These are the people striving, often unsuccessfully, to meet Maslow's basic human needs of safety and security in the shadows of 12,000-square-foot mansions and celebrity residents who choke the small airport with their massive private jets. These clients, men and women whom I treat for a host of relational disorders that manifest in symptoms of depression, anxiety, and substance use disorders, experience the same fundamental pain of isolation as the privileged people they often serve.

The following, and very simplistic, statement best summarizes the simple premise at the heart of my clinical formulations:

At the core of human pain is isolation from others and ourselves. We find relief from this pain in reparative human connections where we are seen and heard as vulnerable human beings.

Pain does not have an economic threshold. Regardless of where you fall on the power and socioeconomic spectrum, you have doubts, fears, and insecurities. At times, you feel the world is unfair and chaotic; at other times, you might feel invisible, not properly seen or heard. Chances are good that somewhere along your developmental path someone whose love and protection you desperately needed let you down, or betrayed your trust. Most people have had at least one traumatic experience, or multiple experiences, that affect how they perceive the world, and it would be challenging to find even one person who could say they've never felt vulnerable or alone.

I certainly have, and in fact, I often still do.

And I'm a privileged, white male born in the United States of America. A man who was raised in a climate of economic expansion and, to date, has never had to live with a war fought on my home shores. I have two doctoral degrees and a professional identity that provide me with more power, property, and prestige than I could have ever imagined. From the outside, I have an enviable life, but the external veneer of my life has not protected me from internal struggles. On a daily basis, I feel disconnected from others and myself.

Many people looking from the outside in would be convinced that someone like me, someone "with more than most" who works alongside people "with everything," would either be immune from life's challenges or have all the necessary resources at their fingertips to counteract the wounds they've encountered from walking through life's brambles.

But that's not the case.

In my work, I've found people who exist in the extreme margins of our society struggle to get care that resonates with the fundamental truth of their being. The bottom 10 percent, if they can access care at all, endure treatment that dismisses them as invisible and labels them *irresponsible, weak,* and *lazy*. In contrast, the top 10 percent have access to an abundance of care, but it's care that sees them as objects, exploits their vulnerabilities, and labels them as *entitled, narcissistic,* and *difficult*.

As it relates to the former, my colleagues, clinicians like Dr. Ilan Meyer, distinguished scholar at UCLA's Williams Institute, and others have provided the field of behavioral health with leadership in working with the invisible and powerless. Through constructs such as minority stress and feminist psychology, these individuals have expanded our notion of what it means to live in the world as a minority of diminished power and created clinical strategies to effectively treat these human beings. My work follows in this tradition of creating specialized treatment for specialized populations but does so for those who live in the world in positions of extraordinary power.

Our map is the same, but the terrain I've chosen to address is quite different.

This shared map is based on principles of unconditional positive regard and congruence that lie at the core of humanistic psychology. What this means is that I must engage in a process to acknowledge the differences that exist between me and the sparkling veneer of my celebrity patients while simultaneously working to value them for who they are at their unvarnished core.

It was a map that was ingrained in me as a graduate student at Antioch University in Los Angeles and as a clinician working with underprivileged people at a free clinic in Los Angeles and at the Lesbian, Gay, Bisexual & Transgender Community Center of New York City. And while this map enabled me to effectively work with human beings very different from me, it also enabled me to begin healing from the aspirational decades of my life, decades during which I rejected my personal truths for social standards of *better, successful, safe,* and *loved.*

This rejection of self is the hallmark of the dark side of privilege.

Simply by virtue of the fact that I emerged from the womb a male in a middle-class American family of European descent, I've been afforded legions of opportunities to succeed in a life that has been defined by other white males who looked like me. Inherent in a privileged identity is a searing compulsion not just to sustain one's privilege, but also to attain even more rarefied and gilded indicia of success, power, and prestige.

The message I received from the family and the world into which I was born was that *being me was not enough.* There were fundamental truths about me that were completely unacceptable. These truths needed to be ignored and rejected out of hand, or I'd be punished and ostracized by my tribe. Then there were other truths, personality traits, and manners that were deemed deficient and required constant improvement, and still others that required me to mimic the affectations and personal presentation of those in the social classes to which I was told I needed to aspire.

Only through my work in the realm of behavioral health was I able to realize that the men and women I'd aspired to become were not immune from the pain of being human. A lot of my clients have "become" something or someone the world deems extraordinary, but this external validation didn't solve their problems. In most cases, it just amplified the fundamental problems they tried to cover over and created new ones. While their success may have originated from a need to be loved and to feel safe, once successful, they felt diminished, unseen, vulnerable, unappreciated, unloved, and objectified.

Over the past decades, I've worked with people who've became powerful by virtue of their successes in the field of entertainment and others through their success in business. A few have attained power through their positions as politicians. Many have their fame and wealth by virtue of their beauty; others have their position simply because of their last name. Most embody several of these categories in their being. Sally, for example, first gained celebrity status by virtue of her beauty. Growing up in rural Ohio, she was given special treatment for her physical appearance. "A rose in a field of dandelions" was how she described herself in her youth. As a successful model in the 1990s, she became famous for her commercial success: "I was a brand." In her late twenties, she married a famous businessman and gained celebrity status as a socialite. "I became the Stepford wife: blond and full of silicone."

As with many of my patients, through my work with Sally, we began to establish our reparative connection on the thread of fragility we shared as human beings, not on the external presentation of privilege that adorned our lives.

•

So back to Sally's important question: *Was* Sally "wasting" her time and money coming to see me? In the space that lingered after Sally's emotionally charged and painfully honest question, I felt my childhood deficiencies emerge. In middle school, my parents had me tested, not for academic talent but to see if I had special needs. "You're funny," my dad would tell me, "but not terribly smart. You should probably go into sales." It wasn't until I found my academic groove as a high school exchange student in Costa Rica, far outside of my family's misperceptions, that I realized just how wrong my father was. Still, those early childhood messages run deep and reappear in stressful situations.

I counted to ten to diminish my reactivity and recalibrated my awareness away from me and onto my patient, Sally. At the end of this exercise, I turned my thoughts over to what it must be like for her to sit across from me—a well-educated and younger man who was judging her. Because I rely heavily on my reactions to my patients—countertransference, as it's known in clinical parlance—I used my felt experience and the thoughts that accompanied it to formulate my response, a response that I hoped would acknowledge the pernicious way our society, and men in particular, see middle-aged women.

"You come to me because the world judges you as a carton of milk with an expiration date. You'd love to change this dynamic but don't know how."

It wasn't a bull's-eye, but it hit close enough to the mark.

Sally, who only minutes before was a tiger going in for the kill, instantly became a deer quaking in the headlights of my answer. Kicking at the golden chain of the Chanel bag lying next to her on the floor, she nervously spun her five-carat emerald-cut diamond solitaire around her painfully thin finger. While she fidgeted, I cleared my throat, preparing, but unprepared for a follow-up intervention.

"I see," she finally responded, bitterness dripping like a lemon rind from her two simple words.

"*Do you?*" I asked as firmly as I could, hoping to hold her in the intensity of her emotions while moving her toward a deeper, more authentic connection.

Sally moved her glance around the room—her ring, the bag, the warm glow of the summer landscape painting hanging over my desk. The latter seemed to console her. Finally, she cast her softened gaze toward me.

"I do." This time, Sally delivered her line not with tart disdain, but rather as a human being finding relief in an authentic connection.

Authenticity. Peace of mind. Connection. Repair. Enhancement. These are the goals of the unique brand of therapy I practice with all my clients. But with the highly successful patients I treat, the fame, power, external recognition, and material wealth they've acquired makes it harder for us to achieve these goals. While success and attainment bring adoration from the outside in, they don't protect these patients from feeling isolated or from suffering from depression, anxiety, and a host of addictive and relational disorders.

What and whom these people possess, the accolades they receive, the dizzying levels of success they achieve—these do not produce the peace of mind, the connection, or the happiness they thought they would. Their power, while producing a certain type of freedom, enslaves them in other ways.

I've also learned that, once attained, the very success to which these patients aspired can turn against them. We need only look to the legions of celebrities who've succumbed to the perilous side of fame to see how fortune plucks out the vulnerable and unprepared. From Marilyn Monroe to Whitney Houston, Heath Ledger, Phillip Seymour Hoffman, Prince, George Michael, Robin Williams, and Kate Spade—the list is endless and seemingly grows longer with each minute that ticks by on the incessant clock of life.

In addition to the extraordinarily successful patients I treat, many more come into treatment seduced and pummeled by a compulsive search for the fame, power, and fortune that elude them. These people live their lives in a diminished state, desperately chasing a dream that heckles them from the other side of a gilded gate, a gate they can't climb over and fail to break through.

Other patients I see in my practice become obsessively engaged in status or celebrity worship to their detriment. They believe they'd be better, more lovable, of value in the world, if they had Elon Musk's entrepreneurial skills, Pamela Anderson's breasts, Oprah Winfrey's billions, Vladimir Putin's dominance, or Meghan Markle's husband. Twelve Step literature is full of references to this phenomenon—it's known as the search for power, property, and prestige.

For many celebrities—as well as those aspiring to become celebrities, 1-percenters, or a member of the elite—the pursuit of power comes with a negative impact on their physical, emotional, or spiritual life. These people diminish their bodies with drugs and alcohol, disordered eating, and self-mutilation. They destroy their relationships through emotional and sexual infidelities, sexual addiction, narcissism, and a host of other personality presentations. They often run through their wealth by reckless and compulsive spending. And last, but far from least, they destroy their spirits by living for an unattainable dream sold to them by manipulative commercial interests.

Throughout this book, you'll meet human beings who've been personally and relationally diminished by the *power* inherent in their identity. Their power could have come from wealth, fame, pedigree, a particular social role, or their physical beauty. In all these instances, there is a central, defining feature they possess—or that possesses them—that makes them stand out from the crowd, different from the masses. At the same time, as a result of being *different, special,* these people are robbed of essential features of their humanity and viewed as clichéd objects. With their agency and humanity defined by the society around them, these individuals have—at the same time—more power than most of us can ever imagine and no real power at all. They have everything and nothing—but they need more. They embody a fragile sense of power that can break at any time.

Through these encounters, you'll learn, just as I've learned by sitting in my therapist's chair, which traits enabled the survivors to transcend destruction and which traits doomed others to demise and death. Along the way, you'll be given insights to deepen your relationships, find grounding in a chaotic world, and change and grow into a better, happier, more contented human being while creating a better, more compassionate world for you and your children.

The clinical issues and patient stories I've included in this book—imposter syndrome, substance abuse, depression, narcissism, infidelity, and more—reflect the patterns I've seen most frequently in a treatment setting; they've also been most impactful on my evolution from an overweight kid who was told he wasn't terribly bright and who believed the salve that would heal these wounds was formulated from external successes to a fraying middle-aged man who has found incredible peace of mind and contentedness in vulnerability and authenticity.

However, before you meet these men and women, it's important you become better acquainted with me so that we can build an alliance of our own.

•

Change and growth are difficult. This I know firsthand. My life and career as a therapist have been journeys of transformation and a search for authentic relationships, all driven by a desire to contribute to the world in a meaningful way.

Why and how has this need for meaning and connection led me to concentrate on the psychological needs of celebrity men, women, and families? Like most meaningful accomplishments, this work came to me after decades of attempts and failures, losing sight of the shore and learning to trust my intuition.

Through my struggles with feeling lost and alone, untethered and vulnerable even as a privileged white male, I've been able to embody the humanistic stance needed to connect with people who live in extraordinary psychic pain. This stance requires an unconditional positive regard for the many ways a patient manifests their unique identity. It demands I meet the patient where they are in their life, rather than thrusting my expectations on them, and it requires me to draw on basic tenets of feminist theory to work with my patients as fellow travelers rather than approach their pain with the superiority of an expert.

Through my intellectual curiosity, my need for meaning, and my hunger for scientific data, I cobbled together a catalog of degrees, licenses, and certifications. It took me decades to find my academic niche through my PhD research, wherein I explored the experience of people who live as minorities in positions of power in our society.

My dissertation was informed by work I did both in Los Angeles and New York City, where I earned my clinical hours to become licensed as a marriage and family therapist. In both cities, I had the privilege of sitting with human beings in psychic pain but at very different ends of the economic spectrum. In Los Angeles, I served as an intern at the Hollywood Sunset Free Clinic. On the East Coast, I served as a clinician in the mental health clinic of the Lesbian, Gay, Bisexual & Transgender Community Center of New York. In both of these settings, I worked with people who our culture treats as "throwaways." These were people who identify as transgender, HIV positive, or sex workers: human beings who struggled not only to meet Maslow's deficiency needs for physical safety, but also to find acceptance and love.

On the other side of the power spectrum, I've worked around the world as a consultant to several of the industry's most elite and distinguished residential treatment programs.

In my own practice as a licensed marriage and family therapist in New York City and Telluride, Colorado, as well as my work as a consultant to ultra-high net worth individuals and families in Malibu, London, Paris, Zurich, Geneva, and the Middle East, I'm constantly engaging with people who live in the world in positions of elite power and called to dismantle the destructive systems in which they exist. Even though these individuals have an abundance of ways to fill Maslow's deficiency needs—things like healthy food and safe shelter—they suffer from a void in their higher being needs, things like self-esteem, meaning, and connection.

Nearly all of my patients—regardless of their status or position in life—have suffered through some sort of emotional or physical trauma in their developmental path. The impact this trauma has had on their central nervous system profoundly affects the way they perceive the world and their place in it.

The ornaments of my present life are eclipsed by the influence of the challenges in my past. So before moving forward in this book, I'd like to take some time to tell you who I am, where I started, and how the scars I still carry inside of me were set in place.

•

In *Game of Thrones*, a show that captures the competitive zeitgeist in which we live, Tyrion Lannister is a dwarf who uses his family's privilege to fight against the prejudices he endures as a result of his physical features. In one of my favorite moments of the series, he gives the following sage advice: "Never forget what you are. The rest of the world will not. Wear it like armor, and it can never be used to hurt you."

I embodied that advice early in life.

By the time I was ten, I'd been told in so many ways, in so many words, that in addition to not being terribly smart, I was seen as "fat" and "a sissy." I was an outsider in the world into which I had been thrust.

While the cool kids in my neighborhood wore 501s and Levi's cords, I was wobbling around in my "husky" jeans—a traumatizing and mortifying label that came along with the indignity of having to visit "The Husky Shop" at the JCPenney store in York, Pennsylvania. I was also overly sensitive. Just *watching* the schoolyard fights between my classmates made me cry. While the boys were brutal, the girls were vicious. When they slapped at each other, pulled out clumps of hair, and called each other names beginning with the letters c and b, I'd fall apart. I just couldn't understand the vitriol, and the violence that ensued from their hatred seemed senseless. Life back in 1978, in Fallston, Maryland, where I grew up, felt tough enough; why amplify the emotional pain with blackened eyes and bloody noses?

From a very young age, I perceived life as aggressive and harsh. I found my physical environment garish. Lights were too bright. Noises too loud. Just hearing the siren of an ambulance somewhere off in the distance sent me into a state of panic. Needless to say, sensitive Paul had a challenging time coming of age in the rough-and-tumble world of rural Maryland.

My parents, concerned with my overly sensitive nature, thought I needed outside help. "You've got to toughen up," they'd advise. But I couldn't.

Today I know that people like me are genetically wired for hypersensitivity. It's our limbic system that causes our condition. We're not weak or devoid of willpower and strength. In fact, just the opposite is true. My oversensitivity and perception of myself as an outsider have made me an incredibly effective clinician. The very traits that were viewed in my youth as liabilities are my greatest assets today. But at the time, I was forced to live in the discomfort of "growing up" and to rely on other people's misplaced attempts to help me. At the top of the list of these people were my parents.

Incredibly kind and generous people, my parents lived in

fear that their youngest son would succumb to the bullying he received from others for being weak and evidencing behaviors that were pejoratively referred to as effeminate. Their solution, to enroll me in a boxing class at a local YMCA, proved disastrous. I remember putting on the boxing gear in a trance, the smell of acidic sweat burning my nostrils as the bile of my stomach dashed up into my throat. "Just keep moving," I repeated over and over to myself as I climbed into the ring like a zombie.

Once in the ring with my opponent, I immediately crumbled. No amount of self-talk could motivate me to swing at the genetically gifted young man who existed somewhere in my line of vision. So I stood in the ring like a statue, immobilized by fear, and did the only thing I could. I started sobbing.

"He started crying before the bell even rang," explained the tattooed coach to my embarrassed father. "No way in hell this kid's cut out for this." And he was right. I wasn't cut out for it. But rather than lessening my struggles, my boxing experience at the Baltimore Y added to them. It confirmed what deep down I'd suspected for years—that I was unlovable, an aberration in a chaotic and unsafe world.

But while I was overly sensitive, I wasn't stupid.

We may bang ourselves around, developing destructive ways of coping, but eventually we weave upholstery that protects us. The forces that get us moving are an awareness that something needs to change, exhaustion from the pain of being stuck, and the courage to move, albeit haltingly, in a reparative direction. In recovery speak, this is referred to as having a "moment of clarity," "hitting bottom," and getting "into action." If we're lucky, we find a secure base from which we can begin to try on new ways of being with others and ourselves, and although we want to believe this base will come from power, property, and prestige, it must be found in a vulnerable and authentic relationship with ourselves and at least one other human being.

In my case, the ache of my moment of clarity came when I realized that to survive my circumstances, I'd need to change them. Darwin noted that in nature, the most successful species are not the strongest but rather the most adaptive. Although at the time I had never heard of Darwin, much less read *On the Origin of Species,* I intuitively heeded nature's call. So instead of trying to match the brute force of my peers, I adapted and found friends I could actually play with. I also found interests more in line with who I was at my core. Some of those interests allowed me even some momentary escape and fantasy.

While the neighbor kids played outside with footballs and yard darts, shot BB guns, caught toads, and tortured cats, I found my sanctuary in the basement in my family's three-bedroom rancher. With its faux walnut paneling, brown linoleum floor, and white dropped ceiling, the "club cellar" (as my mother called it) became my safe harbor. It was cool in the summer and warm in the winter, and it soothed the bite of the outside world like baking soda and vinegar soothe the piercing sting of a bee.

Anchoring me in this harbor was an object that became my best buddy. Magnavox was his name, and we escaped the present and explored future possibilities together. With the flick of a switch, Mr. Magnavox gave me the comfort and acceptance I desperately needed. He didn't judge me as weak or ask me to become a person I wasn't. He showed me a world beyond my present existence and introduced me to a world of potential.

Cut off from the rejection and chaos of life just up the

creaky wooden stairs, I'd spend hours fantasizing I was Fonzie on *Happy Days* or another sibling crammed into the Brady Bunch's immaculate split-level home.

Although I was physically alone in my adventures, I wasn't alone in my method of escaping the snags that arise in the fabric of life. Upstairs, my mother shut out the horrors of the Vietnam War by losing herself in glossy magazines, breathless over Liza Minnelli's glamour and Elizabeth Taylor's dalliances. My father, stressed by his mid-management job, devoured news of John DeLorean's start-up, while my adolescent brother fantasized he had John Travolta's moves in *Saturday Night Fever*. By living in the perfect and charmed lives of celebrities, we escaped the painful realities of our own.

•

There's a fine line between a temporary coping technique and immersing yourself in the worship of power and celebrity—to the point of feeling incomplete until you've attained it.

Since leaving Maryland decades ago, I've learned the need to soothe one's self in celebrity wasn't limited to the Hokemeyer household. In fact, our draw to celebrity is primal.

The reasons for this are several.

For starters, human beings are *tribal*. We instinctually arrange ourselves in hierarchical structures and follow the directions of powerful and narcissistically oriented leaders. In our capitalistic and materialistic world, these leaders are often determined by the success of their commercial endeavors. The world got a reminder of our predisposition to these tribal structures when Donald J. Trump was elected the forty-fifth president of the United States of America, which speaks to the extraordinary power inherent in celebrity and our human need to be led by larger-than-life characters.

Second, human beings are *aspirational*. In the fight to survive, we're constantly looking for ways to self-improve and attract a mate with resources who will subsequently enhance our gene pool. The acquisition and display of power, celebrity, and success provide a model for doing just that. Data collected by marketing firms have found a phenomenon known as the *lipstick effect*. During economic slumps and times of crisis, such as 9/11, women spend more money on products to enhance their appearance, believing that such products will increase their opportunities to find a mate to protect them (Persaud and Bruggen 2015). This is one of the reasons why millions of naturally beautiful women augment their bodies to unnatural proportions, longing for the seductive power of Angelina Jolie, Beyoncé, or one of the many Kardashian sisters. Men, too, are not immune from these aspirational forces. Plastic surgeons make a fortune from chin implants and other surgical enhancements as men strive to emulate Brad Pitt's facial features or Chris Pine's enviable hairline. In fact, males are the fastest-growing segment of the cosmetic enhancement industry. One study found that approximately 70 percent of men are open to and interested in a variety of cosmetic surgeries to enhance their personal and professional opportunities (Technavio 2017).

Third, the worship of celebrity, beauty, power, and attainment is archetypical; it's not restricted to any particular time frame. As a vessel of expression, such worship is universal and has been present in the human experience throughout the ages. It's in our faces in our Western culture with our emphasis on external appearances and material success, but it exists in some manifestation in nearly every culture around the globe. Over time, it's increased exponentially as technology has evolved to allow cross-cultural expression.

Fourth, celebrity mirrors the current zeitgeist. During the Great Depression, when the spirit of America was at its lowest, America became obsessed with musicals dominated by a young and charismatic Judy Garland. The 1950s gave birth to the civil rights movement. In those turbulent times, we grounded ourselves in the humor of Marilyn Monroe and processed our discontent through the rebellious James Dean. The 1980s, marked by the AIDS epidemic and the acknowledgment of global warming, heralded in the celebrity of megawatt musicians— stars who captured our fascination on the newly launched and wildly successful MTV. Leading this charge were the electric Michael Jackson, Whitney Houston, and Prince—stars we've lost far too soon due to drug addiction.

Our modern age, characterized by economic insecurity and class division, is defined by celebrity of the "everyperson" created through reality television and the Internet. Although the basic format of reality television is not new, what *is* new is how a once good-spirited look into human vulnerabilities has become exploitative and unapologetically malicious. In contrast to Allen Funt's good-humored escapades on *Candid Camera*, the reality television shows of today are full of emotional disregulation, vitriol, and degrading depictions of people who suffer from addictions and personality disorders.

But perhaps the most culturally destructive feature of reality television has been its ability to blur the line between what's real and what's fiction. While fiction and fantasy can be effective coping mechanisms—mechanisms that have enabled millions of human beings to endure terrible hardships—we're living in an age where what is being sold as reality is not real. Techniques such as "frankenbiting," where participant dialogue is remixed to create a fictionalized account of what was said, are common. The most widely cited example of alternate reality is the Kardashian empire. Famous simply for being famous, the Kardashians have dominated mainstream and social media for decades with the "fabulous" banality of their lives—they are like us, but not us. The trouble is that we're no longer sure what's real and what isn't. Many people struggled to figure out if Kim's $10 million, seventy-two-day marriage to Kris Humphries was a union inspired by love or ratings. Of late, the Kardashian spotlight has turned to the youngest of the clan, Kylie Jenner, whose meteoric rise on the *Forbes'* 100 list has made headline news in traditional business and news outlets. But is she a billionaire or not? The data is conflicting. As of July 2018, *Time* magazine placed her net worth at $50 million (Calfas 2018), while *Forbes* placed it at $800 million (Robehmed 2018), and that number grew in 2019. Unfortunately, in our modern world, fact checking doesn't really matter.

And certainly we can't ignore the malignant impact the Internet has had on our individual and social well-being. At the time of this book's publication, Facebook is under scrutiny for disseminating false information that may have compromised our democracy. On the beach where I used to live in Malibu, I constantly observed visitors spending enormous amounts of time gazing not out to the sea but rather into their smartphones, contorting themselves to capture a perfect selfie to post to one of their social media accounts. Yes, the Internet and the various sites that it hosts, like YouTube, Instagram, and Facebook, have democratized the media world, but at a cost. We're giving away the most personal and private details of our lives to technological oligarchs who are selling them to the highest bidders.

Most of our popular culture right now mixes what's real with what's not. The one thing we *do* know, however, is that reality television and social media are money-making machines. With a reported worth of over $1 billion, the Kardashians have profited handsomely. According to *Business Insider*, at $16.5 million, twenty-six-year-old Daniel Middleton was the highest-earning YouTuber for his daily posts on his expertise in the online game Minecraft (Lynch 2017). And with huge amounts of money come huge amounts of power.

Unfortunately, this power isn't always being used responsibly.

Fortunately, we've begun to see a backlash and a rallying cry that enough is enough. When Logan Paul posted an insensitive and salacious video of a suicide victim in Aokigahara, the Japanese suicide forest, the public responded with a swift and negative reaction. One outraged person going by the name Ariona posted the following on Twitter:

> Suicide is not a joke. Suicide is not a way to gain views. suicide is not to be taken lightly. what logan paul did is not acceptable. if you're struggling, please take your health seriously and please seek help. your life is worth so much. you are worth so much. [sic]. (Ariona 2018)

Clearly, the Internet holds great value in allowing everyone to have a voice, but will the costs exceed the benefits? Like many scholars studying the impact, I think it's a bit too soon to tell.

One thing that I do know is that the Internet is changing our personality presentations and the personalities of our children.

Today, with the pervasiveness of the Internet and reality television, as well as the ease with which seemingly average people start earning huge amounts of money, radically transforming their lives, power has entered a whole new stratosphere of seduction. And it's drawing our children into its erotic grasp.

Recently, one of my patients shared a story about her seven-year-old son's obsession with YouTube videos and her concern that he was becoming a narcissist. My patient and her husband had taken their son to Aspen to ski for the holidays. Unfortunately, her memories of his first skiing adventure were defined not by her pride in his athletic prowess, but rather by her horror in his narcissist rage. "Oh Mommy, you're not doing it right!" he screamed while she attempted to capture the event on her smartphone. "Get me making a right turn; it looks better."

"Are we raising a new generation of pathological narcissists with all this technology?" she anxiously asked, knowing the answer, but not wanting to admit it was true of her son. It's one of the many questions we as a society must address in order to redeem ourselves from our growing obsession with the seductive and destructive force inherent in our desire to attain power, beauty, prestige, and perfection.

In the pages that follow, we'll explore the psychological lives of women and men who live in positions of elite power. And in spite of this power, whether their power has been derived from their talent, wealth, beauty, or surname, they've found it's not enough to protect them from the pain inherent in being human.

Through clinical case compositions, you'll experience the world on the other side of the gilded gate through the voices of the men and women who live there. You will sit, just as I've sat as their therapist, and experience the full impact that the power of celebrity and wealth has had on the human beings who live—sometimes suffocated, sometimes inflated—inside these labels.

To begin this journey, it's important for me to explain the structure of this book. Each chapter begins with a narrative of my personal journey as a human being struggling to find personal meaning and reparative connections. While initially I resisted the often-unflattering self-disclosures inherent in these revelations, my editor convinced me to include them. "How can you claim to be such a proponent of Jung's basic tenet that in order for a patient to heal, the therapist must be impacted, without providing the readers with an insight into your personal struggles with wealth, power, and celebrity?"

She was right. And while I'm still uncomfortable with these revelations, my work and the clinical formulations created from them are the direct result of what I've learned through my personal imperfections as a privileged white male and lettered professional trying to map new clinical terrain.

My personal narratives are followed by a meta-level review of the empirical data as it relates to the topic being discussed. The trained lawyer and academic in me felt it necessary to support my clinical observations with science and facts.

The last and, for me, the richest experience in writing this book is a case vignette where I explore the topics discussed through a narrative dialogue between my patients and me. Here, it's critically important to point out that while the issues being addressed are real, my editor and I have taken great measures to protect the confidentiality of the individuals and families I've treated and to honor the trust they've allowed me. The intention of these vignettes is to offer you, the reader, an opportunity to see that the power you may long for is not enough to protect you from the pain of being human. They're also intended to show that the way to transcend this pain is through a reparative relationship with another human being.

The ultimate takeaway from this book is that a meaningful and fulfilling life is based on integration rather than abandonment of one's celebrity identity. To be happy and contented in life, we need not relinquish our wealth and power, nor downgrade our dreams and aspirations. We must, however, break through the hard and cold veneer of life's gilt and establish warm and nurturing relationships with ourselves, key people in our lives, and the communities in which we live. For time eternal, we've been told that wealth, celebrity, and the power inherent in them are barriers to enlightenment. The Buddha left his position of privilege and his castle to find enlightenment, and we have been told for centuries that it's easier for a camel to get through the eye of a needle than for a rich man to enter heaven. But this just isn't so. When properly grasped, the power inherent in an elite identity can be channeled in highly productive and rewarding directions for not just those who possess it, but the world in which they live. As such, one of the things this book shows is that one need not renounce one's wealth and lead a life of asceticism or even follow the middle path to attain enlightenment.

People *can* live in a place of material abundance and elite labels *and* heal from relational disorders that include substance and behavioral addictions, personality disorders such as narcissism and borderline personality disorder, and mental health issues such as depression, anxiety, and bipolar disorder. You don't need to leave the castle to find enlightenment. With the proper insights and relationships, you can find it within the castle walls. Simultaneously, it's time we understand and address why so many of us think and feel we aren't enough *until* we live behind the castle walls, how having the castle doesn't "fix" the person or prevent issues from arising in life, and that while life behind the castle gates seems gilded and perfect, the truth is the people who live in those big, beautiful homes are actually *people*—just like you and me.

1.

Ambition

The Costs and Rewards
of Our Celebrity Addiction

*I have absolutely no pleasure in the stimulants in which
I sometimes so madly indulge. It has not been in the
pursuit of pleasure that I have periled life and reputation
and reason. It has been in the desperate attempt to escape
from torturing memories, from a sense of insupportable
loneliness and a dread of some strange impending doom.*

— EDGAR ALLAN POE

"Dr. Hock-o-muir, I need you to stop moving in your seat and
look straight into the camera," a voice from somewhere out in
TV land crackled in the microphone lodged in my ear. I sat
as still as I could, freezing and incredibly anxious. Not even
an hour earlier, I'd been warm and cozy in my office, looking
forward to a quiet evening at home. The universe, however,
held other plans. As I was writing notes from my last session,
my phone buzzed, marking the arrival of a message.

"Hey can u do a cable news show?" asked the PR agent
with whom I worked.

Ugh, was my immediate reaction.

"When?" was what I replied.

"2nite!!!! 7 pm."

I looked at my watch and realized it was in less than an hour. *I really don't want to do this,* I thought.

"Topic?" was how I responded.

"Tragedy on the Taconic!!!! Diane Schuler. Drove drunk, killed her kid!!!!!!!!" I loved my PR agent and was always amused by her copious use of exclamation points, but her vivacious punctuation couldn't whitewash over the highly disturbing topic.

For some reason, over the last several months, I'd become an authority on mothers who killed their babies. Prior to this story, it was a mother who, in a state of psychosis, drove her minivan into a lake, killing herself and her children.

I didn't want to do the story, but again, my fingers betrayed my desires.

"Love to do it. Thx 4 thinking of me!"

"G8t!!!!!" My agent responded back. "We'll send a car!!!!!! Can you be here in 30?"

"Absolutely. Thanks for the car."

"K. Need talking points."

Producers always ask for talking points. They outline the expert's position on the topic in three or four sound bites. Over the years, I found they seldom use them for purposes other than feeling confident you can at least construct a sentence and have one cogent thought.

"Done! See you soon. Thanks again."

Thirty minutes later, I was sitting alone in the studio booth waiting for the segment to begin. As I sat, my initial reaction to the story returned with a vengeance. I didn't want to do it.

Instead, I wanted to pull out my earpiece and run out the door.

Why am I doing this? I asked myself. *This is ridiculous.*

My stomach churned and my pulse raced. The room was unbearably cold. I started to shiver.

A producer from somewhere far away—Atlanta, I believed— bellowed through my earpiece, "Dr. Paul, get ready."

I readied myself the best I could.

"And in ten, nine, eight . . ." Only seven more seconds till I'd hear the bombastic music marking another segment of headline news.

I drew in a deep breath and held it. *Now let it out slowly.* I began to use the very mindfulness techniques I use with my patients.

Where are your feet? Focus on your feet. I felt myself calming, but still I wanted to run out the door, down the hall, and out into the Manhattan streets toward my liberation.

"Three, two, one! And we're live!"

The segment began with a clip of the incident, the horrors of the event, and people's reactions to it. The question on everyone's mind, of course, was how a mother could do this to children. It's a complex question. Not one that can be adequately addressed in two or three sound bites. But that's exactly what I was expected to do.

"Joining us from New York City is Dr. Paul Hock-o-muir, a licensed marriage and family therapist and addictions specialist."

Not surprisingly, the host, a bubbly young blonde in a bright fuchsia top that revealed an abundance of cleavage, screwed up my name. Hosts usually do. My last name is long. But it's not terribly complicated if you slow down and actually read it, Hoke-a-meyer. In the realm of our twenty-four-hour news cycle that's broken down into two-minute sound bites, however, slowness is a luxury not afforded.

I wanted to correct her, but decided to follow restraint of tongue.

"So doctor, how could this happen? I mean, a mother killing her own child . . . and her brother's children as well? Help us understand this." The bubbly blonde's energy shifted. She expected me to supply her—and millions of her viewers—with a succinct answer that addressed the complexity of this tragedy in less than fifteen seconds.

William James, one of the most brilliant psychologists, physicians, and philosophers of the late nineteenth and early twentieth centuries, wrote at length about dealing with the complexities of life. He advised that the mastery of complex issues requires "a large acquaintance with particulars" (James 1902). As this applied to my present situation, dealing with the complexities of this news story meant I would need to spend hours—days, actually—getting insight into this woman's world. The only information available to me was what I could read in the car between my office and the studio.

And it wasn't much.

The event had taken place only a few hours before, and the details were sketchy. I hadn't treated this woman, and I was certainly not privy to the intricacies of her life. Ethically, the Goldwater Rule, a standard that prohibits clinicians from diagnosing public figures and people they haven't treated, barred me from diagnosing her.

I needed to think fast and address the generalities.

This is insane; why am I doing this? The question I asked myself all evening long returned in my brain with a thunder.

And then I heard myself speaking.

"Addictions are complex. They make people do things, horrible things, things they wouldn't do if they weren't under the influence—"

I intended to go on, but the host interrupted me.

"Are you excusing this mother's behavior?"

The vivacious host was angry. It was clear she was playing to an audience who had no understanding of addictive disorders and was determined to see this as a deplorable action by an irresponsible woman.

F. Scott Fitzgerald said that "the test of a first rate intelligence is the ability to hold two opposing ideas in mind at the same time and still retain the ability to function" (Fitzgerald 1945). While I am under no illusion that my intelligence is "first rate," Fitzgerald's articulation of accepting opposing thoughts is a standard to which I aspire. It's also one that I use in working with my patients.

The one thing that was clear about the situation in the studio was that I had to convey that the tragically deceased woman could be a loving, compassionate mother *and* a human being who suffers from a substance use disorder. I attempted to explain this to the host and our audience.

"Addictions are insidious and destructive. Mothers do not set out to intentionally drive drunk and kill their children. But addiction hijacks a person's judgment and perceptions. It's incredibly difficult to understand, but addictions don't discriminate. They impact women and men, mothers, grandmothers, doctors, teach—"

"Well thank you, Dr. Hock-o-muir, our time is up." And with her quip, the monitor turned to black.

Through my earpiece, I could hear her prattling on: "Just plain tragic. How could a mother do this to children? And in other news . . ."

I jerked the earpiece out of my ear and threw it on the desk. Rage and insecurities filled every cell in my being. *They completely ignored the talking points I sent over. I sucked. I didn't get the chance to talk about research that shows mothers are under incredible stress and are not properly supported in our society. Or that women are physically different from men and have a harder time processing alcohol . . . or that women's access to treatment is exponentially more difficult for financial and family reasons— none of which are their fault. . . . I looked like a fool. . . . This is ridiculous. I'M NEVER DOING IT AGAIN!*

As I hurried out of the room, a twenty-something production assistant brushed past me, escorting in the next guest for the following segment. "Thank you, Dr. Paul." The words came out of her mouth but rang hollow. As she assisted the next guest into my still-warm chair, she mouthed the exact same instructions she gave me ten minutes earlier: "Here Dr. X, put this earpiece in your right ear and look directly into the monitor in front of you. You can't see them, but they can see you . . ."

My stomach flipped in disgust as the door closed behind me.

I rode the elevator down to the cavernous marble-clad lobby and exited onto the frenetic Midtown Manhattan sidewalk. An immaculate black Mercedes S-Class idled for me at the curb. Suddenly, my focus shifted. No longer was I fixated on the unpleasantness of the last thirty minutes. Instead, I became elated with the status of the car and intoxicated by the mere thought of my impending escape in it. *These cable news folks are classy.*

As I slid into the back of the sumptuous chariot, my phone alerted me of a new text message:

"Hey!!!!!!! I just saw u on the news!!!!!!! You looked amazing!!!!"

The message was from an old high school classmate living out in rural Pennsylvania, York or Hanover. I'm not quite sure which. The geographic details don't matter. What does matter is how her comments distorted my recollection of the event and instantly generated in me a feeling of euphoria and elation. It also distorted my view of myself as a chubby high school kid worried about getting beat up in the parking lot after school. A few seconds on national news made that once-powerless kid feel vindicated and omnipotent.

But only five minutes prior, I had felt intense disdain at the experience and swore it off *forever*. Now the endogenous opioids produced by my brain completely erased my negative recollection and made me hunger for more of the very experience I swore off.

Drunk on dopamine, I shot a text message out to my PR agent. "The segment was GREAT. See if you can get me on again tomorrow!"

The American Society of Addiction Medicine (ASAM) describes addiction as "a primary, chronic disease of brain reward, motivation, memory, and related circuitry."

ASAM's definition of addiction continues:

Dysfunction in these circuits leads to characteristic biological, psychological, social, and spiritual manifes-tations. This is reflected in an individual pathologically pursuing reward and/or relief by substance use and other behaviors.

Addiction is characterized by inability to consistently abstain, impairment in behavioral control, craving, diminished recognition of significant problems with one's behaviors and interpersonal relationships, and a dysfunctional emotional response. (American Society of Addiction Medicine 2011)

This definition certainly had relevance to my momentary brush with celebrity and the intoxication I felt from being validated by a luxury car and a friend from my inglorious past.

Like an adolescent boy, I became ruled by the most primitive part of my brain: its mesolimbic pathway (MP). Known most commonly as our reward circuitry, the MP ensures our survival as a species. Through it, we're driven to seek to eat, have sex, socialize, and find validation by the world around us.

If this was my reaction to the lowest possible level of celebrity, think about what happens to people with real power and celebrity when their central nervous systems get flooded by the hormonal surge that accompanies being validated or admired by millions. Seduced by these physiological rewards, they obsess about maintaining the euphoria—especially if they overcame so much to attain it—and become panicked at the ever-present possibility of losing it. And in this place of fear, they make unhealthy decisions to compulsively chase it.

In addiction-speak, we refer to these experiences as *tolerance* and *withdrawal*. *Tolerance* refers to the need to constantly up the level of engagement to get the same baseline level of satisfaction. So one segment on cable news wasn't enough for me. My addictive brain told me I needed to be on national news weekly, daily, hourly. *Withdrawal* refers to the emotional thud that occurred when my dopamine rush subsided. Back in my office in Sutton Place, out from behind the tinted windows of the Mercedes and the computer-generated hug I received from my long-lost classmate, I experienced a crushing low that called out to be medicated. Being Paul, a clinician on the Upper East Side of Manhattan, was no longer enough. My limbic system wanted much more.

Neil Lasher, a fifty-year music veteran and executive of Sony Music Publishing, described the seduction of celebrity as follows: "You're adored by millions. You drink in the applause. You're told daily, hell, hourly, how talented and wonderful you are. And then there's the money, the gifts, endorsements, the sex and drugs—just thrown at you. And you need more and more, constant admiration. The problem is, there's never enough" (email exchange with author, 2019).

This insatiable hunger for more is what causes most celebrities to self-destruct. This phenomenon is most pernicious in children who attain success very early in their lives. Their central nervous systems get calibrated to a hyper-elevated baseline of normal that is impossible to sustain, and they lack the intellectual sophistication to discern reality from fiction. Older celebrities are not immune to the stress and pain caused by a marquee name short-circuited. Unlike their younger peers who fail to mature, these older celebrities get frozen in icebergs of public validation.

•

"He'll never make it over to see you. Do you make house calls?" The voice on the other line sounded desperate and exhausted. I detected an accent in his voice but couldn't quite place it.

I subsequently learned the caller was a talent manager named Scott. The patient was a middle-aged celebrity named Jonathan.

I wasn't surprised Scott made the call. Celebrities have teams of people attending to every detail of their existence. The rationale is that it preserves the artist's creativity and enables him or her to focus on work. Perhaps this is true, but up to a point. The unintended consequence of this dynamic is that, over time, it transforms exceptionally competent adults into dependent infants who become paralyzed by self-doubt, enslaved to direction from others.

In the realm of mental health disorders, we call this unintended consequence *enabling*. In contrast to actions and intentions directed to support these individuals in becoming highly functioning, autonomous human beings, enabling leads to dysfunction that deepens destructive behaviors. So instead of growing up and taking charge of his or her life, the enabler gets trapped in excessive caregiving, and the person enabled gets trapped in being broken and in need of repair.

Although it was too soon to see where Scott ranked on the enabling scale, odds were he rated high.

Scott continued: "He . . . well, he's become unbearable. We just secured a gig. The first one in over a year, and he's destroying it. They're trying to let him out of the contract. He's dead if they do."

His use of the word *dead* caught my attention. "So what exactly is the problem?" I needed Scott to be more specific.

Scott sighed before answering. "It's what always gets him into trouble, his bloody ego. He thinks he's the King of England, and these days he's lucky to hang out in the court.

His narcissism is killing him." I finally located Scott's accent as British.

I was taken aback. My presumption was that Jonathan was suffering from one of the many traditional faces of an addictive disorder: drugs or alcohol, sex, compulsive spending. The calls I receive from most of my celebrity patients—or their handlers—reveal that they usually are. This case, however, brought me up short. It also alerted me to my need to be hypervigilant in my prejudgments of the men, women, couples, and families who come to me for treatment.

For it's easy for us to forget that we professionals, like the patients who come to us for help, are human. We're not immune from the host of prejudices and unconscious reactions we manifest toward the people we treat. These exist at every level of a psychotherapeutic engagement, but they become acute when the work involves celebrities and other powerful patients. We fantasize about the lives they lead based on the messages we've internalized about success. Rather than deluding ourselves that we're above these prejudices or denying they exist, we need to identify them and actively incorporate them into our work.

"I get it," I responded, because I did. Narcissism is one of the personality disorders I have a wealth of experience in treating. Not only has it been empirically found to be higher among powerful patient populations, but it's also nearly always present in the host of relational and addictive disorders in which I work (Szalavitz 2013).

But just to be clear, I was compelled to ask, "What's his drug and alcohol use like?"

Although my question was a bit leading, I intentionally

fashioned it as best I could to be open-ended. If Jonathan was using, I didn't want to shame him for it.

"Bloody 'ell. I wish he'd use something! Swears off the stuff. Says it interferes with his performance. Truth is, he's afraid it'll interfere with his waistline. He's a vain one he is."

"Does he know you've phoned me?" I inquired to see just how open Jonathan would be to my visit.

"Yes, we did a bit of an intervention. Me, his agent, lawyer, and girlfriend du jour. We pitched you as a coach. Sorry, mate, but he liked the idea. It worked 'cuz you're a lawyer and a shrink."

I felt compelled to clarify my credentials. "Well, I'm not licensed to practice law. I did in the past and I have the degree, but—"

Scott interrupted me.

"Right, mate, whatever you want. We came up with a list of names, a long one if the truth be told. You're not the only bloke we considered. There's no shortage of shrinks in Manhattan."

Being right-sized by Scott stung, but it also made me chuckle. Everything he said was true. There's certainly no shortage of therapists in Manhattan. Unfortunately, few of them are trained to deal with celebrity and powerful patients as a culturally distinct group that requires specialized clinical skills and interventions.

I appreciated his directness and honesty.

More importantly, Scott's comment illuminated the dynamics of the system in which I was being asked to participate. His comment revealed an overstressed and hypercritical network that was being ruled—and I suspected terrorized—by a narcissist. It also indicated I had some leverage to work with. Yes, it seemed Jonathan was motived by purely outside pressures, but that was enough. Vanity has gotten a lot of people started on a new and greatly improved path. Sure, ultimately it's an inside job, but in this world in which we live, let's not pretend the outsides don't matter. They do. And they especially matter among the higher socioeconomic classes and those desiring class transcendence.

I was relieved to hear that Jonathan expected my arrival and wouldn't feel ambushed by my showing up in his living room. Jonathan's willingness to see me was the first step in what I hoped would become a complex and elegant waltz in which we negotiated the cadence of the therapeutic alliance.

Plus, I have no interest in or talent for surprise interventions. Yes, there are cases where they are necessary, but their long-term success rate is dismal. I'm a therapist, not an interventionist. As such, I need to align myself as best I can with my patients from the beginning rather than throwing a net over them and dragging them against their will toward a goal that's been shoved down their throats by others.

Heather Hayes, a top interventionist who works with celebrity patients and families around the world, agrees. According to Hayes, "Unless safety issues are of paramount concern, it's critical to utilize an approach with ultra-high net worth patients that emphasizes respect and transparency" (email exchange with author, 2018).

"Yes, of course. I make house calls," I responded.

Early in my career, it became clear to me that it was imperative to meet patients where they are. This certainly applies to their emotional state. With celebrity and ultra-high net worth patients, however, it frequently applies to their physical state as well. As a result, I've worked with patients in their offices, spent time with them during family vacations, traveled with them on their private jets, and on many occasions, worked with them in their homes. This flexibility is central to my stance as a client-centered psychotherapist who practices through a feminist lens of collaboration. I don't consider it an extra service, but rather a service that's at the heart of culturally competent care.

"Where can I find you guys?"

I wrote down the address Scott gave me.

I knew the building well. It was one of the grand architectural dames lining Central Park West.

"What's a good time?" I asked.

"Morning," Scott replied instantly. "Before he starts into the day."

"How about ten or ten-thirty tomorrow morning?"

My suggestion was met with a long pause.

"Earlier?" I asked, uncomfortable with the silence.

Now it was Scott who chuckled. I took it as a good sign. At least he still had a sense of humor.

"Well, later actually. Mornings don't start here until about teatime."

The details of the situation came into sharper focus.

"That's fine. I'll come when you're finishing the crumpets. How about 2:00 p.m.?"

I intentionally built in a cushion. For elite patient populations, time is often an abstract concept. The truth of the matter is when you own the plane, it takes off when you arrive at the tarmac, not when United decides it will leave the gate. When I suggested to one patient that he set an alarm to arise before noon, he retorted, "Alarm clocks are for little people." I humorously suggested he shrink himself a bit and find one.

Hopefully, Scott didn't consider clocks beneath him and could pull Jonathan together for our scheduled appointment.

I hung up the phone. But before placing it in my bag, I did an online search of my newest patient.

Jonathan's name pulled up over thirty million hits. For some reason, this surprised me. Even though I knew he'd had a big career, I hadn't heard or seen much of him in well over a decade.

But while I was unaware of his comings and goings, an entire industry built on meanness and shame hadn't missed a single step of his journey. Their most recent postings chronicled Jonathan's infantile meltdowns in various restaurants and retail establishments around New York City, London, and Ibiza. I focused on the latest and most disturbing. Taken the night before, it showed Jonathan arguing with the *maître d'* at one of the Upper East Side's poshest restaurants. A group of patrons stared aghast at Jonathan and his wafer-thin date. The caption that ran with the image was vile and malicious.

Schadenfreude, the feeling of joy that one derives from the misfortune of others, was alive and thriving on the Internet— that was made clear by the abundant entries devoted to Jonathan's long-term decomposition. In fact, there's an entire media industry devoted to chronicling the fallen celebrity. Even IMDb.com, the website created to serve the entertainment industry, has a page devoted to reporting the descent of individuals among their tribe. Titled "Stars Who Faded from A List Stars to B List or Became Washed Up," the listing is not only mean-spirited, it's also downright wrong, for it demands that a Hollywood career must follow the pitch of a ladder rather than the trajectory of a jungle gym with its ups and downs, twists and turns (royals198569 2013).

I was thinking about the unfairness of these mean-spirited websites as I strolled across Central Park toward my meeting with Jonathan the following afternoon. With his building in view, I stopped at the edge of the park and admired its grandeur. The building stood like a fortress under a clear blue sky. In looking at it from my perspective, I got the sense that, while evils may happen around it, they dared not enter the building's shelter.

Feeling upbeat and confident, I crossed the street and entered the building. In the wood-paneled vestibule, I was met by not one, not two, but three imperious doormen. The eldest of the assemblage, a frail-looking, wispy-haired man who looked as if he were installed with the building's foundation, snipped, "May I help, sir?"

"Yes, I'm here to see Mr. Jonathan X."

Upon hearing the name, the frosted blockade melted slightly and a clipboard emerged bearing a list of preapproved names.

The velvet rope of privilege, I thought.

"Oh yes, sir, but of course. May I announce your arrival?"

I gave them my first name, but withheld my last. "Tell them Paul is here."

In working with ultra-high net worth and celebrity patients, the pinnacle of discretion is required. Even though the staff appeared dedicated, and I assumed Scott had given them my last name, the confidentiality of my patients belongs to them, not me. Plus, one never knows when even a trusted insider will turn and seek to profit from salacious information. Any search engine would reveal too much information about my practice and me. The last thing either one of us wanted was a mention in Page Six of the *Post*.

Ticking off my name from the list, I took on the position of a visiting dignitary. "Right away, sir."

The eldest of the lot directed me to Jonathan's apartment.

The number and its location, a low floor in the very back of the building, surprised me. My expectations had Jonathan occupying a sprawling penthouse, or even a duplex—one with numerous terraces capturing a stunning park view.

As I traversed deeper into the building's subprime real estate, my anxiety began to get the best of me. There were so many emotions feeding my reaction that I found it difficult to determine the root of what I was feeling. I stopped two doors away from Jonathan's to regain my composure. *Calm and composed. Grounded and focused,* I repeated over and over while breathing in and out deeply for a count of ten.

Once I'd calmed myself down, I continued on my journey.

The door to the apartment was ajar when I approached it.

Inside I could hear heels clicking on a bare wooden floor.

My hand half knocked, half pushed the door open. As the view widened, I slowly took in the contents of the postage-stamp-size room. Again, it was not at all what I was expecting. Although the building was majestic, this particular unit was humble, small, dark, and cramped.

"Oh, lovely, you found us." An overweight and balding man with sweat on his brow rushed up to greet me. I quickly surmised it was Jonathan's manager, Scott. And while Jonathan was nowhere in sight, I heard motion from behind a closed door that I assumed led into the only bedroom.

"Have a seat. Can I make you a coffee?" I declined the caffeine and searched for a seat that looked like it was meant for grown-up occupation.

And then, like the curtain of a grand stage rising, the creaking door to the cave-dark bedroom opened.

Jonathan came bounding through the door. With his clean-shaven face and bleached teeth blazing, he extended his manicured hand to greet me like a long-lost friend.

I detected mascara and foundation.

"Hey there. Thanks for coming over. I've heard great things about you. You've got an amazing reputation in this town, and it's a tough town. Boy, you're handsome too. I bet the ladies go crazy for you—maybe a few of the men. Can we get you something?"

I was an audience of one, but the apartment was so small that it was a sold-out show.

I looked out of the corner of my eye and caught Scott rolling his eyes in disgust—or was it adoration? The line's often quite thin between the two.

"No, I'm good. Let's have a seat and figure out what's going on here." I attempted to take charge and deflect Jonathan's pandering to my ego, but I failed. Instead of heeding my words, he steamrolled right over them.

"Well, I'll tell you what's going on here . . ." Jonathan started in.

I retreated to a chair that might have been comfortable for a teenager, but that was entirely unsuited for me, a middle-aged man with cranky knees.

For the next twenty minutes, Jonathan gave a bombastic performance.

He pontificated about his integrity, talent, and impeccable work ethic.

While he was stunningly brilliant, his colleagues were amateurish, vindictive, and malicious. No one accorded Jonathan the respect he deserved. Simply by virtue of showing up, he was performing a favor not just for the cast and crew, but for the entire nation as well.

About ten minutes into his dialogue, I got the message. Jonathan felt that he was a victim. Then, like everyone else in his life, I tuned him out.

To make use of the time, I occupied myself by focusing on the details of his apartment. I'm always on high alert for the unspoken details of a person's life. There's so much to glean from a person's home. As I frequently meet people in offices or locations that are for all intents and purposes *scrubbed* to present an image, I'm restricted to analyzing the details embedded in the clothes they wear and the accessories they use to adorn their bodies. Being provided access to Jonathan's home was a great privilege and an opportunity for clinical observations. I wanted to take full advantage of it.

The unit—tiny and suffocating—must have been part of the service quarters when the building was erected. His choice of accommodations told me he'd rather invest in looking good than in feeling comfortable. With its low ceiling, minimal light, and nonexistent view, it was an apartment you'd want to escape from rather than settle into. The art—and I use that term loosely—was nothing less than an homage to a former time. Old photographs and magazine covers of a young and handsome Jonathan stared back at me from every direction. The spectacle brought to mind one of my favorite lines from the classic film *Sunset Boulevard,* in which the character Joe Gillis tells Norma Desmond, "You're a woman of fifty, now grow up. There's nothing tragic about being fifty, not unless you try to be twenty-five."

Unfortunately, Jonathan suffered from the same delusions as Norma—that human love equaled object worship.

Avoiding Norma's and Joe's tragic endings meant finding compassion rather than disdain for Jonathan's deeply entrenched personality presentation. I was under no illusion, however, that the work would be easy or flow seamlessly, or that our trajectory would be linear.

Treating narcissistic patients, especially those who've been drinking in celebrity's seductive elixir for decades, is incredibly challenging. So challenging that Freud mistakenly believed that personality disorders became so entrenched by middle age that it was hopeless to treat them.

Today, however, we know Freud was wrong.

This realization stems from the scientific discovery that our brains, at all stages of our development, are elastic. And while deeply entrenched personality disorders cannot be surgically removed like tumors, they can be softened to enable the afflicted to enjoy a richer, more meaningful life. The key to this softening is going upstream to see when and how the personality disorder was embedded, and then working in the therapeutic relationship to provide the patient with a new relational experience that dislodges and diminishes the original template.

I was deep into these thoughts when the first act of Jonathan's performance ended. He stared at me expectantly, awaiting the applause he felt he'd clearly earned. I sat and stared back at him, hands folded in my lap, detached by his performance.

Finally, I responded.

"That's exhausting."

I intended my two simple words to capture the enormity of his personal complexity.

Clearly alarmed, Scott looked at me, then glanced frantically toward Jonathan; he was awaiting Jonathan's response but dreading his reaction.

I suspected my comment would garner discomfort, but a clinician's role isn't to be a constant source of sympathy and comfort. Patients need to be confronted with uncomfortable truths and challenged in their distortions. To move my patients in a reparative direction, I need to be honest with them—and with myself.

I also needed to tread lightly with Jonathan in our first encounter. Just as Jonathan was auditioning for me, I was auditioning for Jonathan. The questions about me that were going through his mind were the same ones that all powerful patients need to figure out before they engage in treatment: Was I smart enough? Was I successful enough while not being too successful to invoke envy or competition? And most importantly, was I trustworthy enough to be given the privilege of holding their unbearable truths?

But while I needed to walk lightly, I also needed to show him I was human and that his humanness had an impact on me.

And his presence was impactful.

Jonathan's compulsive striving for validation, which grew like a weed from a marsh of inadequacy, choked the life out of him and those around him.

I needed to let Jonathan know I felt his exhaustion in a

kind and gentle but also direct and unambiguous way. I didn't need to sympathize with the indignities Jonathan suffered or take sides. Most of all, I didn't need to tell him to be grateful for his life. With elite patient populations, this last intervention only adds to the shame of having so much and feeling so little.

What I needed to do was to let Jonathan know he was *seen* and *heard* as a human being rather than the *constructed* object of his celebrity. In so doing, I could open up the possibility of his being in an interpersonal relationship that was not just safe but also reparative and beneficial.

●

The capacity to just sit and feel the intense emotions that arise from an honest interpersonal engagement is at the heart of the psychotherapy I practice. The key is to acknowledge, feel, and bear witness to these emotions while modeling the capacity to tolerate the discomfort that arises from them. This approach requires confidence in one's clinical skills and a willingness to take calculated risks in patient engagement.

Early in my career, I would have been ruled by my own insecurities and rambled on. I would have felt compelled to sound intelligent, to come up with some elevated theoretical rationalization for my patients' plight. I'd mirror back their every word or adorn it with an established clinical formulation. In so doing, I was like flip-flops on winter feet—uncomfortable and overly ambitious.

With celebrity patients, the therapeutic engagement happens more slowly than with patients who live in states of diminished power. This is because these patients, in their state of elevated power, are prone to challenge and question the guidance of a professional they feel is beneath them. It's also a dynamic that has less tolerance for discomfort. While all human beings are hesitant to engage with anything that pinches and leaves blisters, people who've reached the rarefied realm of worldwide success—a feat that so defies the odds that it is akin to winning the lottery—have a diminished capacity for tolerating interpersonal discomfort.

This degree of hyper-agency is one of the three cultural markers that, through my research, I've found to define elite patients.

Through hyper-agency, these men and women can manipulate the externals of their lives to avoid any discomfort. While most of the world has to learn to tolerate inconvenience and unpleasant circumstances, the powerful can buy their way out of it. You don't want to fly across country commercial? No problem; within an hour you can be idling in your private jet. You want to avoid the inconveniences of a snowstorm in Manhattan? You can head down to your villa in Palm Beach. You don't like the way your therapist is challenging you? You can fire her and find another who will allow you to manipulate the relationship to suit your comfort and ego or crow that you're much smarter than any therapist.

For this reason, the most effective clinical interventions aren't the ones that *sound* impressive; they're the ones that resonate deep in both the patient's *and the therapist's* core as *feelings of connection*. But practicing at this level of intensity and exposure is exhausting. It requires treating professionals to be fully present to their patients. For me, this means maintaining a small clinical practice that has been as few as three and at most ten patients, couples, or families that I see in the course of a week.

The willingness to fully experience the patient's emotional pain is especially important for human beings who live at the remote ends of the socioeconomic and power bell curve. The powerless of our society need to know that someone sees them as having value to add to the world. The powerful need to be seen as human beings rather than mere objects of value.

Why? These disparate groups are objectified, labeled, and manipulated by the world around them but for very different reasons.

In our tribal, hierarchical, and patriarchal society, we've been acculturated to see the weak and the impoverished as being of lesser value to our society and to push them out of our tribe. To do this, we reduce the fullness of their being to one dominant label, a label that allows us to attack their character. For minorities who live in a state of diminished power, these labels include *lazy, welfare recipient,* and, of late, *immigrant.*

Conversely, we see the powerful and wealthy as being the recipients of luck and unearned privilege, as thieves and "robber barons." Again, we reduce the fullness of their being to a single label that defines them as an object of diminished character, an object that is clearly "not us." Once out of our tribe, we can enhance our sense of belonging to our self-identified tribe and use these "others" as scapegoats to explain our and our societies' ills. From a social standpoint, these labels are dangerous. They are at the heart of what has been called a *crisis of connection* that has led to an increase in income inequality, narcissism, anxiety, gun violence, violence against women, and the opioid epidemic (Way et al. 2018). From a clinical standpoint, the privileging of us over them is highly destructive to the patient and the profession.

To ameliorate our tendency to assign labels to others in the realm of psychotherapy, we must consciously strive to see our patients in the fullness of their being. One of the most effective ways to do this is through what is known as the biopsychosocial model of treatment (BPS). At the heart of BPS as well as client-centered psychotherapy, modalities on which I base my brand of treatment, is cultivating unconditional positive regard for our patients.

In 1977, Dr. George Engel revolutionized the field of medicine by stressing that, rather than just focusing on the symptoms of a patient's disease, it was critically important to know the fullness of a patient's life experience. Dr. Engel maintained that to effectively ameliorate suffering, healing professionals must go beyond the surface of their patients' pain and understand the deeper contextual frames within which they live as dynamic human beings. Such perspective requires an understanding of the biological, psychological, and social dimensions of each patient's illness (Borrell-Carrió, Suchman, and Epstein 2004). This approach has so much to teach us—clinician or not. By looking past a person's external veneer and developing empathy for the fullness of his or her being, we can heal and grow beyond the divisive stereotypes that have a pernicious impact on our personal and social well-being.

To be effective, therapy and treatment must work within the contextual frame of the systems in which the patient lives and breathes. One of the greatest disservices treatment professionals and facilities bestow on their patients is to view them as singular and unilaterally damaged entities void of context.

This phenomenon is obvious whenever a patient is brought in to therapy by a family member or some other person who demands that the clinician "fix" them. This approach is particularly acute in celebrity and ultra-high net worth families in which there is an individual who controls the patient's finances. These patients, not ready to be patients, are forced into facilities or brought to therapists' offices to be "fixed." Instead of being open to treatment, they become consumed by the desire, on both a conscious and an unconscious level, to retaliate against the people who've asserted their power over them in manipulative ways. The success rate of these forced clinical engagements is dismal, and some studies show they actually cause harm (Werb et al. 2016).

Therefore, it's of the utmost importance to understand the interpersonal dynamics at play and to consider them as a critical part of treatment before the identified patient is delivered to a treatment frame. In the field of addiction treatment, this is referred to as properly "teeing up" a case. This is why I will rarely agree to treat an individual if other members of the family do not participate in some capacity in the treatment process, ideally as patients on an equal footing with the identified patient.

This is also why treatment, especially treatment for personality disorders, tends to be of a longer duration and requires the involvement of significant relationships in the patient's life. Personality disorders like narcissism and borderline personality disorder typically take hold early in a patient's developmental path and do not develop in a silo. It's unethical to promise these patients and their families that these systemic disorders can be fixed overnight and without the involvement of those who are in relationship with the patient. Typically, however, there is huge resistance by these collateral relations to participate in treatment as fellow journeymen. The roles they're most comfortable in, and ones they have played for years, fall on two ends of a different power spectrum. The first is of a judging superior, wagging a judgmental and disapproving finger at the patient. Refusing to cede any of this power or admit any liability in supporting the patient's condition, they threaten, intimidate, and wield their power in destructive ways to keep the spotlight narrowly focused on the patient. Their position is usually that of a check writer who says literally and figuratively to the treatment professional, "Look, I'll pay your elevated fees, but leave me alone." But writing a check isn't enough, and in fact it only serves to enforce the destructive dynamics that need to be changed. In order for the patient and the patient's family to heal, the person with the financial power must begin to concede it, or else they will all remain trapped in relational dysfunction and personal pathology.

The second and very different position these relational members assume is that of a terrified and pathologically dependent caregiver. In this role, they cede their power to the identified patient while constantly scrambling to mitigate the damage that is erupting around them.

•

As these extremes related to my case at hand, it was a bit too early to tell where Scott fit into this dialectic. Fortunately, the sense I got from my initial meeting with Jonathan was that Scott was willing to actively participate in the therapeutic process. This was evidenced by the fact that he was with us in the room, not quaking behind a chair or rushing out expecting me to fix his problem. The details of their relationships could be fleshed out at a later time.

The first order of business was to determine if Jonathan and I felt comfortable enough in each other's presence to embark on a therapeutic journey together. I certainly felt up to the task, but Jonathan needed to feel that I was competent enough to hold the enormity of his pain and safe enough to be trusted with his vulnerabilities.

For patients who live in positions of elite power, this is a substantially higher threshold to meet—and maintain. These individuals have a heightened suspiciousness of outsiders. They're used to manipulating their world and the people in it to avoid discomfort, and they isolate to protect themselves from emotional and physical intrusions (Hokemeyer 2014). Like the Lannisters, the powerful family in *Game of Thrones*, they've mastered their power game by honing their ability to manipulate those around them while keeping the vast majority of people at a distance, isolating themselves to hold on to their positions and ostracizing anyone who threatens them. Yes, people who possess elite levels of power have figuratively mastered the game of thrones, but once situated in the castle, they find themselves obsessed about the treacherous forces waiting outside the gates, forces that—in their minds—will inevitably slay them.

With this in mind, I was unsure how Jonathan would respond to my reaction that his day-to-day experiences felt *exhausting*. Fortunately, my response didn't cause him to kick me out of his castle, like several other of my powerful patients have in the past.

My expulsion would come later.

Right now, it appeared Jonathan was intrigued enough to continue down the road of our engagement.

Jonathan paused thoughtfully before responding.

"Well, now that you mention it . . . *it is* exhausting." Jonathan seemed surprised by my observation, but lingered in it. Perhaps he'd never been able to articulate the elite power inherent in celebrity as something that has a dark side.

He certainly wouldn't have been my first famous patient who never allowed him- or herself insight into the true costs of celebrity.

Very few ever have.

And why would they? The hard work, discipline, and sacrifice it takes to attain a position of celebrity in any field, much less the fickle world of show business, is herculean.

In other words, celebrity is not a pot of gold at the end of the rainbow that you chance upon. The exhausting journey to get there extracts an enormous toll and an even more expensive price to maintain. Furthermore, to acknowledge the attainment of celebrity entirely diminishes the drive to continue attaining it. Accomplishing and preserving elite levels of success and celebrity demands blind adherence to a grueling path that, as one of my female patients declared, "beats the sh*t out of you."

Perhaps Jonathan expected me to fall in line with the legions of sycophants in his life who blindly affirmed his rages and rants and confirmed that yes, he was a victim. Or perhaps he expected me to be a stern taskmaster, a hyper-controlling agent who demanded he fit into a box and become an object to supply narcissistic needs of my own.

I needed to be aware of these expectations and artfully maneuver to avoid them.

"I'm not really sure how you've been able to keep it together this long," I stated. "Most people would have thrown in the towel a long time ago."

Jonathan looked at me suspiciously. A master player always senses when there's a potential of being played.

"What do you mean?" Jonathan articulated each and every word. His paranoia crept into the room like fog rolling over a beach.

I needed to retreat and allow our visibility to improve.

"What I mean is that for decades, hell I don't know, maybe your whole life, you've been under the pressure to perform, to succeed against incredible odds. I mean how many people make it in your field? The odds are stacked against you."

I could feel Jonathan starting to relax.

I continued to wade out through the shoals, closer toward his truth.

"Listen, Jonathan. You're a celebrity. I know that, you know that, hell, the whole world knows that. Let's not pretend you have some normal life, hanging out with the guys after work, going on a Disney cruise to the Bahamas with your kids once a year. Wondering how you're going to pay for their college. You occupy a very lonely space, you live in a rarefied world, and you get the sh*t kicked out of you for the privilege."

The beach on which we sat got warmer, lighter as the fog pulled back.

We sat and looked at each other, searching.

Although Jonathan had been a celebrity for decades and was easily recognized by millions around the world, I sensed this was one of the rare times he'd felt truly seen for who he was and the pressures he lived with rather than the fiction people demanded him to be.

People see celebrities all the time. There's a whole industry devoted to "celebrity sightings." What you really see, however, is their veneer and the objects that adorn their bodies—their hair, their cars, their "cribs," their handbags, their arm candy. And while this perspective serves the viewer, it diminishes the viewed. Treating a celebrity patient requires the clinician to transcend the veneer and x-ray into the depths of the patient's psyche. In this regard, the therapeutic process must penetrate. Challenge. Inspire. Hold. It must tap into the psychic pain that's shared by both the clinician and the patient and move both incrementally toward a transformation.

One of my favorite quotes about the nature of an effective psychotherapeutic relationship is from Dr. Carl Jung, a Swiss psychiatrist and founder of analytical psychology. It's an overused quote, but with good reason. In *Memories, Dreams, Reflections* (1963), Dr. Jung described the connection that's required in a reparative psychotherapeutic relationship as follows:

> The meeting of two personalities is like the contact of two chemical substances: if there is any reaction, both are transformed.

On that afternoon in Jonathan's humble home, tucked away in the back of a grand building, Jonathan and I connected not in the strength of his celebrity, but in its weakness. I wasn't there as an adoring fan looking for perfection, but rather as a flawed human being, looking for connection.

Over the next two years, I met with Jonathan on a weekly

basis. For the first six months, Scott accompanied Jonathan to our sessions. Although he said very little, his presence spoke volumes. From a psychological perspective, Scott served as Jonathan's transitional object. He soothed Jonathan while Jonathan developed a capacity to trust not just me, but also the therapeutic process.

The notion of a transitional object is not new. It was first articulated by Dr. Donald Winnicott, an English pediatrician and psychoanalyst (Litt 1986). Dr. Winnicott observed that young children used objects to self-soothe while they were separated from their primary caregivers. Typically, these objects were favorite toys or a soft blanket. Two defining features of such objects are their ability to retain their meaning even in the face of anger and that their overall value never changes—unless the child decides to change it (Winnicott 1958).

Although Jonathan physically matured out of infancy about six decades ago, emotionally he remained trapped in his infancy, clinging to objects for a sense of security and comfort. In this regard, Jonathan was like most of the elite power patients I treat. For these individuals, a best friend or closest companion is someone who will withstand their wrath—and never leave them. Typically, these people are on their payroll in some capacity. It could be they are the beneficiary of a trust they control, or a spouse or ex who hasn't developed a capacity to support him- or herself, or a housekeeper or professional who is a paid agent. Through this financial arrangement, all engagement and interaction is affected and controlled by the power held over others.

To maintain this power over others requires constant vigilance and extraordinary expenditures of energy. The more

Jonathan's celebrity faded, the more he grasped for transitional objects to soothe and validate him—and the more depleted he became. The less he was seen as an object of male virility, the more he became seen as a "f*ckup."

Motivated by a toxic combination of desperation and exhaustion, Jonathan made inappropriate choices that diminished his psyche and esteem. Veneer eclipsed authenticity. The cheapest unit in one of the most expensive buildings in Manhattan looked great from the outside but was cramped and uncomfortable from within. The inappropriate "girlfriends" on his arm looked good for the paparazzi but left him feeling like a predator the other twenty-three hours in the day. The collagen he injected in his lips made him look like a cartoon character. His narcissistic rage gave him a temporary sense of empowerment but burnt out those around him.

This last manifestation was evidenced to me when I learned that, at the time of our first meeting, Scott was planning his escape. Like many others before him, Scott had had enough.

"I was heading back to the UK once I had you in place," Scott admitted to me about a month into treatment.

Fortunately, Scott didn't immediately leave; he stuck around for over a year thereafter. During that time, we moved Jonathan's attachment to Scott onto me, and ultimately to himself and healthier relationships.

About six months into treatment, however, Jonathan fired me via email.

"Thanks, you've been great. But I don't think this is going anywhere. We're just covering the same old ground, beating a dead horse."

My dismissal didn't come as a surprise. I'd been expecting it.

In our prior session, we discussed sexual behaviors in Jonathan's adolescence. He and his best friend, Marc, would masturbate together looking at old *Playboy* magazines after school in Jonathan's bedroom. One day, his mother, a devout Christian, came home early from her job and caught the boys in action. She "went hysterical" and condemned them both to "eternal damnation." To add insult to injury, she dragged Jonathan to their pastor for his intervention with the behavior. He insisted on having a community ritual to exorcise Satan, arguing that was "who'd clearly possessed him."

Jonathan's sharing this incredibly hurtful memory with me was monumental in his recovery and our relationship, but it reopened the betrayal, shame, and humiliation he was forced to endure at the hands of his mother and his religious community.

That Jonathan needed some time to regain his sense of agency and control over our relationship was completely understandable. I allowed him his space and time. It was surprising, however, that he was able to do that in exactly ten days.

Less than two weeks later, I was relieved to hear Jonathan on my voicemail. "Hey, Dr. Paul, Jonathan here. Listen, I need to run something by you. Can you give me a ring?"

While I expect to be fired, even serially fired, by patients who present with narcissistic and borderline personality disorders, it still stings when I'm summarily dismissed. Like my patients, and every other human being walking this earth, I get hurt when people I care for reject me. While I try to take to heart the wisdom of William James that we discussed earlier this chapter, it's challenging to hold the initial discomfort of a patient's rejection along with the opposing reality that rejection is a necessary step in my patient's reparative process.

Welcoming some relief from my bruised ego, I immediately returned Jonathan's call.

Ten minutes into our call, where I was giving him some advice on what to buy Scott for a birthday gift, he bellowed, "You know, you're a f*cking smart guy. What do you say we pick things up again?"

Now it was me who needed to be on high alert for ego inflation. Like the Mercedes idling at the curb after my TV interview, Jonathan's praise made me feel on top of my game and willing to forget about the distress and insecurities I felt from his shutting me out of his life.

Three weeks later, I got around to discussing my reaction to his rejection. He needed to hear that his actions had consequences that caused me to feel insecure and inferior.

"Really?" Jonathan was stunned to hear that I was affected by his email.

"Yes, really. You think you're the only one with an ego that's easily bruised in this relationship?" I said with a frosting of humor that revealed the nourishment of truth.

Jonathan smiled. "I guess not."

From that point on, we began to sit together as peers, equals in our imperfections and hypersensitive dispositions. But rather than see these vulnerabilities as weaknesses to be banished from his existence, Jonathan felt the richness of the connection they created between us. It was the planting of a seed in his soul that would eventually grow into a sapling—a fully living being who could bend but not break, feel but not be overwhelmed by his feelings, and grow into a sturdier, healthier human being.

2.

Inadequacy

Imposter Syndrome and Hiding in the Spotlight

I am not a writer.
I've been fooling myself and other people.
—JOHN STEINBECK

The chauffeur greeting me at Zurich's Kloten Airport was tall and blond with piercing blue eyes that radiated from deep within a chiseled face. He was impeccably dressed in a black suit that whispered, "I'm custom. I'm cashmere. And I'm expensive." An embodiment of the rarefied and privileged environment in which I'd just landed, even the sign he rested on the banister to greet my arrival was perfectly executed—crisp, clear, and understated. Instead of using my full surname, the sign read simply "Dr. H." It was an elegant and discrete foreshadowing of the culture in which I was about to partake. Understanding I was entering a world with different cultural norms, I approached the figure tentatively, intimidated and yet seduced.

"Dr. Hoke-a-meyer." He stated my name as a fact with perfect pronunciation.

"*Oui, monsieur,*" I responded intuitively in French, then immediately recognized my error.

Zurich, not Geneva, you idiot. They speak Swiss German here.

I was stunned, but not surprised, by the viciousness of my own thoughts, as well as the tone with which I was castigating myself. I can go from feeling on top of the world to not worthy of being in it with dizzying speed.

My career is a great source of pride for me, as it is for so many people I've worked with as a therapist. Having worked hard and taken risks to evolve my career, I've developed a niched practice of which I'm proud. However, even at this stage of my career, negative self-talk can still rear its vicious head—especially when I'm feeling nervous and intimidated.

I was excited to be flying into Zurich for a work opportunity; it felt affirming and luxurious to be respected enough to have one of my consulting clients send an elegant driver to collect me from the airport and deliver me to the suite they were providing me during my trip. But in the midst of such an opportunity, or perhaps I should say *because* I was in the middle of such an elegant, beautiful situation, the part of me that doesn't feel elegant, beautiful, or polished overanalyzed everything.

I turned a small European dialectical error into an American supersized one. I greeted my contact at the airport with a response in French instead of German. It meant nothing to my driver, but it shattered my psyche like a crystal glass being crushed under the *chuppah* at a Jewish wedding.

With position and attainment, we expect negative feelings of self-worth to go away. When we've accomplished the things we've always dreamt about and built solid reputations, we assume there'd be no reason for such negative emotions to pop up.

But they do.

When a person struggles with negative feelings of self-worth, of having value, and of being worthy of love in their early years, they become imprinted to live in a state of compulsive aspiration. *If I can just catch that lucky break, get rich, or find my way out of Smallsville to a cosmopolitan metropolis, I'll finally feel safe and grounded.*

We assume that, in the process of becoming, transforming, and attaining, the fears that have darkened our pasts will dissipate. But that's very often just not the case.

While feelings of unworthiness often push us in an aspirational direction, personal growth is not linear. It meanders and turns like San Francisco's famous Lombard Street.

Such has certainly been the case for me.

I wish I could say the professional validation I enjoy at this stage of my career has completely filled that void I first felt as a young boy in Maryland and eliminated the harsh voices with which I still lash out at myself, *but it hasn't.* It's definitely helped—but the external success on its own has not been enough to move me in a reparative direction. This is because the internal messages of being less than were encoded in my psyche early in life, and they remain strong enough to drown out the oxygenation that has come from my external markers of success.

While I'm happy with my career, and I'm proud of what I've managed to accomplish, these indicia of success are not enough to protect me from my internal insecurities and thought distortions. The reparation that I have been able to internalize has come from forming new interpersonal relationships and incorporating intrapersonal mindfulness techniques. Central to these tools are the principals of rational emotive behavior therapy (REBT) (Ellis 1994). The basic premise of

REBT is that it's not the circumstances of our lives that cause us emotional distress, but how we perceive these circumstances (Ellis 2001). The main task of REBT is to identify, evaluate, and replace distorted and untrue thoughts with more accurate ones that enhance rather than diminish our emotional well-being (Albert Ellis Institute n.d.). In short, it means stopping the cycle of negative thoughts long enough to clean off the lens of our perceptions.

In my case, I began my recalibration by pulling myself into the factual details of my physical presence in Zurich. I focused my attention on the here and now and re-evaluated the circumstances, and in so doing, I moved my reactions away from the emotional part of my brain and into my cognition.

In evaluating the facts through my prefrontal cortex rather than my amygdala, I realized they couldn't be better.

I was traveling to Zurich as the guest of one of the world's most exclusive residential treatment programs. We were scheduled to strategize about a joint project in London. I'd looked forward to this moment for months and valued the team of clinicians with whom I was about to collaborate. The flight over from London had been a breeze. Unlike air travel in the United States, flights between European countries are seamless. I arrived in one of my favorite cities and was received as a dignitary by a man who looked like he'd be cast as the next James Bond.

Recognizing these truths enabled me to regain my composure.

I continued my recalibration: *Okay, Hokemeyer, pump the brakes on the crazy train. You're nervous.* By calling myself out and incorporating a bit of humor, I immediately felt better. I continued my internal dialogue: *Look, you want to be here, and* *you won't be here forever. Next week you'll be schlepping up to the E train in Manhattan, dodging dog sh*t and puddles.* Although the words I used were a bit more crass than those I'd use with my patients, they worked. My rational voice quieted my irrational feelings.

In my newfound emotional and physical equilibrium, I made my final approach to the chauffeur and extended my hand.

He promptly rejected it.

Ouch. I started to sink once again into a swamp of negative thoughts and uncomfortable emotions but stopped myself short. I glanced back again down at my feet and mumbled the word *stop*. In the pause that ensued, I realized I needed to allow an officious Swiss man to do his official Swiss duty. It wasn't that he didn't like me; it was that he was focused on doing his job. Instead of reaching for my hand, he reached to relieve me of my hand luggage.

"Da bag please, Doctor." I surrendered my roll-aboard with a chuckle.

"Hi there. I'm Dr. Paul. *Und du?*" My German is pathetic, but I thought I'd give it a good old American try.

"Julian," Mr. Gorgeous replied.

Oh, of course, I thought. *Perfect name.* He had the same name and the same seductive quality as the young Richard Gere in *American Gigolo.* I found the connection amusing.

"Dis way please, Doctor." Like the beautiful gold Swiss watch that poked out discreetly from under his starched white cuff, Julian was a model of mechanical precision. I enthusiastically complied, waddling behind him like a duckling obediently following its mother.

As we walked through the lobby of the airport, I continued to savor the details of my experience.

The building was a mastery of honed gray stone, warm brown paneling, and walls of glass that whispered, "Don't worry. Nothing bad can possibly happen here—and if it does, we promise to keep it our secret." In contrast to the run-down and chaotic airports I typically travel through in the United States, such as LaGuardia in New York and LAX in Los Angeles, Zurich's Kloten felt like a museum. The scene that unfolded between its soaring roof and honed marble floor played out like exquisitely rendered performance art, symbolizing understated grace and grandeur.

I savored a moment of gratitude for being part of the collection.

Just when I thought it couldn't get any more privileged, it did.

As the massive glass doors silently slid open to the crisp alpine air, I followed Julian toward an immaculate black Bentley parked at the curb. So shiny and clean was the coach that it mirrored back the glory of the snowcapped Alps far off on the horizon. For some reason, the license plate of the coach caught my attention. It, like everything else thus far in my Swiss excursion, was a composition of restrained dignity and class. In contrast to the loud and garish vanity plates I see around places like Malibu, New York City, and resort towns in Colorado—plates that read FAB1!, HOTMD, and SPOILD—this one consisted of three seemingly arbitrary letters and a number. I later learned that having a license plate with so few characters is one of the highest status symbols in Switzerland (Bernath 2017). The fewest identifiers on a license plate garner the highest value. In a country where nearly everyone is assumed to be über-rich, a license plate with a few characters quietly shows you have social status *and* vaults of money.

Julian opened the back door, and I slid into my seat. Running my hands over the cream leather of the customized coach, I admired the walnut insets and thick plush carpets. Bentley's tagline, *be extraordinary,* ran through my head. But rather than feeling extraordinary, my self-doubt returned with a vengeance. *You're not cut out for this. Why are you doing this?*

Transported back to the Gordian knot of emotions I experienced when I left the TV interview and was intoxicated by the seduction of a well-equipped Mercedes, I realized there was clearly more centering work I needed to undertake before meeting with my client.

Working at this elevated level of professional engagement entails managing lofty expectations and hypercritical judgments. The power dynamics involved with elite clientele are intense and draining, and the risk of being rejected by this group as an outsider, not worthy of entry into the inner sanctuary of their power, is great. In spite of these challenges and potential obstacles, I'm drawn to the challenge of working with any population that is underserved and in desperate need of culturally competent and excellent clinical care. Doing so with success, however, demands I center myself in an artful calibration of confidence and humility.

It's stressful and exhausting.

So why do I continue?

Because walking through my fears and insecurities enables me to continue to grow as a professional who has an obligation to help human beings heal while doing what I can to close the social and political divisions that are destroying the relational well-being of our families and our world. It's a lofty goal, but that's the point. Creating a new paradigm of clinical treatment requires a "think globally, act locally" approach.

And yes, treating patients who live in positions of elite power has exposed me to opulence and luxury I never even knew existed. I've had the privilege of becoming professionally intimate with people who travel in private jets, holiday in mega yachts, and live in homes that could carry their own zip codes. But while in many ways it is glamorous and exciting, it's also had a pernicious impact on my self-concept and self-worth by causing me to suffer from feeling like an imposter, unworthy of walking in such rarefied shoes. It's also shown me that my patients, men and women who live in positions of elite power and privilege, feel the very same core feelings of unworthiness as me.

One of my patients, a middle-aged woman who achieved iconic status by creating an Internet property and selling it for hundreds of millions of dollars, described it perfectly: "No matter how many times people tell me I'm successful, I'm always going to be that poor girl from Indiana playing dress-up in princess clothes."

I've found that, regardless of how a person's status was attained, even the most bellicose self-made titans—when they are truly honest—admit to feeling like imposters, not worthy of their successes. They, like me, still are ruled by the voices of their past that tell them they're insufficient, too fat, not smart enough, not from the right side of the tracks. Yes, they might have done a fantastic job hiding the negative thoughts under a layer of bling and bravado, but a varnish only covers the grain. It doesn't reconfigure it. The key to quieting these voices, as we'll see in chapter 8, is reconfiguring the grain by examining it in a therapeutic relationship with an empathetic other, a relationship that's built on the foundation of a collaborative engagement, in a humanistic stance, and through a Socratic inquiry.

If a person attains a position of elite power without doing this supplementary work, they will find, like Jonathan found, that these internal voices that tell them they're a fraud only grow louder, amplified by the resentment and critical voices of the choruses of haters who want to see them fail. Other professionals have empirically noted this phenomenon as well.

Although not recognized by the *DSM-5* as an official diagnosis, psychologists and other professionals who work with driven and successful people acknowledge that most suffer from what is known as *imposter syndrome*. Clinical psychologists Pauline Clance and Suzanne Imes first articulated the construct in their work with successful women. They observed a pernicious and persistent belief that in spite of their success, these women "believe that they are not intelligent, capable or creative." According to Clance and Imes, while these individuals are "highly motivated to achieve," they also "live in fear of being 'found out' or exposed as frauds" (Clance and Imes 1978).

At the heart of their motivation to achieve is a compulsive pull toward perfection. But perfection is a tricky concept. At its core, it's elusive and subjective. So much so that it's impossible to define or attain. What this means is that people who feel the pull toward perfection are always striving toward something almost impossible to define and communicate with others, which increases their sense of isolation.

One of my patients, an artist who found enormous financial and critical acclaim for his work as an abstract landscape painter, relayed how painful it was for him to turn a canvas over to his dealer for sale. "They couldn't care less that the work's not ready. I mean, the paint's not even dry, and they're shoving it in the back of a van to be delivered to some Russian billionaire." When asked when he last painted a painting that he considered fully finished, he stared back at me, confused at the notion of "finished." "Well, now that I think about it . . . never. They can always be better."

Unfortunately, the compulsive pull toward perfection can lead down a trail of emotional destruction and creative paralysis. The internationally renowned author Brené Brown warns of the destructive force inherent in perfectionism. In *The Gifts of Imperfection: Let Go of Who You Think You're Supposed to Be and Embrace Who You Are*, she writes, "Research shows that perfectionism hampers success. In fact, it's often the path to depression, anxiety, addiction, and life paralysis." She further notes: "Perfectionism is a self-destructive and addictive belief system that fuels this primary thought: If I look perfect, and do everything perfectly, I can avoid or minimize the painful feelings of shame, judgment, and blame" (Brown 2010).

While nearly all of the men and women I've treated in the field of the arts eventually come forward with their fear of being "discovered as a fraud," as Clance and Imes have shown, individuals who are highly motivated to achieve, including those outside of creative fields, often suffer from perfectionism and imposter syndrome. Business executives have talked openly about this phenomenon. Sheryl Sandberg, the author of *Lean In* and chief operating officer of Facebook, described perfectionism as an "enemy" that causes disappointment and hinders success (Russell n.d.). Seth Godin, the world's leading expert on marketing in the Internet age, constantly advocates for his millions of disciples to abandon their pursuit of perfection. According to Godin, "Perfect lets you stall, ask more questions, do more reviews, dumb it down, safe it up, and generally avoid doing anything that might fail" (Godin 2015).

Because imposter syndrome is so prevalent among the celebrities and actors I've treated, its presence in this particular group provides a foundation from which to explore the issue more deeply. Many of the world's leading actors have been brave enough to publicly share how this syndrome has affected them. These include the Oscar-nominated and Emmy Award–winning actor Don Cheadle. In describing how he feels in his performances, Cheadle told the *Los Angeles Times*, "All I can see is everything I'm doing wrong, that is a sham and a fraud" (Lee 2004). Other exceptionally talented and successful performers who have spoken publicly about feeling like an imposter in their success include the brilliant Tom Hanks. In an interview on National Public Radio, he spoke of the connection he felt with a character who suffered from self-doubt. In reflecting back on his own experience of climbing up the ladder of success, Hanks remarked, "No matter what we've done, there comes a point where you think, 'How did I get here? When are they going to discover that I am, in fact, a fraud and take everything away from me?'" (National Public Radio 2016). Other highly acclaimed performers who have shared their struggles with feeling like an imposter under their mantle of success include Tina Fey, Meryl Streep, Robert Pattinson, Jennifer Lopez, Daniel Radcliffe, and Lady Gaga (*Marie Claire* 2016).

As noted by Brené Brown, there is a strong connection between the compulsive pull toward perfectionism and a host of addictive disorders. This is because alcohol, drugs, and dopamine-inducing behaviors like sex and disordered eating quiet critical voices and numb feelings of inadequacy. One of my patients, a well-known television actor, said, "The Xanax keeps me from obsessing how bad I was that day. If I don't take it, I just obsess about the dailies."

But the relief one derives from these self-medicating techniques is short-lived and leads to feelings of worthlessness and despair. This is why the mindfulness techniques I used on my arrival to Zurich, which teach our brains to stop our negative thoughts and replace them with more loving ones, are highly effective. Instead of diminishing us, they imbue us with a sense of agency over our lives.

Through my work, however, I've found a distinct and ironic gender bias in who uses these techniques and how they are embraced. My patients who are attuned to typically feminine traits of privileging their emotions and relationships have a much easier time with these techniques than do my male patients who tend to be self-reliant rather than relational and privilege intellect over emotions and intuition. Those in the latter group find these techniques a bit "airy fairy." They'd much rather pop a pill to fill the cracks in the walls of their psyche than spend the time and energy to enhance the stability of its foundation. Many of these patients who live in the masculine binary go to extreme measures to deny and hide their self-doubt and insecurities through veneers of bravado while squawking about their positions of elite power.

Like peacocks, these men strut around boasting their success and bragging about their wealth, while inside, their internal dialogue is telling them a dramatically different story. Mark was a patient I treated for a mélange of issues, including sexual compulsivity, addiction to prescription pain medication, alcohol and marijuana abuse, anxiety, narcissism, and dependent personality disorder. Underlying each of the issues was the persistent voice that told him he was a fraud, unworthy of his success.

•

I was winding my way back to New York City from Boston on a standing-room-only train in the early evening when Mark's initial call came in. About an hour outside of Boston, near Providence, Rhode Island, I finally managed to wrangle a place to sit. Dropping down into the small seat, exhausted and feeling drained, my phone began ringing loudly. My fellow passengers, clearly feeling just as tired, looked at me with great disdain, telepathically communicating, "Turn off your phone, as*hole." A professorial-looking chap across the aisle went a step further. Pointing to the sign at the end of the coach, he mouthed "Quiet Car" from under his reading glasses.

Great, I thought, *nothing like being shamed at the start of a long journey.*

I searched for my phone in the seemingly hundreds of pockets in my cavernous bag but failed to find it. After what felt like an eternity, the phone went silent and the caller was transferred to voicemail. Relief finally punctured my shame.

I'll deal with it tomorrow, I thought, grateful the phone had stopped ringing.

After five minutes of bumping along, however, my curiosity and guilt about ignoring the call got to me. *What if it's an emergency?* I retrieved the phone from my bag and listened to the message.

A loud and pressured voice began speaking. "Yes. Hello? I think this damn thing's recording." Papers were shuffling in the background. It was clear the caller was distracted. "So my wife got your name from . . . well it doesn't matter who. She said I need to contact you and schedule a meeting. All right then." Click. End of call.

No name. No callback number.

Oh great, I thought. *This one's going to be a handful.* I smiled at the prospect of working with another powerful and demanding patient.

The notion of "difficult patients" is not new or unique to the field of behavioral health. The concept originated in the field of medicine and refers to the clinician's reactions to patients who seek attention and are demanding, aggressive, rude, and ungrateful (Steinmetz and Tabenkin 2001). Many therapists view belligerent, powerful, and narcissistic men and women as difficult patients and willingly or unwillingly punish them for being who they are. In so doing, they commit grave errors. Not only do they send these patients running for the door, they deny themselves the richness of working in the full and honest expression of the patient's experience.

As a result of their status, many of my patients can be classified as difficult. People who occupy positions of elite power in our society are expected to act and look a certain elevated, removed way; as a result, they become hyper-demanding in their lives in order to be seen and heard as human beings with actual needs when they finally reach out for help. A young starlet whom I treated for heroin addiction summed it up perfectly: "Everyone is constantly biting out chunks of my flesh. It not only hurts, but it's also f*cking exhausting. I have to go scream just to be heard. I have to whack 'em in the eye just to let them know I need something. Then of course, I'm the b*tch, the diva!" At the heart of such behavior is a desperate cry to be seen for more than their exterior and accepted for who they are as opposed to what they are when they are in physical and emotional pain. Another middle-aged patient who attained celebrity status as an Olympic athlete said, "When people see me, they see my gold medals. When I really need to have my needs met, I have to scream and create a ruckus. If I don't, I'll just be another has-been, memorialized in a selfie in some stranger's iPhone."

At a clinical level, getting past the gilt of awards, medals, and achievements so that "difficult" patients can be treated for any combination of conditions requires the treating professional to diligently work to establish a connection to the patient through empathy, collaboration, nonjudgmental listening, and respectful curiosity (Steinmetz and Tabenkin 2001).

Pausing and calibrating oneself before responding to a patient's bark is critical to this equation. The professional needs to be in the right frame of mind and body before he or she can develop a fruitful relationship with a demanding patient. With this in mind, rather than immediately responding to the unidentified caller who was looking to be my next challenging patient, I glanced around the crowded cabin and made an executive decision to shut Dr. Paul down for the evening. Hungry, a bit angry, a little lonely, and extremely tired, I was not in the proper frame of mind or body to engage with the caller. A good night's sleep and a proper meal would put us both on stronger footing to begin our psychotherapeutic journey.

•

The next morning, I retrieved the number from my phone and called it. No one picked up. Actually, I didn't expect anyone to. In this day and age of texting and email, telephone conversations—unless scheduled in advance—simply don't happen.

My call went into a mechanical, system-generated voicemail. *No one is available to take your call.*

I left a simple message with my number.

"Yes, this is Dr. Hokemeyer. I missed your call last night. Please call me back at your convenience. Thank you."

No sooner had I placed my phone down when it sprang back to life. I recognized the number as the one I'd just dialed.

"Dr. Hokemeyer," I answered officiously.

"Yes, this is Mark." The voice on the other end sounded gentle and contrite. It stood in sharp contrast to the belligerent voice that left a message about fifteen hours earlier. The voice on the other end of the line continued tenuously, "You said I called you last night."

Oh my, I thought, *Maybe he doesn't recall calling me.* This wouldn't be the first time a patient called me in a blackout.

I responded in a way I hoped wouldn't shame him. "Well, yes, this number anyhow. Someone left a message about his wife suggesting they call me. I'm a marriage and family therapist."

There was a moment of silence on the other end that

pulsated with anxiety. I sensed he was trying to piece together the details of the night before through its fog.

Mark cleared his throat and regained his swagger. "Oh yes, of course. I make a lot of calls at the end of the day. My secretary just gives me a call sheet. Can you spell your last name for me?"

As I went through the spelling of my last name, I heard the clicking of a keyboard. Perhaps he was going through his call log. Perhaps he was returning emails. In any event, his story didn't resonate with me as true. I doubted his secretary would be reminding him to call a marriage therapist. My intuition told me he was stalling and buying time.

"Sounds like you have a busy life." Again, I intended my comment to allow him some room. There are plenty of people in a patient's life who feel compelled to shame them for their condition. My role isn't to shame, but rather to provide a place of dignity where they can heal.

Mark responded after a pause that was filled with more clicking of a keyboard. "Well, yes, I'm busy . . ." (click, click, click). "And yes, it does . . ." (click, click, click) ". . . seem like I called" (click, click, click, click). "Just found my call notes."

"Great. Are you free to talk now?"

"Yes, in fact I am. It's an unpleasant matter."

"That I suspect; people don't tend to call me when it's smooth sailing. But even the best sailors find themselves in choppy seas." I was impressed by my metaphor.

"That's right. Do you sail?" Mark's voice transmuted from mouse to magnate.

"I have in the past. It's a lot of work, though. I'm more of a Jet Ski kind of guy."

I wanted him to know I was human and not afraid to share appropriate details of my personal life. If I expected him to share the details of his, I couldn't be cold and withholding.

"I thought you sailed because you go to the St. Barths Bucket."

Mark's comment startled me. How in the world would he know that? Sure, I was happy to share some of the details of my life, but judiciously, on my terms and where clinically appropriate.

Once again, I needed a second to recalibrate before responding.

"Do I know you from St. Barths?"

Mark's transformation was complete. He now let me know in no uncertain terms he was the captain of this charter.

"No. But I know quite a bit about you."

Suddenly, it became crystal clear to me what all the clicking was about. The whole time we'd been talking, he'd been on the keyboard of his computer, searching the web for the details of my life. The only place I'd ever mentioned St. Barths was on my personal Facebook page; he'd been successful in mining it.

Even though I'm very conscientious and intentional about what I post online, I still feel slightly violated when someone lets me know they've "searched" me. This, of course, is a function of my age. As a middle-aged man, I've come to value privacy. However, so much of our culture is on social media that there are times I willingly surrender privacy for a few seconds of virtual pleasure and a fleeting sense of connection.

I'm still unresolved in the Faustian bargain.

In any event, I was impressed with his cunning. *Aren't you a clever bugger?* I thought.

I also realized he was making a tactical play. While initially caught off guard in what I suspected was a moment of drug- or alcohol-induced haze, he quickly regained his power and was attempting to define the rules of our engagement. It was a playbook my patients have pulled out hundreds of times. In it, he would work to maintain the upper hand, calling the shots from his position of superior knowledge and intellect. If I got out of line, he could maneuver me back in—or terminate our engagement.

I responded as calmly as I could. "Oh right, the power of the Internet. Everyone can google anyone these days. Did you find anything interesting about me?"

"Not really." He too was trying to be cool. Like a professional poker player, he would try to avoid emotional vulnerability at all costs. Emotions are messy, not to be trusted with the randomness of what he suspected a clinical engagement would require. To be successful in this task, he'd need to have a logical, analytical reason for every move he made.

And at this level of our engagement, so did I.

"Can't imagine you would. I lead a rather prosaic life." It seemed best to keep the conversation moving and let him think he had the upper hand, because he did. The truth is that all patients who suffer from behavioral and physical health issues have the upper hand. Free will and internal motivation are essential features of the healing process. If patients aren't ready to change, then they won't. There are simply too many forces in play to keep them trapped in their disease, including defense mechanisms such as denial and rationalization, the sheer terror of change, the power certain diseases have in impacting a patient's capacity to think clearly, and the people around patients who consciously and unconsciously want to keep them trapped in their condition.

"In your message last night, you mentioned your wife. Does this have to do with her, or your marriage, perhaps? Or is it maybe about a kid? I get a lot of calls from parents about their kids." Yes, I was rambling, but I wanted to give him plenty of room so as not to trap him in the role of the identified patient, the person who carries the weight of the entire family's conflicts. We'd eventually get to the fine points of the truth. Right now, I just needed the broad strokes.

"Yes, it's my wife. She's always freaking out over something. Usually women that she's convinced I'm mixed up with." I made note of the fact that he used the plural form of *woman* and referred to them as *that* instead of *whom*. It's always telling when someone refers to others as objects rather than people—even if only subconsciously.

He continued: "This time, it's the sous chef we had on our yacht this winter. I mean, first of all, like I'd screw the help, and second, like I'd screw the help with the kids around."

Perhaps he had a point. Perhaps he didn't. His rationale was weak at best. It was, however, illuminating. It indicated he probably had a history of infidelities that eroded the trust and integrity of his marriage and that he was a man of great financial means who flaunted his wealth and who could quickly be incited to belligerence.

"Right. So what are you thinking? I deal with these sorts of situations all the time. We would need to—"

Mark interrupted me. "Can you get her off my back?"

I smiled and clicked my pen on my desktop. Outside, the

rain formed a river down East Fifty-Eighth Street. An elderly woman with a broken umbrella artfully managed both herself and her white lap dog across it.

I drew my attention back to the call, "That . . . I'm not sure about. We certainly can take a look at it."

"How? I mean listen, I'm not going to come in there and be the villain. Been there, done that. Paid a fortune, and it didn't work. I apologize and apologize. I mean, she's got an amazing life. Never worked a day—"

Now it was my turn to interrupt. "So it sounds like this isn't your first time at the rodeo?"

"No, like the third or fourth."

I shuddered at the thought of being one of several clinicians to be fired for not allowing an infidelity, or serial infidelities, to go unresolved. I found myself losing my patience with him already. I searched for the woman and the dog, but they were well beyond my sight line.

"Okay, here's the deal. You've been down this road before. Why do you think this time it will be different?"

Mark didn't miss a beat. "I don't."

I appreciated his directness.

"So why are we doing this?"

"I need to do something, and my wife says you helped her friend, Mary-something." I recalled Mary-something. She was the wife of a famous film producer whom I helped navigate the ending of her thirty-seven-year marriage with the grace befitting of such a union.

"Okay, so here's what we can do. Let's schedule a time for you both to come in. I have some time next Tuesday at 11:00 a.m."

My suggestion sent Mark into shock.

"I'm not coming in. Why do I have to come in?" Mark's whine reminded me of the time my three-year-old godson found out I'd added ten more dollars to his sister's Fortnite account than to his.

"Because it's your marriage we're going to talk about."

"But she's the one who's unhappy." His juvenile indignation continued.

"My experience with these matters is that it helps to show you have some skin in the game," I said. "It's up to you. I'm sure you can find a clinician who will see just her, but that's not going to be me." I was embarking on a dangerous path. If I didn't get my own arrogance in check, I'd never be able to establish a relationship with him.

Mark continued, more resolved to prove me wrong and put me in my place. "That's ridiculous."

"Is it?" I shot back entirely too quickly.

"Yes. Listen, I run a—"

Now it was me who cut him off. I too had the power of search engines at my disposal, and I too had an ego that could destroy relationships. While Mark and I were chatting, I did some clicking of my own and figured out who Mark was. He looked like a powerhouse.

"You run what looks like an incredibly successful production company. It's impressive—and I have to confess, intimidating." Finally, I began to regain my professional composure. The truth was that Mark *was* impressive and intimidating. If I expected him to eventually share his truth with me, I needed to temper my ego and share my truths with him.

I allowed my heart to return to a faint rather than thunderous beat before continuing. "Congratulations on the Oscars. I can't even imagine what it took to pull that film off."

The beat of our union began to merge into a duet.

"Thank you. Those actors were a handful."

Once I sensed cooler heads were in charge, I continued.

"But this isn't your professional life we're talking about here. It's your personal life. What would happen if you invested, say, just a fraction of the energy you put in your work life into your marriage? I suspect everyone would settle down and you could get back to winning another Oscar, both at the Dolby Theater . . . and at home."

I fashioned my response so there was precious little for Mark to dispute. I also played to his motivations. It sounded like he'd been taking his wife for granted for years, decades probably, while investing 175 percent of his human capital into his work. He needed to see that I saw and admired his professional success and that he could apply the traits that made him successful to other areas of his life that needed attending and achieve a stunning outcome.

"I don't see the point of this."

"I get it." My ego needed to continue its retreat and focus on Mark's perceptions. I proceeded down what I hoped would be a gentler path.

Mark deserved to know his time would be spent in a productive rather than a shaming way. To do this, I needed to set out the terms of our engagement. "Okay, what do you think of this?" I began. "This is not some dark, no-redemption, let's-make-Mark-the-bad-guy-and-kill-him-at-the-end-of-the-film situation. We'll work to change the narrative of your current situation, but in a very contained, structured process. We'll have rules.

The first is there'll be no ganging up on anyone. We'll meet for a ninety-minute session to start. In this first session, we'll see if it makes sense to continue. If you don't feel comfortable with me, or if I don't feel like I can help out, we'll call it a day."

"Ninety minutes?" Mark was incredulous.

"The time will fly by." I didn't think Mark believed me, but he didn't argue back. I continued, "In this ninety-minute session, I'll learn about you and your wife, and you'll learn about me. I'll get your history, and if it makes sense, we'll come up with a plan of action to address your future."

"And then what?"

"And then we'll implement the plan. I ask for a month-long commitment. Three sessions after the initial consult, if we're not making any progress, and you feel like this is a waste of time and money, then we'll end the engagement." I could sense Mark relaxing. Fear, anxiety, and doubt thrive when they are uncontained. My job as a clinician is to provide a container for my patients' emotional discomfort.

I heard someone in the background call out to Mark that his 9:30 meeting was waiting. I looked at my watch. It was 9:45 a.m. Mark grew impatient and relented.

"Well, all right. Let's give it a go. So put me down for . . . when did you say?"

"Next Tuesday at 11:00 a.m."

Mark agreed to the date and time. I would get the details to him by text message and confirm the day before.

•

The following Tuesday at 11:00 a.m. sharp, Sonya, the incredibly intuitive receptionist in my New York City office, rang my office line to indicate a patient had arrived. Standard procedure. She always called when my next appointment was in the lobby, and she always knew when something wasn't quite right.

"*Hola*, Dr. Paul, your eleven o'clock is here."

"Great, send them in the elevator."

"Um . . ." Sonya hesitated. She is a genius when it comes to figuring out when something doesn't quite add up. "*No hay 'ellos' . . . solo 'ella.'*" When Sonya wanted to relay me a message in front of clients, she often spoke to me in her native Spanish.

I can't say I was surprised that Sonya was letting me know there was no *they* who had arrived; it was only *her*.

How patients and clinicians respond to their appointments is highly relevant clinical information. The manner in which these engagements are negotiated and play out illuminate the power struggles inherent in the psychotherapeutic relationship as well as in the other relationships in the patient's life. In this case, Mark's lateness, his failure to send a message that he would be late, and the potential for him not to show at all evidenced his need to maintain control of and wield his power over the relationship. Like a king whose court awaited his every move, Mark viewed both his wife and me as inferior servants who existed to serve him at his pleasure.

These actions through omissions also evidenced what is known as passive-aggressive behavior. Articulated as a clinical construct in 1996, passive-aggression was a phenomenon observed in American soldiers who failed to comply with their orders (Hopwood et al. 2009). Researchers who subsequently studied this behavior found it originates in people who feel vulnerable toward overly demanding and interfering others (Beck and Freeman 1990). Mark indicated in our initial conversation that he didn't want to come in for treatment, and I pushed him. In this dynamic, I was the bossy outsider, an "other" who was trying to control him. If his direct resistance didn't work, he'd find a passive way to act out his aggression and reclaim his authority in our relationship.

I finished up my call with Sonya.

"Okay. Thanks. I'll come down." I hung up the phone and went down to the lobby. It was important that I honor Mark's wife by acknowledging her physical presence with mine.

As I walked out of the stairway door into the lobby, Mark's wife immediately caught my attention. Coiffed and outfitted to perfection, she was the embodiment of wealth and class. Dressed in a cream silk blouse and slightly darker shade of cashmere slacks that were accentuated by a chocolate alligator belt and handbag, she looked like she had just stepped out of the pages of the latest Ralph Lauren campaign.

"Ms. S.?" I asked, knowing exactly who she was.

She extended her perfectly manicured hand; I was blinded by what must have been a twelve-carat diamond solitaire. "Yes. But please call me Susan."

"Pleasure to meet you. I'm Dr. Paul."

"Of course, I recognize you from your website." She radiated confidence in a fragile sort of way, a cool veneer of distance that quaked with vulnerability.

"Do we know the whereabouts of your husband?"

"We don't. I confirmed with him this morning, but haven't heard a word back. Did you?"

"I confirmed last evening. He said he'd be here."

Susan let out a sad and knowing chuckle. "I'm not surprised. He has issues with showing up for anyone but himself."

"I understand." I kicked myself for falling into a trap of siding with the "easier," more gracious patient and made a mental note to pull myself back over the line.

Susan shot me a glance that said in no uncertain terms, *You have no idea.*

Just then, her phone started vibrating. I chuckled that even her choice of phone notifications was subtle and gracious. She looked down at the phone, then back up at me. "Here he is."

As she spoke into her phone, their game of thrones began. Her tone transformed from warm with me to frosty with him. "Where are you?"

I could hear Mark's voice over the line but was unable to make out what he was saying. Susan nodded while he rambled on and distracted herself by admiring the soft coral pink of her lacquered fingernails.

"Just get here," she demanded before shutting down the call.

"He's stuck in traffic, twenty blocks away. Says the traffic is stopped. The UN is in session, blah, blah, blah." It was clear this wasn't the first time Mark had left Susan waiting.

"Okay then, we'll need to wait until he gets here. Can I get you a coffee?"

Susan looked surprised. "Can't we get started without him? Lord knows when—or if—he'll ever make it."

Every ounce of my being wanted to say yes, to move in and save her, but I forced myself to resist the urge. Mark wanted to set this up in a way that would confirm his fears of being ganged up on by his wife and "her" therapist. To walk in during the middle of a session between her and me that had started without him would prove I was incapable of being impartial. At this point, he would be right. I needed time and distance to recalibrate myself back to a position of neutrality.

"We'll need to wait for him to show."

Susan looked exasperated and sat down. She pulled out her phone and began texting with someone I assumed was a friend.

At 11:50, Sonya rang my office phone again. "They're here."

"*Los dos?*"

"*Si, los dos. Mujer y marido. Juntos.*" With Sonya's confirmation that both Mark and Susan were there, together, I told her to send them up.

•

Mark stepped off the elevator first and extended his hand to greet me. "I'm sorry I'm late. The FDR is a mess."

Susan rolled her eyes as she stepped out from behind him. Apparently, she'd heard it all before and wasn't buying his "traffic made me late again" story.

I led the couple down the hall and into my office. As we were taking our seats, I hastened to acknowledge that we were short on time and wouldn't be able to get much done.

"So look, we have forty minutes here. Not much time. We'll need to deal with more of the substance in our next session. Let's use this time to talk about the form."

Mark and Susan looked at each other with confusion. The good news was they were able to connect on something. The bad news was I spoke in a way they couldn't understand.

I rephrased my question: "How can we make sure we show up on time?"

Susan shot back proudly, "I was here."

Now it was Mark who looked annoyed and rolled his eyes.

"Yes, indeed you were. So Mark, this might be a rough time for you to break away from the office. Can we schedule something in the evening?"

That wasn't going to work for Mark. "Evenings are tough for me. I'm in the office every night until around 9:00 or 10:00 p.m. managing things in the LA office."

Susan shot me a look of exasperation.

Suddenly, I was struck with an idea. If Mark couldn't get to my office, then I'd take my office to Mark.

"So let's do this: instead of worrying about you having to schlep up here, I'll come down to you. Susan will meet us there, and you guys can grab a lunch after."

Susan looked like the cat that had just swallowed a mouse, while Mark looked like the mouse that had just been eaten.

In his typical form, Mark tried to object but found himself void of any true objections.

"I . . . I . . . well, I . . ."

Susan took full advantage of his hesitant articulation and closed the deal. "You'd do that?" she asked me. "That would be amazing."

"Absolutely, I'm happy to do it."

Mark remained silent. I took his silence as a "sounds perfect to me," and confirmed our agreement.

"Sorted then. Mark, we'll all meet at your office next Tuesday at 11:00 a.m." Although we had about ten minutes remaining in our session, I figured it was best to quit while we were ahead. I stood up and walked over to open the door before Mark had time to finagle back the reins of the carriage.

•

The following Tuesday, Mark was in his office as agreed, ready, willing, and able. He even provided refreshments—coffee, water, ice, and a Baccarat crystal decanter of what I suspected was scotch. *Be interesting to see how that plays out,* I thought, wondering if Mark would steady himself with a shot or two during our session.

In contrast to the Mark whom I encountered uptown the preceding week, that day's downtown Mark was a different animal. Relaxed and confident in his own surroundings, he had lost most of the rough edges I'd experienced from him in the past. Susan seemed more at ease as well. Suited up as the boss's wife in a floral print dress discreetly labeled Gucci, she floated through the door and took her seat with the majesty and elegance of Grace Kelly.

In our first session, I learned that several of my initial impressions about Mark were right, while several were wrong. Yes, Mark did have a history of infidelities. "I've wandered a few times during our marriage," he readily admitted. There was also evidence of his tendency to drink too much and take anti-anxiety and pain medication during the day. "I have chronic knee pain, and the only way I can get through the day is by popping a few pills . . . and taking a few hits of my medicinal marijuana. By the end of the day, though, I'm wiped out and need a scotch to recalibrate." Not a surprise in the least. What *did* surprise me, though, was how—in spite of his outward bravado—Mark was incredibly insecure and dependent on Susan's approval. Even though Mark had a tendency to speak with great swagger and forced gravitas, he would constantly look over to Susan to gauge her reaction to what he'd just said.

In our second session, I began to understand why. In contrast to Mark's very modest beginning, Susan's was quite elite. The only child of an alcoholic and narcissistic mother, Susan was taught early on that looks definitely matter. "Mother loved her martinis and never met a mirror—or man—she didn't adore. The only thing she cared about was how she and I looked. Early on, I was a reflection of her beauty, so all was well. But as I grew older and matured, I outshone her. I became a threat to her existence." Eventually, alcohol and ego proved to be a lethal combination for her mother. "The end of her life was tragic. No one will openly admit it, but she drank herself to death. She had a staff to dote on her, but trust me, if she wasn't paying them, they would've never stuck around."

Susan's father also had issues of control, narcissism, and addiction. "He was brilliant at making money, but rather dull in his emotions. To be honest, I can't say I really knew who he was, but it was clear what he wanted from me was to be pretty and to marry someone up the social ladder. It was an unspoken truth that I accomplished the first but failed miserably at the second."

While Susan attended the most elite boarding schools and colleges, Mark barely made it to community college. "I wasn't what you call a scholar. In fact, school was never my thing." But what he lacked in scholastic aptitude, he more than compensated for with hard work and self-discipline. The son of a steelworker and a stay-at-home mom, Mark scaled the ladder of success one tenuous grasp at a time: "I got my first job when I was twelve, cleaning out my neighbors' gutters." From cleaning gutters in the fall to shoveling snow in the winter to cutting grass in the summer, Mark found power through the money he earned. "I realized the more money I had, the more I could do whatever the hell I wanted." But, like most men and women who attain power, celebrity, and position by virtue of their financial success, there was never enough to make him feel safe or genuinely validated.

By our third session, I realized Mark simultaneously worshiped and resented Susan's privileged upbringing. Cultured, smart, and beautiful, Susan, with her assets and accomplishments, was Mark's trophy; but his trophy also made him horrendously insecure. During one of our sessions, Mark admitted, "Susan's the one with the brains and beauty in this family. I'm just a step above trailer trash. Just ask her. She'll be happy to tell you." It was also clear Mark was convinced he'd be back in his hometown working a menial job if it wasn't for Susan. "I know I can be a jerk, but the truth is I love my wife and tell her all the time that we have the life we have because of who she is and what she brings to the table."

Over the next month, I continued to see the couple in Mark's office. The arrangement worked out well. In fact, things were going so smoothly I felt compelled to check in and see if my observations were shared and why, in contrast to their past experiences in therapy, we appeared to be making progress.

"Listen guys, I'm not sure exactly how to say this . . . well, without being patronizing or . . . well, I'm . . . I've just observed—"

"*Oy vey*, already, Hokemeyer. Spit it out." Mark grew impatient with my blithering.

"Okay, you're doing really well in this work. I know this isn't your first time in therapy. Does it feel different to you?"

As was his habit, Mark was about to answer, but he looked

over at Susan for the tacit approval he needed and craved from her. Susan turned up her palms, encouraging him to speak.

He followed her directive.

"Well, for starters, you come here. And I really appreciate that you make that effort. I also get the sense we're working as a team."

Susan nodded in agreement.

"You're also really fair and balanced, logical. You think like a lawyer, talk like one sometimes too, which . . . is annoying, but you look like you fit in here."

How quickly Mark moved back into the realm of appearances. I wanted Mark to ferret out why without my directly expressing it. I asked an obvious question to draw him deeper into engagement around the issue.

"Where is 'here'?"

He looked at me like I was an idiot.

"Well, this office."

I nodded, indicating I understood. "So, what does this office mean to you?"

Mark paused while he considered my question. He shot yet another "save me" glance in Susan's direction, but this time she didn't jump in to rescue him.

"Well, it means . . . it means that . . ." Mark stumbled around his mind, looking for an answer. "I guess it should mean I've made it, but to be honest, I'm not even sure what 'made it' means."

"Do you feel successful?"

"Hell, no. What I feel is like I'm back behind the curtain of Oz, about to be discovered as a fraud."

I glanced over at Susan, who sat motionless, staring at

Mark as if seeing him for the very first time. But rather than viewing her husband with an air of haughty disdain, her eyes conveyed compassion.

I needed to secure and expand their connection.

"Susan, you looked shocked."

A normally articulate Susan stuttered.

"I . . . well, I . . . I've never heard that."

"Heard what?"

"Well, that Mark . . ." Susan hesitated, lost for words.

I persisted. "That Mark what?"

"That he feels like a fraud. I mean, he absolutely radiates confidence."

Mark looked over at his beautiful wife like a lovestruck teenager. I suspected it was the first moment in a very, very long time he felt truly seen as a human being rather than the object of power he held himself out to be.

"And what does that confidence do for you?" I wanted to keep the attention on Susan to allow Mark to sit with his vulnerability and feel the value it added to his marriage.

"To me?" Susan grew uncomfortable with my continued focus on her. She fumbled with her vintage Van Cleef & Arpels necklace. "I don't quite understand." She needed clarification to consider the unconsidered—or deeply repressed.

I opened my mouth to speak, but Susan preempted me.

"Well, it infuriates me, if the truth be told."

I had to laugh. "Yes, the truth does need to be told."

Susan stopped fidgeting with her $30,000 necklace and recalibrated herself in the invaluable truth of her statement.

She wanted desperately to be done. But we weren't. We were only halfway through our exploration.

"But that's just one side of it," I started.

"One side of what?" Susan interrupted me.

"The anger. Well, the infuriation, to use your words."

Susan's brow furrowed.

She attempted to take back what she said. "Well, perhaps *infuriation*'s a bit too strong. Annoyance . . . it's more of an annoyance." It was clear anything approaching anger was too vile an emotion for her to integrate into her idealized self, the cultured and gracious person she was convinced she should be.

"But we just established we were telling the truth."

Susan looked sheepish and returned to twirling her necklace.

"Look, anger gets a bad rap," I said. "We think it's an emotion only found in lower socioeconomic classes, in people who have no control over themselves or their lives."

I heard Mark rustle in his chair. Susan returned to fidgeting with her necklace. My mention of social class made them uncomfortable.

"The truth is that anger is a highly valuable emotion. But like other emotions, it doesn't exist in a vacuum. It exists in relationship with others."

"With other trailer trash?" Mark questioned from the sidelines.

"No. Other aristocrats," I shot back.

We sat for a moment enjoying the lightness of the moment before I continued.

"Aristocrats—and you both are aristocrats, by the way— decorate around anger." I knew Mark and Susan found my calling them aristocrats slightly offensive, but I needed to say it. We were, after all, operating in the realm of truth.

I continued, "Anger is just one part, and a completely valid part, I must add, of how you respond to Mark's confidence. But is there something good . . . something positive in it?"

Again, I'd given Susan an unconsidered angle to contemplate. "I don't follow."

"If anger is the shadow, what's the light that balances it?" I asked.

Susan cocked her head and drew her focus inward. She desperately wanted to figure this out.

Finally, she got it sorted.

"Well, I guess the light is that his confidence makes me feel safe."

I felt like jumping out of my chair and hugging her, but resisted the urge.

Mark's head jerked up in surprise. I got the sense that it had been a long time since he had heard anything positive about his ambition from his wife.

I needed to extend this moment for as long as possible.

"Safe?" I parroted back Susan's words.

Susan nodded in agreement.

"Mark's confidence makes you feel safe." I phrased the second bit as a statement rather than a question to drive it home.

"Yes, that's right. I . . . unlike my father . . . well, and my mother to a large measure . . . people who were completely unsafe . . . Mark . . . well, at my core, I know he's there for me. Like a lion, he'll keep away the bad guys."

Mark savored the lion analogy and sat up with the posture of the king in his moss-green armchair.

"Wow. That's impressive . . . and a gift." I validated their connection.

Tears began to form in Susan's eyes. She fumbled with the

zipper on her gray Chloé bag to find a tissue, but Mark saved her the trouble and gently handed her the bright-orange pocket square he pulled from his gray flannel suit. It was the first act of tenderness I'd seen between them.

Over the next several months, I watched their tenderness grow. While at first they sat in separate armchairs for our sessions, subsequent to this tearful exchange, they sat together on the tobacco-brown leather settee Mark had in his office. Instead of ignoring Susan when she entered the room, after that session, Mark stood up and walked over to embrace her warmly when she arrived.

And his kindness was not unrequited.

Susan, once distant and full of criticism, began to express her appreciation for the new and improved Mark. "He even took out the garbage the other day."

Finally, the two of them were operating as a pair, or as Sonya would say, *juntos*—together.

A short three months into treatment, they announced they would finally be spending the winter in a house they had purchased more than five years earlier just outside of Palm Springs, California. They had barely set foot in the house since buying it. "I know it has an amazing view," Mark explained when I asked him about it, "but to be honest, I can't even tell you if it has a garage."

"It has four," Susan was quick to add.

Susan had announced their decision to winter in the desert with the excitement of a teenage girl who had just been asked on a date by the high school quarterback. "Finally, we get to enjoy the house we've both dreamt about for decades!"

"Brilliant!" I responded, genuinely happy for the couple.

"How did this come about?"

Mark responded first: "Susan's been at me for a while now to spend time there. No one's getting any younger, you know."

"Boy, I certainly do," I retorted.

"It's a lovely home, in the Vintage Club. Not sure you know it."

"I do, actually. I dated a realtor in Palm Springs back in my misspent youth."

"You've certainly been around," Mark added.

The three of us smiled.

"You know the saying, 'You've got to kiss a lot of toads . . .'"

In the middle of my comment, I caught Susan and Mark looking lovingly at each other. It was clear that after years of growing apart, Susan had rediscovered her prince, and Mark his princess.

I continued to work with the couple on a regular basis while they remained in New York, then monthly while they were setting up their love nest under the grandeur of the San Jacinto Mountains. The transition was infinitely more difficult for Mark than Susan. "I'm bored out of my mind," he'd complain during our sessions in New York.

"It'll take time," I attempted to assure him.

But unlike times in the past, when Mark would put his career before his marriage, he shared his discomfort with his newly discovered partner and soul mate. And rather than fight against him, Susan held him in a more compassionate embrace.

"I've told him he can come and go as he pleases. We have plenty of unused time on our plane."

But Mark refused to leave his wife's side. "No, we're in this together. This is a new phase of our life, and I want to be fully present for it." And more present he was. In an atmosphere of connection rather than judgment, Mark began to explore his relationship with alcohol and drugs. "I'm not quite ready to go to those meetings," he confessed, "but I've started to taper off the prescription drugs and cut out the alcohol completely."

•

Mark and Susan's story illustrates the challenges people who live in positions of elite power face when confronted with issues of personal intimacy. To succeed in the hypercompetitive world of show business, Mark deemed it necessary to build a castle wall around his psyche. Vulnerability was an enemy he not only intellectually believed, but also felt on a cellular level would kill him. As Mark's success grew, so did the strength of his fortress. At first, it served to protect him from self-critical voices: "I'm not enough," "I'm a fraud who'll be discovered and humiliated," "I'm a little dog playing with the big ones." Later, the wall served to protect him from the hypercompetitive and mean-spirited forces that wanted him to fail and from the incredible stress of investing other people's money in high-risk endeavors. "Films are costing well over $100 million these days, and the expectation is that the investment will be recouped in the first forty-eight hours of its opening. The trouble is, no one knows what's in the secret sauce."

Even though he loved his wife dearly, Mark had assimilated to the dominant cultural message that "nice guys finish last" and that power, property, and prestige are the keys to open the kingdom of nirvana. Deep down, he wanted to have an intimate connection with his wife, a woman he respected and loved deeply, but he simply didn't have the emotional or physical energy to negotiate the artful balance it would require between his personal life and professional identity. Mark attempted to fill the void that was created between them with the external markers of success and power he thought reflected her needs and station in life. He showered Susan with $100,000 diamonds and $20,000 handbags. In so doing, Mark transformed his wife into yet another object that reflected *his* success and ghettoized her further and further into a rarefied and isolated state of being. "That's quite a diamond," I commented during our fourth session together, after noticing a pattern wherein Susan would stare down at her ring whenever she felt discomfort. Mark beamed at my comment. Susan scowled. "It's like I'm wearing Times Square on my hand. It's all people see. I'm surprised no one has cut my hand off to get it yet." Was Mark a "bad guy" or a "creep" because of his way of relating to himself, the significant others in his life, and the world around him? No. He was a vulnerable human being trying to survive as best he could behind what he authentically felt were the enemy lines of the unsafe and capricious world of intimate relationships and show business.

As his clinician, my job was to first help Mark obtain intellectual insights into his situation and provide him with a contained frame in which he could begin practicing vulnerability as a relational asset, rather than feeling it as a liability. In developing more vulnerability, he felt like less of an imposter. For Mark, this was a terrifying proposition. It required him to loosen the reins of control and dip his toes into the waters of vulnerability. Rather than walk away from the challenge, Mark continued to show up for the work.

For a little over two years, we negotiated and created. At

the end of our engagement, was Mark a warm and fuzzy teddy bear who wore his heart on his sleeve? No. He was still guarded, quick to run back into the castle, and at times arrogant and defensive—only less so. It wasn't Mark perfected, but for the health and well-being of Mark, Susan, and their relationship, it was a significant improvement.

It's only in unpacking these dynamics that we realize, no matter the person's background or status, that we are all human beings with insecurities trying to survive in what often feels like an unsafe and chaotic world. Fundamental to seeing this commonality in each other is understanding how we pursue success and status as a protective armor and realizing that yes, while it does keep the wolves at bay, it also keeps us isolated from relationships of authenticity and integrity—relationships that will enable us to repair the damage of our past and author better, more rewarding life narratives.

3.

Vanity

Self-Worth, Vulnerability, and the Narcissism Nexus

*When I look at narcissism through the vulnerability lens,
I see the shame-based fear of being ordinary. I see the
fear of never feeling extraordinary enough to be noticed,
to be lovable, to belong, or to cultivate a sense of purpose.*

— BRENÉ BROWN

The frustration in my voice was thick and icy as I spoke at—not with—the unshaven millennial who smelled like dirty laundry. "I paid well over a thousand dollars for this d*mn iPhone X, and it doesn't work." He'd been given the unenviable task of managing the hordes of tormenting customers descending upon the Apple Store in Santa Monica, California, on a Friday evening. But while his hygiene was sketchy, his comportment and professionalism were pristine.

In this regard, he stood in sharp contrast to me, freshly showered but sporting a polluted demeanor. Even though I'd pulled myself back from a narcissistic meltdown only two hours before, I felt it returning with a vengeance.

Just prior to my arrival, I'd been on the phone with AppleCare for what seemed like an eternity. A woman named Irene, who seemed less than effective at her job during the thick of my meltdown, trundled me through a checklist of interventions. "Power off and power on." No results.

She tried again. "Go to your settings. I'm going to reboot something from my end. We'll get disconnected, but I'll call you right back." At the end of our call, she offered up a cheerful, "That's the darndest thing!" and informed me I'd need to go to the closest Apple Store and talk with a "genius." "They're really smart. They'll figure it out." She also hastened to warn me, "They don't take appointments after 6:00 p.m."

Her comment shot an electric current through my being. "No appointments! You mean I'd have to wait in a line?!"

I picked up the malfunctioning phone for which I'd just paid an arm and a leg and saw it was 4:53 p.m. The only thing it seemed to be good at was providing me with torment. Getting to the store by 6:00 p.m. was outside the realm of possibilities.

It would take me at least an hour and a half to gather myself up and make the drive to Santa Monica.

I glanced longingly at my surfboard, which beckoned from the patio. The sea and sky behind it had just begun to morph into a Rothko painting of navy blues, purples, and pinks. I'd planned on spending the evening in that opus, floating, catching a few easy waves. A piece of fuchsia bougainvillea lightheartedly danced across the deck toward the sea. I wanted to join it, liberated from responsibility.

Standing in line at the Apple Store under fluorescent lights was not how I wanted to spend my evening, and the mere thought of my fate filled me with panic. In less than a second, my panic grew into rage.

I tried to infect Irene with my anger by asking a rhetorical question: "You're kidding me. What am I supposed to do?"

The truth was that I knew perfectly well what I was supposed to do—act like an adult, drive down the coast to Santa Monica, and take my place in the queue.

I thought of several of my patients who take helicopters out to their homes in the Hamptons to avoid sitting in traffic with us mere mortals. An image of me landing on the roof of the Apple Store like Tom Cruise in a *Mission Impossible* film momentarily amused me, but Irene, my customer service agent, pulled me back into reality.

"Paul? Paul? Are you still there?"

"Oh, I'm still here." I repeated my hostile question. "What am I supposed to do?"

Even though I liked her and respected the manner in which she was handling her unenviable job, I wanted a companion in my frustration.

In contrast to the infantile me, Irene was a study in adult composure.

"I know it's inconvenient, but I'd suggest you just go there. I mean, I could schedule an appointment for you, but the soonest I can get you one is next Friday."

"Next Friday! You mean a week, a full week from today?" I was now officially livid. "This is completely unacceptable. I just paid over a thousand dollars for this phone!"

Irene tried to use facts to soothe my irritation. "They're exceptionally busy because Apple is replacing the iPhone 6 batteries for $29.00." I suspected she thought her employers' decision to offer an inexpensive solution to their admission of installing batteries that intentionally diminish the effectiveness of older phones would appeal to my altruism, but it didn't. It only fueled my indignation.

"iPhone 6! You've got to be kidding me. I just threw down serious money for an X, and you're going to put $29.00 batteries ahead of me. You guys are headed for bankruptcy! Dump your Apple stock!"

Irene knew to keep her mouth shut.

I continued. "You need to sort this out! You are going to have to send someone out."

As smart as Irene was, my irrationality confused her. "Out where?" she sheepishly asked.

I was neither sheepish nor confused. I pounded my palm on the wooden slab that serves as my desk and kitchen table "Here! My house. I'll give you the address!"

For the first time during our hour-and-a-half call, Irene had no answer.

As an Apple expert, she certainly encounters entitled people every day, but I could hear her telling her husband when she got home that evening, "Boy, I had a real whack job from Malibu call in today. You'll never believe what he demanded."

It took only a second for Irene's confusion to convert to clarity. "No, Paul, we can't do that."

I persisted. "Well, why not?"

"Well, we just don't have that capability. I guess you can call an independent service . . ."

Finally, my maturity kicked in, and I realized the gig was up. I was acting like a jerk and pulling a perfectly lovely human being into what's known as the narcissistic cycle of abuse (Hammond 2018). Because I paid a premium price for a premium product, I felt like I deserved special treatment. Having my unreasonable expectations dashed, I suffered an ego injury, and in an attempt to assuage my defeat, I became a victim who attempted to reclaim a sense of power over the situation.

Unfortunately, in the process I'd exhausted myself, looked like a fool, forced a kind and professional human being to deal with an unreasonable man, and wasted precious time postponing the inevitable.

It was time for me to make some amends.

"Listen, Irene. I'm sorry. I got a bit out of hand. I just . . ." I stopped myself from rationalizing my actions. I said what I needed to say. What I needed to do now was jump in the shower, put on a clean shirt, and drive myself to Santa Monica.

When young Narcissus fell in love with his reflection, he did more than capture the imagination of artists and poets through the ages; he spawned a term for a nexus of traits that describes one of humankind's most seductive and destructive personalities. Narcissism, as it's known, is characterized by self-absorption, a need for constant validation, a sense of superiority, and an extraordinary capacity for manipulating others. Of course, narcissists don't literally drown in the waters of self-love. But they do find themselves gasping for air on islands of isolation. This is especially true of individuals who've attained improbable levels of success while burning out relationships with the people who've supported them along the way.

•

"I didn't have the emotional space to give to someone else," explained Jonathan, the actor we met in chapter 1. In the autumn of his life, he desperately craved an intimate relationship, but he had no idea how to sustain one. "It's not hard for me to meet someone, but it never lasts more than a few weeks."

When asked why that was, Jonathan could only point his finger at others. "These twenty-year-old women are so self-absorbed. They think that I'm going to be their sugar daddy. Once they find out that's not how I roll, they become b*tches." Fortunately, over the three years he and I worked together, he was able to stop pointing the finger at others and consider his role in the situation.

In this regard, Jonathan was an exception.

Too few narcissistic patients stay in treatment long enough to get insight into their condition. Because the nature of their ailment is to avoid intimacy, they struggle to attach to a clinician who simultaneously holds and challenges them while they learn to tolerate the relational discomfort that comes with an honest and egalitarian relationship. Their fragile egos and hypersensitivity to observations they perceive as criticism prevent them from tolerating challenges to the grandiose fantasies they hold about themselves (Horton and Sedikides 2009).

Ninety percent of the time, the men and women who present with narcissistic personality constructs come to therapy through what are known as external motivations—a spouse threatens divorce, they're court ordered, or they need to manage a public relations crisis. Although they initially approach treatment motivated to "fix" these external situations, in short order, they turn on their heels and run for the door. Unfortunately, this means they and the people in their lives remain stuck in their narcissistic cycle of abuse. This "cut and run" dynamic was characterized by Piet, a middle-aged man who moved from Amsterdam to New York to direct an off-Broadway play.

Like most narcissistic patients, Piet came to treatment under duress. The show's producer, an insightful woman with whom I'd worked on several occasions, had had enough of Piet's adolescent drama and called me. "This one's a doozy. He makes the princess from the last show look like Mother Teresa."

Fortunately, neither doozies nor princesses put me off. Unfortunately, the most severely narcissistic cases, the people who need help the most, generally don't stick around long enough to attach to their therapist and make progress in treatment.

Piet fell into the unfortunate category.

"I don't need to be here," he announced in the first few minutes of our first session. "It's the idiots I'm trying to direct who need to see a shrink."

"I see," I responded while rubbing the furrow in my brow. And while my comment was sparse, it captured a clinically significant observation. When placed in an emotionally challenging situation, Piet automatically digressed into his character pathology of engaging in the narcissistic cycle of abuse, the very same pattern that I fell into with Irene, my Apple agent. It was hard-wired into his limbic system, where it failed to yield to any intellectual reasoning. I prepared myself for when it would be directed at me.

The narcissistic cycle of abuse is a phenomenon articulated by Christine Hammond in her book *The Exhausted Woman's Handbook* (Hammond 2014). In it, she expands on Lenore Walker's cycle of abuse in domestic violence cases. While Walker's cycle consists of tension building, acting out, reconciliation, and calm, Hammond observes that when a narcissist is involved, the cycle of abuse has a similar but slightly modified trajectory (Walker 2019). The four stages of Hammond's narcissistic cycle of abuse are as follows:

- The narcissist feels threatened.
- They respond to the threat by blaming others.
- In blaming others, they assume the role of the victim.
- In the role of the victim, they turn the tables to regain their sense of power.

From what I could gather through my conversations with the referring producer and subsequently with Piet, the play he was directing never came together and was doomed to fail. Feeling threatened and refusing to acknowledge his part in the situation, he lashed out and blamed everyone around him.

Piet described the script as a mess. "It must have been written by a five-year-old," he complained. The actors were entitled and incompetent. "Where did they find these idiots?" He even blamed the theater's HVAC system. "I've seen better theaters in third-world countries; it's so hot in there I can't think straight." Instead of taking responsibility for his shortcomings and redoubling his efforts to make the production a success, he retreated into the role of a victim. "I've done everything I can to make the play come together and, well, they don't like me because I'm Dutch. I'm not all warm and fuzzy like you Americans."

I wanted to respond that they didn't like him *and* he was Dutch, but I held my tongue. It was way too soon in our relationship to challenge Piet that directly.

Unfortunately, Piet never stuck around to engage in therapy or to salvage the play. He canceled our second session and, a week later, packed up his bags in a huff and headed back to the Netherlands, convinced that mercenary and shallow Americans had taken advantage of him. He also vowed never to return. Several months ago, however, I came across a notice that a theater company in Chicago hired Piet to direct a local production of a musical revival. Narcissists burn relationships out, but they're remarkably clever in seducing themselves back into good graces.

But even if he had stuck around and engaged in therapy, could Piet have completely eliminated all traits of his narcissistic personality? The data and my clinical impressions indicate he could not.

While a narcissistic personality disorder can be "softened," it can never be completely eliminated. It's simply too deeply ingrained in a person's psychic makeup. Therefore, successful therapeutic outcomes involve providing patients insight into their condition and working interpersonally to train them to respond differently to themselves, the people in their lives, and the world around them. Through this process, patients don't just intellectually understand but also *feel* the benefits of being in a reciprocal relationship that they don't need to lord over.

Some of my patients find the prospect of this new reality a relief. Most, however, find it terrifying. This is because, at a very significant point in their lives, their narcissism saved them.

Contrary to popular opinion, narcissism isn't a personality trait that people actively pursue. It's a very human consequence of overcompensating for a deficiency they endured early in their developmental path. Heinz Kohut, one of the leading clinicians who practiced what is known as object relations therapy, maintained that narcissism develops in response to a primary caregiver's failure to validate a child's most basic identity needs (Kohut 1966). This caregiver didn't adequately convey to the child that he or she was of value, a person worthy of being seen, heard, and respected for his or her authentic self. This failure of the primary caregiver to adequately *see* this child caused the child to grow up with a poor self-concept and an insatiable need to be validated by others (Watson et al. 1992). So instead of maturing into a confident, secure adolescent and adult, the child embarks on a compulsive quest for outside proof that he or she is enough: pretty enough, manly enough, smart enough, rich enough, famous enough, powerful enough. This is why narcissists present so well. They're incredibly charming, affable, charismatic, and physically attractive (Watson et al. 1992). It's no surprise that narcissism runs rampant among people of elite power.

But are all individuals who rank among the rich and famous narcissists? Not all, but research indicates people with narcissistic tendencies pursue positions and lifestyles that will grant them the power and approval they so desperately crave (Braun 2017). There have been copious articles detailing how CEOs, power brokers, leaders, and politicians with narcissistic traits often rise to the top of their industries; some argue that it's their narcissistic drive that distinguishes them as leaders. The elements and history that create an individual's deep-seated need for approval and power propel these individuals to attain "black swan" levels of success—success that brings about extraordinary social and industrial change—while making them vulnerable to vicious personal attacks.

Elon Musk, a larger-than-life innovator, has had his mental health called into question for a tweet he made about taking Tesla, a company he founded, private (Gelles et al. 2018). While the accusations are cloaked in polite and politically correct terms, he's been called *insane, unhinged, dangerous,* and *unfit to run his empire.* But unlike other leaders who hide behind a curtain of bravado and viciously attack anyone who dares criticize them, Musk has been open about the stresses of his elevated position and the incredibly high physical, emotional, and relational price he's paid to keep it.

And it will come as no surprise that not only industry leaders but also actors, politicians, artists, and musicians tend to score higher on what's known as the Narcissistic Personality Inventory than those in the general population (Young and Pinsky 2006). Several well-known actors have spoken publicly about this phenomenon. Ben Affleck, speaking with *Interview* magazine (Sischy 1997), described the prevalence of narcissism in the entertainment field as follows: "I'd say it's the one quality that unites everybody in the film industry, whether you're an actor, a producer, a director, or a studio executive. You want people to look at you and love you and go, 'Oh, you're wonderful.'"

The compulsive need to be validated is not a trait found only in Oscar-winning actors. Today, one only needs an Internet connection and a social media account to manifest narcissistic traits.

Much has been made about the "epidemic" of narcissism in modern times, particularly among the millennial genera-tion (Twenge et al. 2008). Born between 1982 and 2002, the millennial generation is the first to be raised in a culture of hyper-connectivity as a result of the Internet and social media.

And they've embraced it with *gusto.*

More than 90 percent of millennials have Facebook ac-counts, and approximately 88 percent get their news from the platform (Ellison, Steinfield, and Lampe 2007; American Press Institute 2015). Many claims have been made that social media is fueling narcissism and even suicide rates, but these claims are misplaced. Narcissism is *played out* in the realm of technology, through abundant opportunities to engage in shallow connections with others that are based on vanity, showmanship, and self-promotion, but it's not *caused* by it (Buffardi and Campbell 2008). In fact, a recent study out of the University of California, Irvine, found there can be a benefit in moderate and positive "selfie expression" and that sharing selfies with your friends can actually increase your levels of happiness (University of California, Irvine 2016).

It's important to note that the selfies in this study were taken and used for the purpose of *connecting with others through positive emotions.* This stands in sharp contrast to selfies taken from a narcissistic point of view, which are taken and shared to *impress others with their fabulousness.* The latter show only the polished and artificial veneer of the human experience and can invoke feelings of inadequacy in the recipient, conceit in the sender, and disconnection in their relationship.

The ultimate takeaway from this study is that while technology holds the potential to disconnect, it also holds the power to connect human beings in positive ways. The key is engaging and using social media platforms with the pleasure of connection rather than the sorrow of self-absorption.

Narcissism has also been shown to play a powerful role in the personality and behavior of the very wealthy. In one widely cited 2014 study, the University of California, Berkeley, psychologist Paul Piff reported that narcissism is more common among people of higher income and social class (Cowen 2015). He found rich people were far more likely than those of ordinary means to agree with the statement "I honestly feel

I'm just more deserving than other people."

Why is this so?

Piff speculates that upper-class people have more control over their lives and greater personal choices, which promotes greater independence and self-focus. In contrast, those with fewer resources have less control and are more dependent on others, which leads to less focus on themselves. Piff also found evidence that the sons and daughters of wealthy and well-educated parents are the most likely to exhibit narcissistic characteristics. Does this mean that men and women who have grown up with wealth are more narcissistic than those who have created their own fortunes? Not necessarily. According to psychiatrist Michael Stone, quoted in a *New York Times* article about psychotherapy with the mega-rich, the two kinds of patients—inheritors and self-made wealthy people—have different problems (Konigsberg 2008). Among his patients who were born rich, who suffered "from the neglect of jet-setting parents or from the fear that no matter what they did they would never measure up to their father's accomplishments," he found a high incidence of depression. He observed that the self-made rich didn't suffer in the same way. They could justify their excesses by believing they were entitled to them, and they were less likely to crave closeness to others. Dr. Stone cites a patient in his 40s who "could get gratification through his wealth and move from one model to another. He didn't really need to maintain a relationship" (Konigsberg 2008).

This attempt to find gratification from what money—lots and lots of money—can buy is a phenomenon I see every day in my clinical practice. While I agree with Dr. Stone's observation that there is a distinct difference between people who've earned their wealth and those who've inherited or married into it, I disagree with the premise that money can buy meaningful and lasting gratification from empty relationships.

This was certainly true of George, a forty-seven-year-old man who hit the "technology lottery" in the late 1990s and overnight became, as he put it, "richer than the Queen of England." George used his sudden wealth to buy houses, cars, and lots of sex with age-inappropriate women. "I was living in Newport Beach," he recalled, "at the top of the world literally and figuratively. I had a Maserati, a Mercedes S600, and a Range Rover—all in black. I bought the biggest house on a promontory with a 180-degree view of the Pacific Ocean. It was heaven. For about six months."

"So what happened?" I asked.

George grimaced. "The stuff began to own me. The cars were fun for about a month after I bought them, but f*ck, at least one was always in the shop for maintenance. And the house, I had to hire a staff to take care of it, and then I had to hire someone to manage the staff."

It took George another three years of living the way he *thought* a person of his means should live before he began shedding the layers and layers of material goods and parasitic relationships he'd accumulated. He came to therapy looking for some "coaching" on how to get himself out of a toxic relationship.

"You're a lawyer and a shrink, right?" he asked over the phone during his initial interview of me. "I need someone smart to help me get rid of this train wreck."

No easy task, it turned out. George had overcome his compulsive spending patterns and was managing his money in a sensible way. But when it came to relationships, his narcissism made it hard for him to see the role he played in his misery. Like Jonathan and Piet, he could only point his finger away from himself and become a victim.

The "train wreck" he was involved with was an opioid-addicted, bulimic twenty-three-year-old former adult film star named Tina. Only after he and I struggled through six months of intense therapy sessions did he begin to recognize that he was an enabler, giving Tina money and a place to live. His feelings of superiority toward her and his fantasy that her youth and beauty reflected back his own youthful vigor served George's narcissistic ego, but it did nothing to save Tina from self-destruction. He also began to see that just as Tina was using him, he was using Tina. While her looks temporarily assuaged his deep feelings of inadequacy, the parasitic nature of their relationship haunted him and made him feel like a slimy old man.

As for extricating himself from the relationship, George first needed insight into how his past relationships impacted his present. Armed with this intellectual awareness, he then needed to develop the internal scaffolding to establish boundaries that were clear, consistent, and enforceable with Tina and the other parasites in his life. Eventually he got there, but it took close to two years of practice.

I still see George in therapy—narcissism doesn't yield easily to change, especially when wealth is involved. Presently, George has taken a "break" from relationships. "You know, I think I need to take some time off from dating," he announced at one session. It was an insight George reached on his own and one I completely supported. Before he could have relationships of integrity with others, he needed to start with himself.

Patients who suffer from relational and personality disorders like narcissism don't come to therapy pleading, "Help! I'm suffering from narcissism." In fact, many, like Piet, are astonishingly unaware of their own interpersonal shortcomings. Consider Pamela, a television producer in her mid-fifties, who sought my help because her marriage was foundering, her grown sons wanted little to do with her, and her "friends" had begun to avoid her. The only child of a socialite mother and a father whose immense wealth was of dubious provenance—some said he was a member of the Mob—she could boast of a host of professional achievements that included three Emmys.

And boast she did. Our first three sessions were taken up with entertaining accounts of her genuinely impressive career. But listening between the lines, I heard a tale of Pamela manipulating and bullying her colleagues and subordinates. It was clear to me they regarded her with suspicion, if not outright terror. I also detected a typical personality characteristic of narcissists: Pamela seemed to consider the people she worked with as accessories, without feelings and needs of their own. Did this attitude extend to her family and friends? I was pretty sure it did. In our third session, I got a glimpse of how she treated those outside her professional circle.

"I don't understand why my friend Naomi is mad at me. She doesn't return my calls," Pamela complained.

I looked at her expectantly, encouraging her to go on.

"I invited her and her husband to dinner last Saturday. True, it was a bit last minute. I was having a dinner party for eight that night and two people dropped out. I needed to fill the places. It's a big round table," she explained. "It doesn't work well with six."

"So you needed those two places filled," I repeated back her explanation, hoping she could hear the insensitivity in it.

"Yes," Pamela answered, completely missing my intent. "But Naomi said she had plans that evening. And she asked if she could come for dessert. Of course I said no, because I needed the table filled for the whole evening. And she said, 'Well, if you wanted me there for dinner, you should have invited me in the first place.'"

"Could you understand why she was offended?" I asked.

Pamela looked at me blankly. "No—I mean, it was a nice invitation. There were people there who could help her husband's career—and from what I can gather, he needs some help."

We would have a lot of work to do, Pamela and I. My goal would be to establish a therapeutic alliance with her by first connecting with her on an intellectual level. Once she felt I was a person worthy of her truth, we could then delve into the vulnerability of her feelings and explore how her behavior affected those around her. My hope was that she would learn to see the world from other people's perspectives and that the empathy she would thus gain would help her diminish her narcissism and improve the quality of her relationships.

A narcissistic personality is formed early in a person's life, well before the individual truly understands anything about elite power constructs. In my experience, which is supported by academic research, people who suffer from narcissism have never matured past the self-centered love that enabled them to survive as infants and young children (Ronningstam 2011). This is because they grew up being undervalued, overindulged, or—as I often see in cases like Pamela's—a toxic combination of the two (Mayo Clinic n.d.).

When she was growing up, Pamela's parents surrounded her with every imaginable luxury, including a collection of toys and dolls so extensive it required a separate alcove in the family's huge apartment, tiny custom-made fur coats to match Mommy's, and a chauffeur who ferried Pamela back and forth to school. She was sent to a strict Episcopalian day school, even though the family was Jewish. "My father was probably trying to compensate for his gangsterish ways," Pamela remarked. "Episcopalians had higher status."

At the age of seventeen, Pamela was "treated" to weekly sessions with a personal trainer because her looks-obsessed mother thought the only way she'd "hook" a man was "to be gorgeous."

Although Pamela's father, Lester, prided himself on providing the ultimate protective cocoon around his only child, he had little to do with Pamela himself. The little contact Pamela remembered with her dad included the occasional bedtime hug, a grand gesture here and there, and her regular presentation to his buddies at poker night (in her pajamas, no less). On the other hand, her mother, Sylvia, instilled in her daughter conflicted feelings of superiority and inadequacy. Pamela was the smartest and the prettiest. She could do no wrong. She would accomplish all the things Sylvia had never accomplished. She would be the perfect child.

But Pamela knew she wasn't better and certainly not perfect. In fact, deep within her burned a feeling of being fundamentally flawed and woefully inadequate. Hadn't she fantasized about punching that boy in her class in the face when he made fun of her patent leather shoes? Hadn't she thought about running away and making her parents grieve for her? She also knew she could "do wrong." Hadn't she shoplifted those doll clothes at FAO Schwarz? She didn't get caught, but she was left with deep feelings of guilt.

She was also aware of and confused by the conflicting messages her mother sent her. How could she be the best when she lived under her mother's hypercritical and disciplined watch?

Like most narcissists—and especially those who come from inherited wealth—Pamela grew up wavering between a grandiose self-image and profound feelings of inadequacy. Yes, she knew she was superior to her classmates: Mommy made that clear. And Nanny certainly did as well. But Pamela didn't *feel* superior to anyone.

She was also bewildered by her own emotions. She glowed when her mother heaped praise on her, but that was contradicted when Sylvia would become harshly critical, or suddenly indifferent to the point of emotional and physical absence— off shopping or lunching and seeming to forget she even *had* a daughter. Painfully subjected to the whims of her mother's moods, Pamela struggled to find her own emotional center and in time grew to fear any strong emotions.

Narcissists frequently tell of being betrayed by an important figure in their lives, leading to distrust of close relationships. Pamela's experience with her mother is a case in point. I've heard similar stories from other patients. One woman described being groped by her pediatrician when she was seven or eight. Scared and ashamed, she reported this to her mother, who promised to switch doctors. But her mother either didn't believe her or didn't think this transgression was important. A new physician never materialized, and my patient endured years of improper touching whenever she was taken to the doctor. Her fear of male molestation and especially of doctors persists to this day.

Early on, narcissists learn the world is an unsafe and threatening place. Central to this threat is the overwhelming power of their emotions. For people like Pamela, emotions do not add to the warm richness of their lives; rather, emotions make it chillingly painful. Indeed, I've found that narcissism doesn't discriminate, even if it is more common in some groups than others. Narcissistic people—rich, poor, or middle class—lack a personal sturdiness that enables them to weather emotional storms. They live in fear of being discovered as a fraud, of revealing their true thoughts and feelings to others, and of being rejected or scorned for who they are at their core. They defend against these emotional intrusions by creating impressive exteriors—think of Pamela's dazzling career, Mark's Oscars, Susan's diamonds, and, as we'll soon see, Luke's elegant creations. They are desperate for people to worship them—*but only from a distance.*

Psychoanalyst Otto Kernberg, one of the world's foremost authorities on narcissism, says that narcissists live with "feelings of inferiority and overdependence on external admiration and acclaim." Kernberg maintains that they suffer from "chronic uncertainty and dissatisfaction about themselves, conscious or unconscious exploitiveness, and ruthlessness toward others" (Kernberg 1975).

I've seen Kernberg's observations play out across the world. They are especially apparent in middle-aged men. These patients, who range from the mid-forties to late sixties, engage in behaviors that compromise their health and relationships in vain attempts to validate their existence and keep their true feelings at bay. They work themselves to the point of exhaustion and spend money on expensive prizes that trumpet their success—mistresses, trophy wives or husbands, mega-mansions, cars, planes, and boats. Many pump themselves full of performance-enhancing drugs, including testosterone, steroids, and human growth hormone, all to maintain a façade of strength and virility. They are also no strangers to plastic surgery. While they may look strong from the outside, at the center of their being, a place typically referred to as the "self," they suffer from imposter syndrome, plagued by feelings of being fraudulent, unstable, and incomplete.

Narcissism is by far the single most destructive feature I address in the lives of the wealthy and powerful men I treat. It gives rise to a multitude of damaging behaviors that include alcohol and drug abuse, infidelity, and impulsive financial decisions. It also presents the greatest challenge to treatment, because—as mentioned—in many circles of wealth, power, and prestige, narcissism is considered an asset rather than a failing. As psychiatrist Michael Stone remarks: "Superbly well-to-do people tend to have much less of an impetus to work through things now. They have so many opportunities to seek gratification that they're not hurting in the same way" (Konigsberg 2008). While men from lower socioeconomic classes and limited positions of power are forced to face the destructive nature of their narcissism, which can undermine their careers and their relationships, men of means can justify theirs by citing how well it's served them, their families, and the world around them.

My patient Luke is an excellent example of a highly successful man whose narcissistic bravado hid his enormous insecurity.

The son of an abusive and alcoholic father, Luke made his way out of Kentucky and landed in Manhattan, where he found extraordinary success as an interior designer to the rich and famous. In so doing, Luke defied the odds of his underprivileged roots through a lot of hard work, perseverance, and tunnel vision. He managed to accomplish something that is nearly impossible for someone who was *not* of the manor born—much less a man who came to being in a doublewide trailer.

With his lithe, muscular body and chiseled face that made him look like a movie star, Luke became a superstar of the architectural glossies. He also happened to be gay. Because of his sexual orientation, he'd lost the love and support of his conservative Christian family at an early age. Many years later, he was still severely damaged by their rejection and in deep denial about it.

When I asked if he missed his parents and brothers, he practically crowed, "Not at all! They did me a great service by kicking me out of the house when they did."

Luke was seventeen when his father found him in the basement with a *Playgirl* magazine. Outraged, his father demanded that Luke leave the house immediately. As Luke told it, the move was to "protect my two baby brothers from my perversity and damnation."

Luke's mother stood by and watched. "What could she do?" Luke asked, shrugging his shoulders. "My father was drunk as usual and she wasn't about to suffer his wrath. When he was in that state, you did exactly what he said. There was no reasoning with him."

So Luke left. He packed up his sparse belongings and moved in with a male friend whom he sensed had a crush on him.

"His family was welcoming," Luke said. "And he claimed he was straight, but he loved having sex with me. It worked for a while. At least for the three months I needed to graduate."

Eventually, as with Luke's later relationships, his friend started to feel used and asked him to leave. But rather than recognizing the part he played in the relationship's failure, Luke blamed it on his friend's and the community's homophobia.

When school was over, Luke took his high school diploma, borrowed $200 from an aunt, and made his way to the Neiman Marcus store in Dallas.

"How did you even know about Neiman Marcus when you were that age?" I asked, amazed at his precociousness.

Luke burst into laughter, "Honey, I knew about Neiman Marcus from the moment I emerged from the womb. It was my *raison d'etre!*"

Of course it was, I thought to myself. The two things I knew about Luke with great certainty were that he was very narcissistic and very resourceful. Like most narcissists, he was also charismatic. Both men and women were easily seduced by his flirtations. But while their admiration was intoxicating, it was unsustainable. He was simply incapable of maintaining a long-term relationship with anyone. But his seductive charms also seemed to be diminishing. Now well into the second stage of his life, Luke was beginning to worry he was going to become "one of those pathetic old queens, all boozy and alone, paying for sex from coked-up hustlers." After a few therapy sessions with him, I sensed his fears were well placed.

Like so many wealthy narcissists, Luke was adept at making money. From the moment he left his parents' house decades earlier, he worked, saved, and invested in himself. "I started selling shoes, and now I sell lifestyles. Last year, I billed close to $2 million. It's hard to believe that people want a white-trash hillbilly to tell them how to live, but whatever. I kiss those checks all the way to the bank."

Reflecting back on his humble beginnings, Luke said proudly, "I made ridiculous money selling shoes at Neiman's, and I saved every penny."

By the time he was twenty-three, Luke had socked away "about $10,000" and decided it was time to seek out the bright lights of the Big Apple. "There was no way I could stay in Dallas and sell shoes to those insufferable women with their teased-up beehives and those little pearl-handled pistols in their purses." Not surprisingly, Luke had broken a lot of hearts along the way, including that of David, the man who supported him while he was working in Dallas.

"David actually was shocked when I told him I was leaving. What did he think? That I'd be satisfied for the rest of my life peddling footwear while he taught history at Sam Houston High School?"

Luke lied to his boyfriend, telling him he'd gotten an offer to be an assistant vice president of accessories for Gucci in Manhattan. He called it the "chance of a lifetime." But this was just a story to get David to support Luke's move. "I promised that once I got settled he could join me, but that too was a fib. I was done with him and way over Dallas. Listen, I had a body to die for, a killer wardrobe, and the skin of a twenty-three-year-old. The world was my oyster."

Three days after he told David about his "new job," Luke was gone. He took up residency at the YMCA on Manhattan's Upper West Side, and within three months, he had moved in with Arthur, an older man he met at a gay bar on the Upper East Side known for May–December relationships of a commercial nature. "Easy, breezy," was how Luke described his entry into elite New York circles.

It didn't hurt that his new boyfriend had just sold his family's textile company for "hundreds of millions" and used a considerable chunk of his windfall to purchase a board seat on one of New York's leading cultural institutions as well as a six-thousand-square-foot townhouse on a prime block between Fifth and Madison Avenues in Carnegie Hill.

"I was his trophy boyfriend," Luke boasted, as if he had earned a PhD from Harvard.

For several years, Luke lived life in the fast lane. Busy taking all that was given to him and "being fabulous," it never occurred to him that at some point it would come to an end. "Just when I was about to hit thirty, this jerk came home and said that our relationship 'wasn't working.' I had no idea what he was talking about. I'd given him the best years of my life. My youth. Now he wanted to replace me. *Not so fast,* I said to myself."

Luke resolved to use the situation to his advantage. "'All right,' I told him, 'I'll get out of your life, but first you need to set me up in business.'"

Arthur was eager to move on, and a few million dollars was chump change for him. So he agreed. He started by allowing Luke to redecorate the townhouse.

"I had a year and a million dollars to make it world class," recalled Luke. "It was a reach, but I pulled it off. Everyone wanted to publish pictures of it."

Soon Luke was the darling of the decorating world, securing

the best projects in the toniest locations. But what he couldn't secure was a meaningful relationship with another person and the feeling that he wasn't a fraud. Plus, just as he was using others, he knew deep down inside that others were using him. "I didn't kid myself that these people actually cared for me. What they cared for was what I could do for them . . . how fabulous I could make them look."

Nearly a quarter of a century and millions of dollars later, he was still searching for emotional fulfillment and relational security.

Luke came to see me at the suggestion of another patient, Skylar, whom he described as his "bestie." Over the past year, I'd been helping Skylar deal with two things she didn't want: a wandering husband and a teenage son with a marijuana problem.

Luke would never have sought out treatment but for a traumatic event he couldn't ignore. A week before coming to see me, he had gotten drunk and ended up in what he described as "a sleazy sex club." During our initial consultation, he told me he had no idea how he got there, the shame of the experience still echoing in his voice. "I started out having a lovely dinner with Skylar at Per Se. The next thing I remember I was wrapped in a cheap towel frantically searching for my Rolex in the locker room of this dump. I either traded it for sex or someone stole it." After three days of vacillating between denying that the event even occurred and feeling so depressed over it that he couldn't look at himself in the mirror, he called Skylar, the only person he could trust.

When he was in my office a week later, however, his humiliation had been replaced by swagger.

"Skylar said you have great insights and aren't so bad to look at, either." Luke grinned, revealing an impressive set of very expensive and perfectly veneered teeth.

I sat with his comment for what felt like an eternity before I responded. "Which of the two do you find more important—the substance or the veneer?" I was shocked by the icy tone of my voice and a bit troubled by my unconscious observations about his teeth.

I also shocked Luke, who wasn't used to getting a chilly response to his flirtations. His body tensed, but he didn't give up. He dealt the best cards in his deck: charm and manipulation. "It's just that you look so young and you're so accomplished. I was expecting someone much older."

No patient, gay or straight, had ever made such an overtly flirtatious comment to me. Rather than allow his remark to feed my ego, I saw through it for what it was—a masterful attempt to manipulate me and put Luke in charge of the situation.

"Why do you feel the need to charm me?" I asked. I was not about to become a pawn in his game.

"Well, I . . . I . . ." Luke didn't know what to say—perhaps for the first time ever.

"We're here to talk about you. You're paying me well to make that happen. I suggest you take full advantage of it. I don't need to be charmed. You, on the other hand, need to get some insight into your behavior."

I could feel the blade slicing into his fragile ego. In spite of his considerable wealth, in spite of his superstar status in a highly competitive field, and in spite of his God-given good looks, Luke had to work hard to conceal his shaky self-esteem.

"Wow, you're tough!" he said.

I needed to act fast to direct him away from his devolution into victimhood and toward a position of strength. I also needed to move myself away from feeling exposed and unsafe.

"I can be," I replied with a smile. "Listen, we're here to look at why you feel so unfulfilled in your life and why you can't find a meaningful relationship. Right?"

"Well, I thought we were here to discuss the loss of my Rolex."

"We'll get there."

"I never mentioned that other stuff, about being unfulfilled or whatever. Did Skylar tell you that? What else did she say about me?"

Luke's response was a textbook example of the paranoia and obsession with what others think about them that characterizes people with narcissistic personality presentations. In my practice, I've found that feelings of paranoia are particularly acute among those who make their living in status-conscious fields, such as fashion and design.

I wasn't surprised that Luke would think Skylar would divulge personal information. "No, she didn't tell me," I said. "But let's not forget where you ended up. You must have been looking for connection if you went to a sex club. People don't usually go there if they're feeling content. Are you in a meaningful intimate relationship?"

Luke rolled his eyes and laughed. "If you call the twenty-three-year-old rent boy I screw every couple of weeks meaningful."

I didn't laugh with him. "It doesn't sound terribly meaningful to me."

This time Luke didn't have a sarcastic response.

A good sign.

He slouched in his chair and stared at the art hanging on my office walls.

"That's a Philip Guston print, isn't it?"

"Yes, it is. This is uncomfortable, isn't it?" I didn't add "for you" because the exchange was also uncomfortable for me. Narcissistic and highly successful men are the most challenging for me to connect with. They bring out my insecurities with their tendency toward critical judgments, condescension, and a Machiavellian winner-takes-all approach to relationships.

"Very," he replied.

Another good sign. He was capable of being honest.

"Therapy can be hard work. You don't know or trust me. That will take time—it may happen, and it may not. You had a traumatic experience that I don't think was an isolated event. There's a huge amount of shame and guilt around it—really crappy feelings. Feelings you don't like. No one does. I certainly wouldn't."

Luke nodded. If I could give him nothing else in our first session, I hoped to show him he was seen and heard as an autonomous individual who could walk out the door anytime he pleased, while holding out the possibility of a reward greater than walking.

"Lord, what did I get myself into?" he asked, not really wanting an answer.

"In life or in therapy?" I resorted to Therapy 101. Answer a question with a question.

Luke let out a slight laugh. "Now that's a good question."

"Thank you. So let's start with therapy. I take it you've not done this before?"

"No, I've definitely not done this before. Skylar swears by

it and she's really been able to change her life."

I wanted to say that what she had really changed was her perception of her life and that I helped her pick out a better pair of glasses, but I didn't want to talk about Skylar's treatment or continue muddying the waters. Instead, I went back to the fundamentals. "So let's start with the basics."

"Please."

"Therapy is about understanding and breaking patterns that are self-destructive and that you've outgrown. It's reparative. We all start out strong, but life intervenes and we hit potholes that flatten our tires. This—this therapy—will help you fix the tires and get back on your journey."

"Well, I do find myself a bit deflated."

"Everyone does from time to time."

"But I've been in rough places before and I got myself out. When the market crashed in '09, I nearly went bankrupt, but I just worked like a dog and, well, in short order I was back in the game."

"Yes, you're a brilliant businessman. You nail the numbers side of things, but the relational things . . . maybe not as much."

Luke pushed back, "Skylar and I are buddies. We've been besties for years."

I wanted to argue with him and let him know that Skylar actually hung out with him for comic relief, but I held my tongue. Such a response would have been highly unethical, mean-spirited, and destructive.

I sidestepped his comment and jumped back into my explanation of the psychotherapeutic process.

"Self-destructive relational patterns begin in relationships and are healed in relationships. It's just finding the right relationship to do that. I hope that your therapeutic relationship with me will be that relationship."

"That's a lot of relationships!" Luke observed with a double shot of humor. I felt my face turning as red as the bottoms of many of my patients' Christian Louboutin pumps. He relieved me from my discomfort. "Lord, I just wanted to find my $12,000 watch and figure out how to drink normally again."

Okay, here we go again, I said to myself. Another member of the elite power tribe scared to give up a destructive behavior they think is helping them. I've seen so many of these cases over the years.

"It's a bit more complicated than that. How old are you?" I responded.

"None of your business," Luke shot back. "I'm a Gemini. That's all you need to know."

Now it was my turn to laugh. "Okay, I won't go near that one."

"Good! See, Skylar was right. You are wise for your age."

Suddenly, the tension left the room, and we shared a feeling of lightheartedness and connection. This moment marked the critically important beginning of our therapeutic alliance. That alliance would fade and reappear over our course of treatment, but it provided the invisible cord that tethered us together.

The greatest challenge of treating patients like Luke, who are both powerful and narcissistic, is getting them to stay in treatment long enough to do solid psychotherapeutic work. They're used to controlling their emotional state and are wary of handing it over. Plus, their narcissism has served them well—allowing them to push themselves to succeed in spite of the enormous odds against them. Understandably, they're skeptical about giving up these aspects of their character. As a result, patients of elite power are prone to go missing when the real work of therapy begins. They cancel sessions at the last minute and pay for them anyway. After all, what's a few hundred dollars when you're worth tens or hundreds of millions? Otherwise, they justify their absences for a host of reasons. The excuses are always plentiful, impressive, and often season—and vanity—related. I've heard everything from "I'm traveling for work next week," to "I'm spending the holidays in Aspen," to "I had a peel yesterday, and I can't possibly be seen in public."

Many therapists let these absences go by. They like getting paid when their patients cancel and are too impressed or intimidated by their patients' jet-set lives to challenge them. But this complicit stance is the opposite of what these patients need. What's required for them to grow is a relationship that artfully but firmly confronts them with uncomfortable truths and unflattering realities. They need to be reminded that therapy requires consistency and commitment. They also need to be made aware of their patterns and how their absences create resentment and distance with the significant people in their lives—including their therapist.

Mark, the executive I introduced in chapter 2, personified this pattern. Although he was motivated when we were in session together, he would miss months of treatment due to his work schedule. Rather than let these absences slide by, we spent many hours talking about what they meant to him and the tradeoffs they entailed. We figured out ways he could stay engaged in the therapeutic process while he was out of town, through homework assignments and HIPAA-compliant Internet sessions.

As for my opening session with Luke, we had about ten minutes left, and I wanted him to leave with clarity, direction, and hope. I also wanted him to keep coming back to do the deep and difficult work that would be needed.

"So let me try to explain how this typically works," I said. "We start in the here and now—and take a look at what comes up between us." I continued in this vein, carefully explaining how handling the snags in our relationship would ultimately help him deal with those obstacles in the real world.

Luke cocked his head to the right and frowned. I knew he was confused. Perhaps I'd given him too much information. The truth was he made me feel nervous and vulnerable. When I'm in this state, I tend to ramble.

"We're going to work on your issues within this therapeutic relationship, and we'll see how you interact with me." Luke seemed to understand, but his confusion was replaced with skepticism. As smart and successful as he was, he was woefully ignorant when it came to the give-and-take of intimate relationships.

Sigmund Freud said that for a person to be fulfilled in life, he or she must master a balance between love and work. Luke, like many of my patients, was way overweighted on the work side of this equation. This overweight typically happens at critically important points in the lives of people who suffer from narcissism, including their middle-age and late-adult years. These patients think that professional successes can substitute for the love they've strategically avoided—or never received—when in fact they desperately needed it.

But it can't.

By the time many patients find themselves in my office, they are in a state of material abundance but emotional scarcity.

Freud described love as a generosity of spirit and regard for the well-being of others. This mutuality is in sharp contrast to the narcissist's self-focused and superficial needs. Freud spoke of work as a moderate effort that enhances a person's capacity to love—not an obsessive and all-consuming industry that focuses solely on material gain.

It's true that many careers are fulfilling and exciting apart from their remunerative value. But the point Freud was making concerned balance between those all-important sources of satisfaction: love and work. Destabilizing that balance by becoming a "workaholic" can turn out to be an addiction as harmful as alcoholism or drug abuse. Often, too, it signals that something is wrong on the love side of the equation. My patient Pamela, the television producer, told me that after one of her fourteen-hour days on location, she came home to find her husband deep into his third martini. "Well, home from the wars, are you, my darling?" he said, trying not to fall over as he greeted her. Then he reminded her of the oft-quoted quip: "Nobody on their deathbed has ever said, 'I wish I'd spent more time in the office.' But maybe you'll be the exception."

It doesn't take a degree in psychology to see where Luke fell along this continuum. Ideally, he should have been in the stage of life where he was using his elite power to give back to others. But Luke had never offered his time or resources in a genuinely altruistic way or to mentor newcomers in his field. While his external self glittered with his professional success, his relational failings tarnished his inner self. Moreover, he'd accumulated material riches beyond anything he'd ever dreamed, but he lacked the joy that comes from tenderness, emotional vulnerability, and charity toward others.

In fairness to Luke and other narcissistically driven people, it's important to point out that he never *set out* to be a cold and loveless man. His personality evolved in response to the serial rejection he received at the hands of his family and community. To survive, he turned away from the vulnerability of intimate relationships and into an aspect of life he could master and control.

Michelangelo reportedly once said that to create the pure beauty that became David, he simply "chipped away at everything that wasn't David." But Luke, like Jonathan, didn't chip away at anything; instead, he piled on layers of artifice. If a shirt or sweater didn't have a designer label on it or cling to his once-taut body, he didn't wear it. He doused himself with too much cologne and Botoxed away any trace of what would have been rugged handsomeness. While his goal was to appear young and desirable, he actually made himself look painfully unnatural, unapproachable, and out of reach.

In creating a treatment plan for Luke, Jonathan, and Mark, and for other patients who suffer from narcissistic personality presentations, I never expect they will be born anew, completely freed of their narcissistic traits. As I mentioned earlier in this chapter, not only are narcissistic personality styles notoriously difficult to change, but there is also the reality that the ambition, discipline, and drive that comes out of them has often served my clients well. In Luke's case, he was a talented decorator who was gifted at managing his accounts and attracting new clients. Surprisingly too, considering his interpersonal deficiencies, he managed to hold on to his clients—mostly women—with a potent mix of flattery, reassurance, and a punishing regime of hard work that never "shut off." It wasn't difficult to picture him in action, proclaiming, "Of course you love that couch—you have such wonderful taste!" To ask him to lose these parts of himself would be a great disservice to his welfare and compromise the integrity of our therapeutic alliance.

Instead, I needed to look at the aspects of his narcissism that enhanced the quality of his life. For Luke, these were his drive to improve his station in life and enhance the aesthetic lives of his clients, his strong work ethic, and his passion for the creative process. Once we identified these strengths, we could then apply them to the deficient areas of his life—to explore sobriety, to deepen his existing relationships, and to encourage him to steward others in their personal and professional pursuits. Welcoming a challenge, Luke embraced this plan enthusiastically. Like other narcissistic people of elite power, he loved mastering tangible goals. In addition to keeping him engaged in therapy, this work gave us the space and time to delve into the deeper aspects of his personality through a collaborative and inquisitive interpersonal process.

In contrast to making immediate changes in his behavior, exploring the structure of Luke's personality required a subtler approach, grounded in our strong alliance. I helped him intellectually recognize that he got stuck in the adolescent phase of his development and was paying dearly for his failure to mature emotionally.

"So you're saying that I'm still that hot young stud back in Texas?" Luke said with a wink.

"Emotionally," I responded firmly.

"Damn. . . . Do you think I can get back the body?" he asked.

I shrugged my shoulders and responded with truth tinged with humor, "That's above my pay grade. But I do think I can help you enjoy where you are with the body you have."

Luke, ever the sharp wit, responded without missing a beat, "I'll pay for the upgrade."

Gradually, we processed his physical reality, but before we did, we needed to establish the baseline of what he had become—a self-absorbed middle-aged man who was terrified of getting old and was enslaved to other people's opinions of him.

Famed psychologist Erik Erikson wrote that in order for people to remain "psychologically alive," they must resolve the aging of their bodies and souls with grace and dignity. Guiding Luke toward that resolution was a vital—and rewarding—goal of our journey. The steps in his reparative direction were small and started, not surprisingly, with his external presentation. The conspicuous labels that adorned his clothes slowly disappeared and were replaced with luxurious fabrics and classic tailoring. He stopped dyeing his hair and was even considering backing off on his Botox injections. "I've had so much work done on my face, I'm afraid one day I'll wake up and it will be around my ankles. I'm going to take a break from it all." He began spending his Saturday afternoons at a dog shelter in Sutton Place exercising the dogs that lived there awaiting their fate, and he spent his evenings at a very popular AA meeting. "The guys are a whole lot hotter than the ones at any bar," he said. While Luke was not a man reinvented, he was a man repaired— and renewed. He also realized he didn't have to renounce his success or the elite power inherent in it to enjoy a happier and healthier life. The key to his reparation was staying in therapy long enough to realize that external success alone is not enough and that there was real value in his capacity to feel vulnerable and authentic in an interpersonal relationship.

4.

Dominant

Exploring Sex, Eroticism, and Power

Everything in the world is about sex except sex.
Sex is about power.

—OSCAR WILDE

On October 7, 2016, I awoke to a sapphire blue sky in Santa Fe, New Mexico. The hotel in which I was staying, the Inn and Spa at Loretto, upgraded me to a room with a balcony, and I was savoring my good fortune. I'd planned on spending a leisurely morning sipping coffee and catching up on the news. After a few minutes of taking in the piñon-scented air, I turned on the television. Within seconds of powering up the remote, the bliss of my morning was lost to a new world reality. In my face was Donald Trump crowing that he had the power to grab a woman by her genitals.

Now known as "Pussygate," the infamous conversation between Donald Trump and Billy Bush ran nonstop around the world. Never before had such a blatant display of hubris, aggression, and degradation of women by a political candidate been documented and widely disseminated (Drum 2016).

Watching the clip made me feel physically sick, emotionally distraught, and spiritually dirty. Even its inglorious name is dishonorable and demeaning to women and our families.

I turned off the TV and walked out onto the balcony to regain my equilibrium. Down in the lot, a sparkling black Ford F-250 pickup backed out from a parking space. I spotted a "coexist" sticker on the bumper and a gun rack in the back window. *Now that's the America I love,* I thought, *a fierce spirit of individual rights coupled with a fierce respect for others.*

As my horror quelled, my hope blossomed.

Surely this event would be the death knell to patriarchy and the privileging of elite male power that's inherent in it. As the truck disappeared from my view, I envisioned an America uniting across class divisions in its outrage toward the scandalous abuse of power.

I was deluded.

Prior to this moment, the mere whisper of a scandal of this magnitude would have halted a political candidate's advancement and shamed them into obscurity. But in our modern state of populist anger, it didn't. It marked the return to Machiavellian politics, where the ends justify the means and morality is abandoned for grasps of power.

The *Access Hollywood* tape became historic, not for what it ushered out, but rather for whom it ushered in. Just over a month later, Donald Trump—a man who has referred to his own daughter as "a piece of ass" and bragged about grabbing a woman by the crotch—became the forty-fifth president of the United States of America (Politi 2016).

Modern populism, it seems, worships an aggressor with swagger.

Years later, I'm still asking the questions I asked on that physically bright, but emotionally dark morning in New Mexico:

Where are the consequences? What happened to our family values? Why have economic pursuits trumped moral ones?

And I still don't have an answer.

Whatever a person's preferred political party, the *sexual politics* that played out across the United States with the 2016 election led many people to choose partisan sides rather than analyze or address the gender, equality, and moral issues that were at hand. I manage my anger, my fear, my anxiety, and my depression over the state of ideological division and moral regression in America by reminding myself that our narrative of social justice is still being written, and that as Dr. Martin Luther King Jr. stated over fifty years ago, "The arc of the moral universe is long, but it bends toward justice" (Hayes 2018). But even though I'm able to temporarily reframe my thoughts, my outrage frequently returns over how an abuser of elite power was granted an infinite amount more.

Yes, there was an outcry, but in the highest echelon of public power, not much seems to have changed.

The #MeToo movement had a moment of glory and raised public awareness around sexual violence against both women and men, but the noise it made has faded.

A handful of men in positions of elite power in the realms of business and entertainment were asked to pay dues, tokens in an economy of privilege. Billy Bush, a witness to Donald Trump's misogynistic boasts, was fired from his position on *TODAY* but received a payout of millions. According to supermarket tabloids, Matt Lauer is living as a "recluse" in the guesthouse of his $36.5 million mansion in Southampton, New York, after showing a colleague his penis and giving a sex toy to another (*In Touch Weekly* 2018). Harvey Weinstein is awaiting trial for a raft of sex crime charges against (at last count) eighty-seven women and, after posting a million-dollar bail, is free to live between his homes in Connecticut and Manhattan (Baker and McKinley 2018). Higher up the elite male power scale, the Catholic Church is finally being called to take responsibility for decades of covering up thousands of sexual assaults by its priests (Goodstein and Otterman 2018). The pope is saying the right words, but there will never be enough action to repair the damage caused to the victims and their families.

We keep thinking Icarus has flown too close to the sun, but he hasn't.

If you're having a hard time making sense out of this quagmire, you're not alone. It's hard to believe the level of splitting, also known as black-and-white thinking, that's occurring in the American psyche around the topic of elite power and sexual aggression. During a 2018 lecture I delivered in Greenwich, Connecticut, on the topic of the psychotherapeutic treatment of elite patient populations, the former president of Silver Hill Hospital asked me what I thought of the new political reality. I responded that we're living in dark and dangerous times in which our collective psyche has manifested in a borderline presentation. In this morally vacant state, nuances of behavior are discarded for simplistic decrees, and complex, rational thinking is eclipsed by bland pronouncements. Statements such as "fake news," "lock her up," and "build a wall" stimulate our limbic system while shutting down our executive functioning. In this state of hyperarousal, we lose our capacity for rational thought and make decisions against our moral well-being.

Modern populist rhetoric resonates because it appeals to a deficiency in Maslow's most basic needs, which in our modern age are grounded in economic survival. Driven by these primal needs for safety and security, we don't simply overlook but elevate sexual aggressions that result from the elite male power of our president, a man upon whom we've projected fantasies of celebrity and whom we've pardoned with forgiving statements such as "Oh that's just how he is" and "He's the president, so his actions are presidential."

The ease with which we've turned a blind eye to sexual injustices toward women in the wake of our fear, anger, and aspirational greed being stoked by a celebrity leader is terrifying. As long as he and his court are allowed to ride roughshod over women's sexual dignity, our moral and psychological well-being will devolve to baseness not seen since the dark ages of world wars and ethnic and religious genocides. The #MeToo movement and the holding of a few powerful men accountable for their actions is a start, but it's a grain of sand that's gotten lost in the toxic beach of elite male sexual aggression.

•

The world loves a celebrity mug shot, especially when it involves a DUI—and a sexual misstep. When it involves a celebrity with a history of both, the Internet chatter around it becomes as animated as the latest release by Pixar. Such was the case on Memorial Day 2017 when a mug shot of Tiger Woods found its way into virtual commerce. Asleep in his Mercedes on the side of the road by his home on Jupiter Island, Florida, Woods was arrested and thrust back into the searing spotlight of celebrity gossip.

Like many other celebrities, Woods is no stranger to the perils of motoring and sexual indiscretions. Nearly a decade earlier, his private sex life became public when he crashed his Cadillac Escalade in the wake of an argument with his former wife, Elin Nordegren. What emerged after the crash was a narrative of infidelities with women who were deemed far below his status as a celebrity with megawatt charisma.

The question on everyone's mind, of course, was how a man with so much at stake—a stunningly beautiful wife, multimillion-dollar endorsements, two young children—could risk it for a few hours of sexual pleasure?

The question is not unique to Woods; it's so common that it's attained an archetypal status. From Debbie Reynolds and Eddie Fisher to whispers about Brad Pitt and Angelina Jolie, the celebrity world is full of larger-than-life stories of stars who sexually wander out of the bounds of their primary relationship, then pay an extraordinary price for their indiscretions. And it's not just Hollywood and sports celebrities whose talents get overshadowed by their peccadillos. With the exception of our current president, many a male political figure has seen his career tarnish and implode under the weight of his sexual infidelities. John Kennedy is arguably better known for his affairs with Marilyn Monroe than for his handling of the Bay of Pigs. Bill Clinton is better known for his affair with Monica Lewinsky than for his ability to balance the federal budget (Jackson 2008) and Arnold Schwarzenegger for fathering a child with his housekeeper than for his role as governor of California. And while Anthony Weiner became infamous for sexting with minors, we can't recall exactly what political office he held.

So back to the billion-dollar question: "What was he (and occasionally, she) thinking when they wandered, and why do we all care so much?"

To answer this question, we need to step away from the tantalizing gossip for just a moment and explore rational thinking through the physiology of the human brain.

Like other bodily functioning, logic and reason involve a series of chemical and electrical reactions. Monitoring this rational thinking is the region of brain known as the prefrontal cortex. This is the part of our brain that enables us to make rational decisions, to consider the consequences of our behaviors, and to modulate our social interactions (Yang and Raine 2009). It involves higher-level decision-making skills and is most developed in mature and educated human beings.

Sex and other survival drives, like ambition and a concept known as the "will to power," involve a more primitive part of our central nervous system. This is the part of our physiology that's collectively known as the limbic system.

Most people can negotiate between the impulsive pulls of their drives and the rational part of their brain and arrive at a responsible, constructive outcome. So a potential mate may provoke sexual arousal, but the person is able to run a cost-benefit analysis of the engagement and realize it's simply not worth it. They'll say to themselves, "Yeah, she's smoking hot, but getting romantically or sexually involved with her just isn't worth the price."

Many have the good judgment to discuss their attraction in confidence with a friend, which further stabilizes their reactions to the situation. The simple act of stating and asking something along the lines of "I'm turned on by my kids' nanny, and I get vibes back that she's totally game for a hookup, but I don't think it's a good idea to get involved—what do you think?" can go a long way to defuse a highly charged situation. So, rather than act on their impulses, they think through them, consult with a confidant, and avoid both personal and relational destruction.

Unlike most middle-class people, who have strong relational support systems, the rich too often have social networks defined by isolation and inauthenticity. As such, they lack the social scaffolding that keeps their primal drives from overwhelming their rational judgment. This chronic problem becomes acute when they suffer from a host of psychological challenges including narcissism, substance use, and mood disorders such as depression, anxiety, and bipolar disorder. Like rust on a steel beam, these conditions further erode their judgment and cause them to engage in irrational and self-destructive behaviors.

Yes, people celebrated for their elite power might have personalities big enough to support reality television shows, garages full of exotic sports cars, and trophy homes around the world, but these provide only a veneer of protection. Deep down, they're terrified that someone will discover they're actually weak and ineffective.

Many self-medicate this emotional vulnerability with the elixir of their success. They become so intoxicated by their power that they feel entitled to their sexual exploitations. This is especially true of men and women who attain power, renown, and celebrity status by virtue of their success in financial endeavors. Traditionally, this financial excess was viewed as the purview of East Coast financiers, but with the extraordinary wealth being generated from Silicon Valley, it has found its way out west. The toxic and elite "bad-boy geek" culture that's grown in Silicon Valley has come to dominate many news cycles and is perhaps best exemplified by Uber and its former CEO Travis Kalanick. With an estimated market capitalization that once reached $120 billion (Hoffman, Bensinger, and Farrell 2018), Uber became infamous for the misogynistic culture, bad-boy excess, and violence against women that flourished under Kalanick's leadership (O'Brien et al. 2018; Kleinman 2017).

As a clinician who works in New York City and London, two of the world's financial capitals, I treat a large number of individuals who lack the scaffolding to hold the enormity of their success. In the privacy of my office, I'm privileged to hear their tales of excess told not out of hubris but as a means of relating to me the details of their lives. Other times, however, I overhear these tales out in the commerce of my life.

Several years ago, I was getting dressed after my 6:30 a.m. yoga class when I was drawn into a conversation between two thirty-something wonder boys. Both men resembled Greek gods. It was easy to picture them as prom kings and quarterbacks at their prep schools and Ivy League colleges. However, their clean-cut looks stood in sharp contrast to the profanities that spewed from their mouths.

"It was sick," the dark-haired one said to his blond friend. "The new bottle chick from Pink Elephant was f*ckin' on fire. She hooked us up with a table of Russian models who just wanted to pour Cristal and c*ck down their throats." I recognized their references to a popular downtown nightclub and ultra-expensive champagne. They were oblivious to me as they prattled on in their elite brand of street slang.

"Yeah, she's smokin' hot," replied his blond friend, casually slipping into his $1,300 John Lobb double monks. "She totally hooked me up in Southampton at Dune. Fourth of July weekend there was more Russian p*ssy at our table than flies on sh*t. That weekend set me back thirty large."

"Sounds about right," the "gentleman" with the dark hair said, admiring himself in the mirror and running his fingers through his hair. "I haven't looked at the Amex yet, but I'm sure that's what I'm in for."

For most of us, the thought of spending $30,000 for a weekend of partying and sexual excess seems outrageous, but for a shockingly large segment of alpha males in New York, Hong Kong, Las Vegas, London, Dubai, and Los Angeles, this is the price of an evening of elite power.

In fact, a cottage industry has arisen in large metropolitan areas consisting of "bottle girls" and VIP concierges who sell alcohol marked up by nearly 2,000 percent and procure a variety of services for men with lots of money. The most infamous of these bottle girls was Rachel Uchitel, who went from being the international poster girl for grief and loss after her fiancé's death in the September 11 attacks to being one of Tiger Woods's mistresses and to eventually exposing her struggle with addiction on *Celebrity Rehab with Dr. Drew* (Smith 2009). In the process, she has also become a wealthy woman. She reportedly made around $500,000 for her appearance on *Celebrity Rehab* and, according to Celebrity Net Worth, has accumulated a net worth of around $10 million (Celebrity Net Worth n.d.).

Many of these high-striving men who—like my locker-room companions—suffer from narcissism seek out sex of this sort in an attempt to validate themselves. What I find most surprising about this over-the-top behavior is that any of these men could date just about any woman he wanted simply by asking her out. They're good looking, well schooled, and rich. So why do they choose to buy expensive sex from escorts and pay for the affections of silicone-enhanced women in nightclubs?

The easy answer is they suffer from narcissism and view emotional vulnerability as their Achilles' heel. Early in their lives, their egos were painfully injured, and they vowed to never be emotionally exposed again. To compensate for this perceived weakness, they've decorated the exteriors of their lives but failed to create the internal architecture to support the weight of the gilt that covers them.

But sex is a form of relational expression. So to fully understand sex relative to elite power, we must look at it through a relational lens.

Sex that leads to love requires vulnerability, especially if you're involved with someone you genuinely care for and view as a peer. As Viktor Frankl observed in *Man's Search for Meaning*, "(S)ex is a vehicle of expression for love. [It's] a way of expressing the experience of that ultimate togetherness which is called love" (Frankl 1959).

But men and women who've failed to internalize their elite power into their self-concept or their interpersonal lives view the equalitarian togetherness of which Dr. Frankl wrote not as an asset, but as a liability that can destroy them. To guard against this destruction, they turn their sexual relationships into transactions. In the form of a transaction, they reduce their sexual partners to objects over which they can exert their power and control.

Of course, this works most effectively if money changes hands. Reducing sex to a commercial exchange transforms it into something that can be quantified and used to assuage personal insecurities and relational doubts. They outmaneuver their fear of being objectified for their wealth, their celebrity, and their beauty by a pre-emptive objectification of others.

The more a person pays, the higher they perceive their control over the transaction to be. Public personas like Eliot Spitzer and Tiger Woods didn't pore over Craigslist or Tinder to find the kind of sex they craved. Neither did Brenda, whom you'll meet later in this chapter. They went straight to the deluxe services of high-end escorts and discreet purveyors to satisfy their needs and paid hundreds of thousands of dollars for sexual services. In this way, sexual conquests become nothing about love and all about control and domination.

•

The use of escorts by a rich, powerful, and beautiful man was one of the central issues I worked on with Marcelo, a law student from Brazil. Marcelo came from a wealthy family in Rio—his father owned an oil and gas company—and he was living a lush life in New York while attending law school at NYU. He came into therapy after crashing his Porsche during a drunken weekend at his uncle's house in Miami. "My mother is flipping out," he said in his heavy Portuguese accent. "She says I must see a—how do you say?—shrink. She read about you on the Dr. Oz website."

Tall and muscular, with piercing green eyes, Marcelo, at twenty-six years of age, had what can only be described as a sexual energy that was innate and organic. He was the kind of person who left both women and many men simply breathless. After meeting him for the first time, my receptionist said, "He is so gorgeous, I blanked out when he came in the door. He asked me where the bathroom was, and I couldn't remember!"

At first, Marcelo was more interested in manipulating his parents so as to keep his trust funds flowing than he was in committing himself to therapy. But his attitude changed once we started unlocking the secrets of his complicated sex life.

It didn't take long for me to discover that in spite of Marcelo's external beauty, he suffered from imposter syndrome. Although externally he projected strength, internally he felt emotionally fragile and undeserving of the awe the world bestowed on him. Instead of seeking out young women from his own social class—and he had plenty to choose from—he paid dominatrices thousands of dollars to lock him in a cage and beat him with a leather whip.

Appeasing his parents may have first led Marcelo to therapy, but he eagerly took to the psychotherapeutic process and made it about his healing and nothing else. "Wow, that went fast," he commented after our first session. After a few more sessions, it became clear that Marcelo desperately needed help. He hungered for a relationship that let him talk about how uncomfortable he was in his own skin—without seeming ungrateful or conceited.

When I asked him if he considered himself attractive, he said, "I guess so. People tell me that I am, but I don't always feel it, and people definitely respond to me in a certain way that can make me feel uncomfortable."

"Do you feel attractive right now?" I asked.

"I actually feel fat," he said, to my surprise. "Like I'm

poured into these jeans." He grabbed a handful of skin in his midsection and pulled on it.

Like many other people who are objectified for their external beauty or for their wealth and power, Marcelo was terrified of losing what he and others viewed as his relational currency. The question that constantly haunted him was "Who or what will I be once my looks or money are gone?"

He craved intimacy based on something other than his physical attributes but didn't know how to find it. "People look at me like I'm some sort of god, which I'm not. It's a huge amount of pressure. And what happens," he asked, "if I get fatter than I already am, or, God forbid . . . old?"

Marcelo's fear and anxiety led him to a website dedicated to bondage, discipline, domination, submission, sadism, and masochism—known colloquially as BDSM. "I like getting lost in the Internet," he said. "It helps calm me down, and I just happened upon this kinky website." In no time, Marcelo was hooked by the conversations he found there. Within a month, he had ventured into a BDSM event at an abandoned warehouse in a rough-and-tumble section of Brooklyn. There he met Cat, a professional dominatrix.

"I know it makes no sense, but I feel free when she puts me in a cage," he admitted. "I don't have to fill these—what's the American expression?—large shoes." The pleasure and release Marcelo found in his sexual adventures is an experience shared by other highly successful and well-educated men and women who find the experience of being dominated by another person emotionally and sexually cathartic. "I love it when Cat is in control," Marcelo explained. "I completely lose myself and, strangely, I feel at peace."

But the price Marcelo was paying for this peace was way out of proportion to the moments of release he got from his anxiety. Not only was the financial toll tremendous, but he was also paying heavy emotional premiums. "Sometimes after Cat and I meet, I'm so tired I can't get out of bed. I lie there curled up in a ball. Everything feels so heavy and dark."

My first order of business with Marcelo was to get him relief from his debilitating anxiety and depression. I referred him to one of New York's best psychiatrists, who put him on a carefully titrated cocktail of medications. While we waited a few weeks for the meds to kick in, Marcelo and I began to search for events in his past that might have laid the foundation for his unhappiness. It took a while, but six months into treatment, Marcelo revealed that when he was four or five, his governess would sexually stimulate him while she was putting him down to sleep.

Marcelo had told only one other person about the governess: a former girlfriend. She made fun of him for being "so sensitive" about it, and she subsequently broke off their relationship. Marcelo was humiliated—it had taken a lot of courage for him to make this disclosure—and he took her rejection as a sign that he was flawed and deserved to be punished.

Once I had this critically important background, I formulated a treatment plan to correct his cognitive distortions about women, punishment, and sex and subsequently to help him *feel* what an intimate relationship with healthy boundaries felt like.

Did it help that I was a man? I believe in this case it did.

Many people ask if it's important to see a therapist of one gender or the other. My response is always "it depends." The two main factors I consider in making this determination are the patient's presenting issues and the ability of the clinician, regardless of his or her gender, to engender trust and hold the psychotherapeutic frame around the patient's issues and personality. As these considerations applied to Marcelo, it was important that, in the initial stages of his treatment, he worked with a male therapist or with a female therapist who was a lesbian.

This is because the first few months of treatment are critically important to the long-term effectiveness of the therapeutic engagement. While all emotional and relationship issues require trust in the clinician, dealing with sexual issues of any sort, especially those grounded in a sexual trauma, requires an extraordinary amount of trust in and vulnerability with a therapist. During this time, patients are on high alert for signals that the clinician is worthy of their truth and can handle the enormity of their pain. While there are many straight women therapists who could have effectively worked with Marcelo, Marcelo would never have tolerated the initial stages of the therapeutic process with them.

Numerous studies have demonstrated that the gender of the therapist matters to the patient's outcome. Most of these studies have focused on the female identity expression of the patient and the therapist. Not surprisingly, these studies show women therapists are more empathetic and enjoy more successful outcomes for their patients—especially patients who are also female (Kirshner, Genack, and Hauser 1978). But the statistical data tells only one part of the complicated and highly nuanced art of the psychotherapeutic relationship, especially in matters related to sex, sexual orientation, and sexual expression. The more interesting and important data come from the felt experience that occurs in real time within the sanctity of the professional encounter.

For Marcelo to transcend his bravado, he needed to step outside of his game of sexual cat and mouse. He needed to feel that there was no sexual tension in the room. Most of all, he needed to soften his narcissistic ego to speak of experiences that simultaneously filled him with shame and made him feel acutely alive. Eventually, this is exactly what Marcelo was able to do. It took three months before he finally admitted he was into bondage and paid for sex, and another three before he alluded to the sexual molestation. About a year after we began working together, I could see that his brain had made progress in decoupling the wiring that connected sex with humiliation. He put together a small group of female peers whom he enjoyed for their intellect and humor rather than their sexual abilities.

A year and a half into treatment, Marcelo became involved with a young woman he met in his constitutional-law study group. "She's smart, funny, and beautiful in a way I never thought I'd find attractive." It was clear to me that he felt safe and loved in her presence—and he didn't need or want to be "punished" for his attraction to her. He had formed a truly *intimate* relationship with another human being whom he viewed as a peer rather than as an object.

·

The connections between elite power, money, and sex are certainly not new. Prostitution, objectification, fetishism, and transactional relationships are phenomena that transcend time, race, religion, and culture. What is new, however, is the degree to which extreme wealth alters the way sex is thought of, consumed, and executed, and how these evolutions have expanded to include a consumer base of women.

But before we explore the ways in which women's relationships to sex have changed, let's look more closely at the sexual experience of men of great financial means outside the rarefied world of bottle girls and sexual procurers.

According to a recent survey by Prince & Associates, a marketing research firm that specializes in global private wealth, men of high net worth report that their wealth and status afford them better and more exciting sex (Kerner 2012). No surprise there: Men with higher status tend to attract women, who themselves gain status from their association with powerful men. And with all this power flowing so freely, it stands to reason that libidos are enhanced. But celebrity males—and particularly the narcissists among them—are also frequently characterized by arrogance and the conviction that they are more deserving or entitled to a hypercharged sex life than other people. After all, other people simply exist to satisfy their needs. But as we've seen time and again, this attitude of narcissistic entitlement can provoke powerful, wealthy, and/or famous men to make destructive sexual decisions. We need to think back no further than Luke, the wildly successful decorator who got drunk one night and landed in a "sleazy sex club"—sans his Rolex.

Marital unfaithfulness in varying degrees is known to be a hallmark of the rich and famous. According to social psychologist Justin Lehmiller, a faculty fellow at Harvard University, "Research has found that power and wealth are linked to a higher likelihood of infidelity" (Kerner 2012).

Underscoring this claim, the wealthy men who claimed they had "better sex" in that recent survey defined it as "more-frequent sex with more partners." Wealthy women, in contrast, defined "better" sex as being of a "higher quality," with no mention of multiple partners (Kerner 2012).

Over the years, I've become known as an authority on infidelity—both the usual kind, where sexual contact takes place, and emotional infidelity, in which a partner directs his or her romantic energy toward a person outside the primary relationship but doesn't have sex with him or her. In spite of my extensive experience, the thick layer of denial and rationalization that surrounds infidelity always amazes me.

Lionel and his wife, Rebekah, are striking examples. The much-admired CEO of a major publishing house, Lionel cut a vigorous figure at the age of sixty-seven. More than six feet tall, with thick salt-and-pepper hair and deep laugh lines that fanned out from the corners of his eyes when he smiled, he looked more like a gentleman farmer than a husband who wandered outside the agreed sexual bounds of his marriage. But looks can be deceptive. Lionel had spent the last thirteen years of his life maintaining a mistress in a pied-à-terre across Central Park from the palatial East Side duplex he shared with his wife.

"So you had no idea?" I asked Rebekah, a chic and petite woman of an indeterminate age.

"None," she responded, with more conviction than was required.

I looked at her with the furrowed brow I get when I'm unable to hide my skepticism.

"Now let me get this straight. For the last thirteen years,

your husband took the dog for a three-hour walk most nights, had a slush account to which you were not allowed access, spent all Jewish holidays home with you but all Christian holidays away on 'business' (while Lionel and Rebekah were Jewish, the mistress was Catholic), and you haven't suspected anything?"

She sighed deeply before allowing, "Well, maybe I had an awareness."

"Maybe you didn't want to know," I added too quickly. *Ouch,* I thought to myself. *That was harsh.*

"Of course, I didn't want to know," she snapped back, rightfully annoyed with my crass persistence. "What wife wants to know her husband has a mistress?"

Her point was an excellent one.

Certainly no wife who is terrified of being a divorced middle-aged woman would desire such knowledge, I thought to myself. Rebekah was better at reading my mind than picking up her husband's clues. "There was a lot to lose here," she added.

"There certainly was," I responded. "But there's also an enormous amount to gain."

Rebekah wasn't convinced. She sighed deeply and added, "Well that's easy for you to say."

Again, she made an excellent point.

While I could sit in the comfort of my office and make clinical observations and platitudes, Rebekah was the one who'd have to face the incredibly painful realities of her life and walk through them.

But Rebekah wasn't the only one deeply defensive about the affair. In the joint sessions I had with the couple, I found that Lionel was also in denial. But while Rebekah's defenses helped her close her eyes to harsh truths, Lionel's defenses were based on grand and narcissistic delusions.

He argued that he was French and that all French men maintain mistresses. He rationalized that he wasn't an adulterer, just a polygamist who supported multiple wives.

"But you're Jewish and of Dutch descent," I responded when I realized what he was saying.

He pretended not to hear me, so I persisted. "I've never heard of a section in the Torah that allows for multiple wives. I thought that was a Mormon thing." Again, no response. Finally, he looked down at his razor-thin Patek Philippe watch and responded in a derisive tone, "According to ancient Jewish law, only a king is limited to the number of wives and/or concubines he can have. That number is eighteen. Everyone else can have as many as they like. Up until a few generations ago, deeply religious men often had multiple wives."

Oh, my, I thought. *This guy's really arrogant—and really smart. He's certainly trumped me on Jewish law.* I was at a loss for words, and so was Rebekah, whose jaw dropped as her husband spoke. But before we could fashion a response, Lionel pre-empted us. With an air of self-satisfaction, he proclaimed, "This is going nowhere. Rebekah insists on getting a divorce, so I'll have the rabbi draw up a *gett*," referring to a Jewish divorce decree.

Rather than admit any culpability or assume any responsibility for his actions, Lionel went through a costly and humiliating divorce. And in the end, it was Rebekah who thrived as a result of the decision. My comment about her having a lot to gain was glib, but she proved me to be right. Nine months after her separation from Lionel, she was a woman transformed.

"I feel twenty years younger. I'm sleeping like a baby, and

my life has actually improved. Fear kept me in that relationship for way too many years. I wish I'd left decades ago."

She started actively dating as soon as the divorce finalized and ended up marrying another successful—but this time faithful and attentive—man.

Lionel didn't fare as well. You might expect that he'd simply cross the park for good and live happily ever after with his mistress. But you would be wrong. A month later, their relationship was history. For him, forbidden fruit was far more delicious than the kind he could consume in the open.

Despite the pain it inflicts, infidelity is a world away from coercive sex, which is by no means foreign to the rich and famous. It used to be thought that rape and other forms of sexual abuse were confined to the so-called lower classes—think of Tennessee Williams's Stanley Kowalski, the iconic brute in *A Streetcar Named Desire*. But research in recent years has revealed that upper-crust sexual aggression is far more common and dangerous than most of us, including psychotherapists, had ever imagined. Date rape on Ivy League campuses is on the rise, despite the fact that these high-status students could easily obtain consensual sex. Once again, it's a matter of narcissism and the will to power; these young men expect women to satisfy their needs regardless of the women's own needs and preferences and feel entitled to objectify them.

This abuse of power isn't confined to the campus. In 1987, the notorious case of children's book editor Hedda Nussbaum, whose common-law spouse, attorney Joel Steinberg, beat her beyond recognition and murdered their illegally adopted daughter, brought the horror of upscale intimate terrorism to public attention. In her landmark book "*Not to People Like Us*," psychotherapist Susan Weitzman delves deeper into this type of domestic abuse, laying bare one of the most devastating social problems faced by upscale wives, many of them educated professional women. These battered wives rarely report the emotional or physical abuse their husbands inflict on them, in part because they are convinced, rightly, that the authorities will be less than sympathetic. "You have all that money; you can take care of yourself" is what they hear from social workers and criminal justice officials. In effect, they are revictimized by the very people whom they look to for help.

•

When we think of people who pay for sex and objectify or abuse their sexual partners, we usually think of men like my potty-mouthed pals at the gym. But, as I hinted earlier, recent research and my clinical experience indicate that women are catching up to their male counterparts in their infidelities and sexual exploitations. One study found that over the past ten years, the rate at which women have been cheating on their husbands rose 40 percent and is now nearly equal to that of men (Giacobbe 2016; Schonfeld 2013). And rich and famous women are outpacing their less prosperous sisters. The study by Prince & Associates that I cited earlier found that nearly 75 percent of the women surveyed said they'd had affairs, in contrast to 50 percent of the men. One of the key factors in this rise is the increase in women's income—and thus their power and autonomy to exercise their sexual freedom in ways that were once largely limited to men.

These findings are consistent with my clinical impressions. Among the elite women I treat, I see a much higher rate of infidelity than in my middle-class patients. What's more, I am seeing sexual exploitation—and even a willingness to pay for sex—that begins to rival that of my male patients.

Several years ago, I treated a woman I'll call Brenda, whose adult response to childhood oppression manifested itself through destructive sexual expression. An attorney named Richard, who was the gatekeeper on a trust her late father provided for her upon his death, referred Brenda to me. In my years of treating trust fund heirs and heiresses, I'd never met anyone quite like Brenda.

Richard began his phone call with a compliment. "I heard you speak at The Breakers in Palm Beach last October on your research on wealth," he said. "Good talk. I've been following your work since then."

I was flattered.

"Thank you," I replied, pleased that my presentation had been heard—and found to be useful. He began to describe the plight of his client, a woman in her forties who lived with her fifteen-year-old daughter in Greenwich, Connecticut.

"I'm afraid the whole matter is a bit embarrassing," Richard said.

"For you or the client?" I asked, trying to inject some humor into what was obviously an uncomfortable state of affairs.

He responded with a chuckle, "Well, for us both, it seems."

I was relieved he had a sense of humor. A bit of levity goes far in dealing with the intensity of the work.

"Fair enough. But just so you know, I've heard a lot, and there's not much that shocks me."

"Good, because this one's a doozy." He hesitated. "There's really no elegant way to say this. So I'll just spit it out." He paused for what seemed like a minute. "Apparently my client has a thing for peeing on men." Another pause. "She hires them from some sort of 'service' in Manhattan."

"Ah, water sports," I replied, proud of my knowledge in these matters.

"Excuse me?"

"Urinating on another person for pleasure is known as water sports. The formal name is urolagnia. It's not as uncommon as you'd think."

"Well, it's pretty uncommon in my world," he said. "Anyway, this particular night things got messy in a big way. The guy she hired ended up overdosing on heroin in her bathtub. My client freaked out. Called her daughter, who was spending the night at a friend's, and said she had to come home immediately."

"Oh my, this *is* messy."

"Hold on. It continues. The girl has no way to get home— her friend's parents aren't there to drive her. So she does the only thing she can think of, which is to call 911."

"Oh my."

"Yes. The police and the paramedics show up. Just in the nick of time. The guy was purple. Five minutes later, he would have been dead. Only now it's a scene straight out of *The Wire*. The friend's father comes back, and the daughter insists he take her home."

"Lord, I guess there's no Uber in Greenwich?"

"Well, now there's a thought I've not considered. I'll leave that interpretation to you."

"Let's just say the trauma impaired her judgment," I said.

"Sounds like a solid interpretation. In any event, the father takes her home. When they arrive, the house is surrounded by police cars, ambulances, flashing lights—we're talking Greenwich here, not Baltimore. The daughter rushes in and sees this mess. Calls her father, who's out of town on business."

"Your client is married?" I asked.

"Separated, but definitely still married. The husband—well soon-to-be ex-husband—is drunk most of the time and always traveling for business. He runs a fund that owns trailer parks—I mean mobile-home communities. There's amazing money in these parks. In any event, he's completely wasted when the daughter calls. He's slurring his words, and so the daughter just hangs up on him."

"Poor kid. Well, there's no shortage of clinical opportunities here."

"And should I tell you who the client's father is . . . or was? He died about twenty years ago now, may he rest in peace."

"Please. I suspect he was a big deal."

"Yes," he replied, and proceeded to tell me the name of one of the most successful and beloved celebrities of the twentieth century.

"You're right. That matters a lot."

"Exactly, and it continues. Mom, my client, is hauled off to jail, and child protection gets called. Mom spends the night in the county jail, and I spring her the next day. The daughter gets sent down to her grandmother's, my client's mother's, in Boca. Mom's mortified beyond belief, and for the past three days, she has been holed up in New York in a suite at the Surrey, burning through cash—cash that she really doesn't have."

"And cash she's expecting the trust to fund, I'd imagine."

"You got it."

"So that is quite a stew you've got there."

"It certainly is. Any suggestions?"

I always have suggestions, but they come to me faster when the cases are less complicated. This case presented so many issues that I wasn't sure where to begin. I needed more information.

"What's your relationship with the mom—her name is Brenda, right? What are the dynamics?"

"Yes, Brenda. Well, it's obviously strained right now, but I've known her for her entire life. Her father and I go way back. I basically managed his career. Kept the sharks at bay, and let me tell you, there was no shortage of sharks."

"There are still plenty of sharks, it seems."

"Oh, yes."

"I don't recall reading about this. Was the press involved?"

"Thankfully not. We've got a lot of goodwill in that community."

"Okay, back to Brenda, you've got a good relationship with her?"

"Yes, she's a great kid . . . kid . . . she's almost fifty, and I still see her as a kid. She's been through a lot. It wasn't easy for her growing up under her father's fame. I'm kind of like a second father to her."

Brenda has to be overwhelmed with shame, I thought. *Not only must she deal with her daughter's, her mother's, and her husband's disapproval, but also the judgment of her "second father," a man who also holds the purse strings. No wonder she chose to hide out in a five-star hotel.*

Instead of sharing these thoughts with Richard, I decided that a "soft intervention" was in order. It was a risk, but Brenda had no intention of coming home any time soon. Before a decision was made to cut off her money—a reaction I seldom condone—we needed to see if we could get her to come around on her own volition.

I shared my thoughts with Richard. "So what would you think about showing up at the hotel tomorrow?"

Richard was taken aback. "Well, I—"

I cut him off. "You wouldn't go alone. I'll go with you."

"You'd do that?"

"Yes. Listen, it's a risk. She may not even open the door, but since you have such a long-term relationship with her and she's at risk, I say we give it a whirl."

Richard agreed, and we arranged to meet at the hotel the next day at 3:00 p.m. There was no answer when we called Brenda's room, so we settled down in the lobby and waited. Around 4:30, she sailed in through the revolving door, toting an armful of violet shopping bags from Bergdorf's.

"That's her," said Richard, jumping up and heading toward Brenda.

If I had pictured a whip-wielding dominatrix in black leather and stilettos, I was quickly proven wrong. Brenda looked no different from the other designer-suited women passing through the lobby.

She was surprised and angry to see us, but I sensed she was also relieved.

"What are you doing here?" she asked, raising her voice ever so slightly. "Are you stalking me?"

"We're not stalking you. We've come to help," Richard said.

The "we" got her attention.

"Who is he?" she demanded, pointing a coral-tipped finger

in my direction.

I waited for Richard's lead. He was the one who had the leverage to get her into treatment.

"This is Dr. Hokemeyer. We need him to help us sort out the situation."

Well done, I said to myself. Richard handled everything brilliantly. He didn't add to Brenda's shame by saying that I'm a licensed family and marriage therapist whose expertise is in treating high net worth individuals with addictions, narcissistic tendencies, and sexually deviant behaviors. He joined us together by using the pronoun *we*, presenting me as part of a solution as opposed to an outsider.

Brenda looked me up and down with a combination of contempt and curiosity. I could see she was too tired to fight much.

"I certainly don't need a doctor. This is insulting."

A desk clerk who was handsome enough to be an actor or model emerged from behind the mahogany reception to offer assistance. Brenda waved him off.

"Maybe we can find somewhere more private," I said, slightly above a whisper.

Brenda looked around the lobby. Other people were beginning to stare.

"Let's go up to my suite," she suggested, searching the pockets of her full-length mink for the key. "I need a scotch and a Xanax."

What shocks most people about this story is not that it's a mélange of drugs, infidelity, prostitution, fetishism, wealth, and sex, but that the protagonist is a woman. While we accept that wealthy men pay for sex and dominate their sexual objects, we have a hard time acknowledging that women also have a destructive relationship with their "will to power" that causes them to sexually exploit others.

Nietzsche's concept of the "will to power"—the need to strive, succeed, and dominate—is a phenomenon that's as old as time. It's a force that has propelled our human race forward, but it has also come at a cost: the exploitation of others. In *Beyond Good and Evil*, Nietzsche wrote: "Life simply *is* will to power. . . . 'Exploitation' . . . belongs to the *essence* of what lives, as a basic organic function" (Nietzsche 1966).

While we've typically considered the will to power as it relates to male patterns of aggression, times are changing. And they're changing quickly. For the first time in our history and culture, women are becoming more financially independent.

Most of my female patients don't rely on a man to support them. They've earned their wealth, inherited it, or acquired it through a divorce. My practice is just one slice of a much larger pie. Women's increasing wealth is an international phenomenon.

Numerous statistics confirm this trend. An article in *Forbes* reported that "the number of wealthy women in the United States is growing twice as fast as the number of wealthy men"; that "45% of American millionaires are women"; and that "48% of estates worth more than $5 million are controlled by women, compared with 35% controlled by men" (Stengel 2014). Women control nearly 60% of the wealth in the United States (Kransy 2012). Additionally, "60% of high-net-worth women have earned their own fortunes" (Stengel 2014).

When it comes to sex, this burgeoning prosperity has important implications. With financial independence, women feel empowered and often eager to assert themselves sexually.

When this impulse is driven by sensuous and erotic motives, it's healthy and life affirming. But when the motivation is anger, resentment, fear, inability to establish true intimacy, self-loathing, imposter syndrome, narcissism, or any of the patterns we've covered so far, sexual assertion comes out in destructive and self-sabotaging ways.

The latter was the case for Brenda, who became my patient—not entirely willingly—one week after our encounter at the Surrey. By our fourth session, I realized that her sexual exploitation of the men she hired was related to the intense anger she harbored toward her father, her brother, and her soon-to-be ex-husband.

When I asked Brenda about her father, she said, "Everybody loved him. But he was a bastard. Yes, he made a good living, but he got rich because he was cheap. Squeezed a dollar so tight it would cry."

"So money was important to him?"

"Important? He worshiped it. It was his god. The reason he got up in the morning and didn't come home at night."

"Do you feel he loved money more than you?"

"Absolutely." She didn't need to think about that one.

"So talk more about the role money played in your childhood."

"I'm not sure I understand what you mean."

"Yes, it's a complicated question. Money is complicated. I think of it as an energetic. It has the power to do great things, and yet it can be very damaging."

Brenda's arm tightened around the throw pillow she was holding. "I would definitely say it caused more harm than good in my family."

"How so?" I needed to walk her through this slowly.

"We lived in a fancy building on Park Avenue and had a house in the Hamptons, but the apartment and the beautifully landscaped property were a pretense. Inside we had secondhand and broken-down furniture. My dad would scream if we left the lights on or kept the refrigerator door open for too long. God forbid we would have air conditioners out in Long Island. They had one in my parents' room, but my brother and I had to sleep out on the porch during the summer and got eaten alive by the mosquitoes."

"Sounds terrible."

"Very. My dad was a control freak, especially around money. Once I came home with a new album I bought at the mall with my friend. I'll never forget it, Peter Frampton's *Comes Alive*. Do you know it?"

"'Show Me the Way' is still one of my all-time favorites," I replied as the song ran through my head.

Brenda smiled.

"Well, my father went nuts. He made me return it that same day. I was furious and humiliated. Never mind that I bought it with my money. Money that I made babysitting."

"Did you always work?"

"Yes, I had to work for everything. One time, when I was fifteen and had my period, he wouldn't let me buy sanitary napkins. As a punishment for even asking, he made me iron all of the shirts in his closet—and there were, like, hundreds. I was outraged. I spit on the white ones and peed on the colored ones."

"Seems like you still are."

"Still are what?"

I wanted to say "pissing," but didn't. "Angry," I hastily added.

She thought for a moment. "Yes, I guess I am."

"And so where was your mom during all this?"

"Doting on my brother. He was the prince, the boy protégé. He could do no wrong and was handed everything on a silver— no, make that a platinum—platter."

"How's your relationship with him now?"

"Not great. He moved with his family to Santa Barbara . . . or maybe it's Montecito; I'm not sure which, but rest assured it's the most expensive, fanciest town up past Malibu."

"Probably Montecito, then. It's like the Beverly Hills of Santa Barbara. Oprah has a big spread there."

"Well then, it's Montecito for sure."

"Does he work?"

Brenda let out an angry chuckle. "Right. Work is for little people, and he's quite grand. I'm not quite sure what they do out there. Lots of tennis, bike riding, and polo."

"So tell me about the trust."

"What about it?"

"What does it mean to you?"

"My father left me $7 million in trust when he died. It's been well managed by Richard, and even though I draw 5 percent a year from it, it's grown to over $10 million, I think."

"You think?"

Brenda winced. "I'm not quite sure."

Typical, I thought. *Another woman who was told by the men in her life not to worry about money.*

"And your brother?"

"What about him?" Her body tensed. It was clear that she resented him.

"Did he get the same amount?"

"I'm not sure. I doubt it."

"How could you not know?" I asked, genuinely curious, but way too judgmental for the situation.

Brenda was getting more and more angry with each of my questions. She glared at me and responded, "Because no one told me, and whenever I ask, I get a runaround."

"Wasn't there a reading of the will?"

Brenda's anger grew. I thought of retreating back, but I wanted her to move into her anger rather than suppress it.

"You mean like in the movies? Hell, no. I was just told what I got and expected to shut my mouth and be grateful."

"Do you think he got more or less?"

"What is it with you and this f*cking will? Are you afraid I don't have enough money to pay your fees?"

"No. I'm afraid we'll be avoiding important data if we don't address it. It's clearly a charged topic."

Fortunately, my instincts were correct. Brenda and I had a strong enough therapeutic alliance to support the relational stress I put us in. She continued on bravely.

"More, definitely more. I'm certain of it. He has a very grand lifestyle, and from what I can tell, he's not generating any money through any efforts of his own. I think he just cashes checks. I do know that whatever he got, he got it outright."

"Outright?"

"Yes, outright. There's no trust, no Richard to watch over things. No budgets he has to submit. No approvals for the expensive cars he buys, or trips he takes, or tuition he pays to his kids' fancy schools."

"How do you feel about that?" I asked, kicking myself for using such a clichéd intervention.

"*Feel?*" she asked, squinting her eyes and frowning. The subjects of money, her father, and her brother were highly charged. I needed to go deeper into them at some point in our future, but I hoped I hadn't proceeded too fast. I decided to trust my intuition and continue.

"Yes, feel. You must have some reaction to the trust and how it was set up. What it represents. How it impacts your life."

She frowned more deeply and stared at a coffee spot on my rug.

"Who spilled coffee?" she asked.

"I did. I'm a klutz."

Brenda smiled, indicating some of the tension had been released.

"But we're not here to discuss my sloppiness. Can we stick with this?"

"F*ck."

"Yes, f*ck. It's uncomfortable, but it's important. So back to my sloppy and clichéd question. How does it make you feel?"

Brenda looked up from the floor and stared directly into my eyes. "I hate it. It infuriates me every time I have to call Richard and beg for money that's mine! I hate that Richard, who gets paid to manage me, has to approve every dime that I spend. It's insulting. And why did my brother get the money outright? I'm not smart enough to manage my life? So what's that about? I'm Bernie Madoff, and my brother is Warren Buffet? But there's always been a double standard. My brother was the prince, the favorite child for sure."

"It's certainly infantilizing." Subconsciously, I must have felt the need to use a fancy clinical word to compensate for my sophomoric "feelings" intervention.

"Infant what?" she asked. It was clear my clinical jargon annoyed her. Instead of being offended, I encouraged her to continue.

"What did you feel when I used a word you didn't understand?"

"You confuse the hell out of me," she barked. Her anger was increasing, and I welcomed it.

"Go on."

"F*ck you and all your degrees. Big lawyer turned fancy therapist."

"Very nice," I replied calmly.

"Oh, f*ck you again. I bet your wife hates you too. You're probably lousy in the sack. More smoke than fire, Doctor Sensitive."

Ouch. The smoke comment stung, and she was way off on the wife thing, but we were getting somewhere.

"So I'm yet another man who disappoints . . . and tries to control you?"

"You bet. I should fire your incompetent and overpriced ass."

Great. Now we were getting into the money, power, and sex connection.

"But you can't," I said, knowing this would fuel her anger. "The trust is paying me, and you have to see me in order to have access to the funds. Richard made sure of that."

Suddenly Brenda's rage ignited. She took the throw pillow that was propping up her arm and threw it at me. I caught it and held it tight and watched her wrath explode.

Her whole body began to shake. "F*ck you, f*ck you, f*ck YOU," she screamed so loudly that the hair stood up on my forearms.

I tossed the pillow back at her. She caught it and clutched it to her chest.

"Now breathe in deeply," I instructed. It was time to show that anger would not kill her and that it could be therapeutically expressed and safely contained. I also needed to show her we could transcend our conflict and remain united in a reparative rather than a destructive relationship.

She looked at me with terror but followed my directions.

"Hold your breath in, and then let it out slowly."

Again, she complied.

"Do it again, only this time, extend the exhale."

While this process was uncomfortable for us both, it was a critically important part of Brenda's treatment. For starters, it allowed Brenda's anger toward powerful men to manifest itself toward me in a safe and contained space. Second, it provided her with some concrete tools to move through her anger constructively. Lastly, it allowed me to plant in her psyche a seed of cognitive understanding that anger could be expressed in a relationship rather than destroy it.

We continued in this way for about fifteen minutes while Brenda regained her equilibrium. Once grounded, I offered an observation: "You handle direct anger a lot better than sideways anger."

"Wow, you're right," she laughed. "It actually felt good." She sat for a few more seconds, working through some of what just happened, before asking, "Can we do that again next session?"

For the next five months, breathing exercises played a prominent part in our work as we tackled highly charged issues around money and her sexual expression. We talked about how her father and brother's dismissiveness made her feel a multitude of uncomfortable emotions, including sadness, humiliation, and anger. We discussed how her brother's current lifestyle felt insulting and how her father still controlled her from the grave. We also worked through the betrayal she felt from her mother and the resentment she felt toward the world for having been born a woman, a gender that relegated her to an inferior position in it.

The goal, of course, was to give Brenda cognitive insights and a reparative relational experience so she could see how fragile she felt toward money, fame, and men. Once she had a baseline level of understanding these issues, I helped her find healthier ways to emotionally and physically express her feelings and sexuality, move her life in a more fulfilling direction, and avoid the raft of negative consequences that resulted from her misdirected use of power. Until she intellectually understood how facts from her past interacted with feelings from her present, she remained trapped in a destructive behavioral loop, which was amplified by the power inherent in her elite identity.

In contrast to people who live in diminished states of power, Brenda had wealth that enabled her to purchase what she thought she needed to avoid discomfort while her famous surname allowed her to remain in an elevated state of isolation. But while Brenda's social class enabled her to keep tucking the destructive consequences of her sexual behaviors up in the eaves of her seemingly perfect world, eventually their weight crashed down on her and her family in a highly destructive and most inelegant way.

It is here that we land on one of the primary motivations of change: having to bear the consequences of one's behavior. My work in the intimacies of the psychotherapeutic relationship with powerful patients has shown me that while the effects of their sexual comportments may take a while to catch up with them, they eventually do catch up. Unfortunately, the damage caused by these behaviors spills over into the lives of those who live tethered to them. For this reason, it's important for us—as global citizens living in a zeitgeist of sexual hubris and relational betrayal—to resist the urge to normalize these behaviors and continue to push back against their carcinogenic forces. The best way to do this is to redouble your efforts to maintain dignity in your relationships and to speak out against the degradation women are forced to endure at the hands of male bullies. To turn a blind eye or rationalize these behaviors away will undermine the foundation of our relationships, our families, our communities, and our democracy.

5.

Resolve

Understanding Wives Who Stay

Grit is sticking with your future day in, day out, and not just for the week, not just for the month, but for years.

—ANGELA LEE DUCKWORTH

"Come on, Paul, they're about to introduce you and Kathleen . . . your first dance as a married couple."

My brother stood outside the bathroom stall clinking the ice in his gin and tonic. The frustration in his voice increased as his patience with me diminished. For the last ten minutes he'd been trying to coax me out of hiding and join the 450 guests who'd gathered in Youngstown, Ohio, for the nuptials of a beautiful medical student and a promising young lawyer.

"Yeah, okay . . . give me a minute to pull myself together."

My brother chuckled and chided, "You've had twenty-two years to get your sh*t together. If it ain't happened yet, a few more minutes aren't going to make any difference."

I stood with the cool metal of the beige enclosure against my back and stared at the stained ceiling tile that looked exactly like I felt, once white and clean, but now tarnished by my own betrayal. Staring down at my black leather shoes, I felt physically present but emotionally removed. I was numb to what should have been one of the most joyous days of my life.

"What in the hell did I just do?" I asked myself while downing my own gin and tonic. I placed the empty glass on the stainless-steel toilet tissue holder and steadied myself. Outside, the band began cueing up the song "Daddy's Little Girl." The melancholic and contrived melody only served to heighten my anxiety and anger. I felt trapped but was moved by my father's sage advice, which I repeated over and over to myself in my head: "Buck up and soldier on."

Drawing in a deep breath, I turned the corroded lock of the door and joined my brother.

I stared into the mirror that was directly in front of the stall I'd finally just emerged from and gave myself a final look-over. "Let's do this," I commanded to my own reflection.

My brother just shrugged his shoulders and smiled.

"Okay," he responded, feigning enthusiasm for my suddenly urgent mission.

Bounding out of the bathroom, I made my way through the ballroom doors and marched confidently onto the dance floor. Following the clichés wrapped up in the song I resented, I tapped my newly minted father-in-law on the shoulder and took my wife in my arms. But instead of cherishing that moment as the start of my life with a true partner, it remains burned into my memory as a question: "How am I ever going to get myself out of this?"

Less than two years later, the question I dwelled on during my wedding dance found a painful answer. The woman to whom I had pledged my lifelong devotion became a human being I referred to as my ex-wife.

There were several reasons why my marriage didn't work. The primary reason is that we were mismatched but too young and too driven to accept this reality. I thought we could bulldoze our way through the internal features of myself that made my wife and me incompatible and that our external accomplishments would carry us through the stresses and strains of life and marriage.

They didn't and never could.

I also had set up inauthentic goals for our marriage. As you'll see later in this chapter, marriages that survive the inevitable challenges placed in their way do so because the partners have long-term goals that have a deep resonance and meaning to them. At this point in my life, I was too young, too unaccepting, and too unresolved in essential truths of my being to take a long-term view of my life and set goals accordingly.

I want to say that I suffered more in the divorce than did my ex-wife, but that perception is a reflection of my own narcissistic ego, which took a brutal beating in my marriage's failing. For the first time in my life, I'd allowed myself to be vulnerable with another human being, and when my truth finally came to the light, I felt not just betrayed but vandalized by her, her family, and my professional colleagues.

As a marriage and family therapist and as a divorced man, I believe that marriages are infinitely easier to enter than to exit. We spend precious little time thinking through the reasons to go into them and ridiculous amounts of financial and emotional capital getting out.

Without a doubt, my divorce was one of the most painful experiences I've lived through to date. Unlike the deaths of my parents, events that were expected and planned for, my divorce from my wife had no family and cultural support.

There's no hospice or palliative care for a toxic or withering marriage that's dying on the vine. No cultural affirmation or religious redemption exists for a man or woman who struggles to be liberated from a marriage that limits his or her growth or kills his or her soul. In fact, many conservative religions shun members of their tribe who dare divorce their spouses, causing the divorcing person to lose not just the person whom they once trusted as their soul mate, but their families and communities as well.

This cultural judgment is pronounced in the religion of celebrity, where we savor the opportunity to opine on the men and women who live under the scorch of the spotlight. Typically these opinions take the form of several "How dare you?" questions. The first "How dare you?" question we commonly ask is "How dare you leave?"

Gwyneth Paltrow attempted to announce her divorce from her husband and the father of their children with grace and dignity by calling it a "conscious uncoupling." In choosing these nonblaming words, she was brutalized by the public. Few could accept that a megawatt celebrity would act in the realm of her private life with personal agency and maturity—especially at a time where by her own admission she was at an emotional bottom. Instead of applauding Paltrow for her decision and approach, the public projected their hostilities on her for what they perceived as hubris. "How dare she not grovel in the wake of her marital failure?" was the war cry that met her as she attempted to, in her own words, "Check [her] own sh*t at the door and put [her] children first" (Chester 2017).

The second "How dare you?" question asks, "How dare you be happy?" These judgments are projected on the celebrities we curse with the fate of leading doomed romantic lives. Celebrities we've put at the top of this list include Jennifer Aniston and Julia Roberts. The tabloids are replete with images of these megastars sobbing, mascara streaming down their cheeks as headlines scream from above: *Jennifer dumped again! Julia's marriage is OVER!* For some reason we can't accept that these intelligent and extraordinarily talented women can have meaningful relationships and fulfilling family lives.

The third manifestation of the "How dare you?" chastisement manifests through a damned-if-you-do-damned-if-you-don't genre of thinking. Although we could never truly know the intimate details of anyone's individual life or the dynamics of their relationships, we're quick to ask, "How dare you stay?"

The most famous example of the "How dare you stay?" phenomenon is, of course, Hillary Clinton. When it came to light that her husband, Bill, had an affair with Monica Lewinsky, it was not Bill who paid a price of unpopularity, but rather his wife, Hillary. After his impeachment proceedings in 1998 and 1999, Bill's approval rating reached its highest point at 73 percent (CNN 1998). Hillary, however, never recovered. And her intimate decision to remain in her marriage continues to haunt her.

Twenty years after the Bill and Monica affair came to light, Hillary was asked by the hostesses of the popular talk show *The View* to explain why she chose to remain married to Bill in the wake of his infidelities. Hillary responded directly, "I hear that people say, 'They have an arrangement.' *It's called a marriage.* There have been a lot more happy days than sad or angry days, and I am very proud and grateful that I am married to my best friend" (Savitsky 2017).

In a world where the extraordinary pressures of being in the public eye can crush celebrity marriages in months, Hillary Clinton has remained committed to her marriage for more than four decades. The Clintons have stayed together for better, for worse, for richer, for poorer, in sickness and in health. Hillary has not run from the challenges of a long-term, high-powered marriage but has continued to negotiate them.

And in spite of the public backlashings she's received over her decision to stay, the research in the field of marital therapy supports her decision. As it relates to couples who work through infidelities, the evidence shows that when infidelity is brought out of the shadows, the prognosis for its treatment is exceptional (Gordon, Baucom, and Snyder 2004). Research further shows spouses who stay together and work through infidelity are happier and healthier over the long term. One leading study found couples who worked through infidelity recovered quickly and often had higher rates of marital satisfaction than spouses who did not have to negotiate its challenges (Atkins et al. 2005).

Helping couples successfully navigate infidelities in their marriages is rewarding, but it's never easy. It involves providing a frame for imperfect human beings to struggle—often inelegantly—to modify the terms of their marriages to suit the power dynamics of *their* lives rather than conform to the objective expectations of the religious and cultural institutions that surround them. In this regard, successful marriages are very much as Hillary stated in her interview on *The View*. They're arrangements between two mature and intelligent adults who understand that most marriages—69 percent, according to one of the world's leading marital researchers—entail "perpetual" problems that will never be fully resolved (Gottman and Silver 2000). In these marriages, *success* is defined by learning how to arrange these problems into the narrative of the marriage with respect for oneself, one's partner, and the relational entity. The human beings in the relationship "dare to stay" because they've accepted the reality that, like the individuals who make them, marriages are imperfect entities that need to bend and sway with life's tempests and twists.

The message that marriages are a dynamic mix of challenges and rewards is one that is fortunately making its way out of the realm of marriage counseling and into the field of domestic law. In the last decade, there has emerged a small but growing number of international divorce lawyers who see their role not as a hammer used to crush an errant spouse but rather as a sieve that helps couples sift through the overwhelming facts and feelings that are baked into the marriage soufflé.

The pioneer in this regard is Michael Rowlands of the London firm Kingsley Napley. For the last three decades, Rowlands has helped spouses answer the "shall I stay or shall I go?" question with his razor sharp wit and humanistic heart. According to Rowlands:

> When you remove or relegate "love" and replace it with practical considerations, decisions sometimes appear easier—economic (am I better off leaving or staying?); social (what are my future odds in the dating game?); family (are the children better off with two parents living together?).

But while these considerations are important, they must be considered in tandem with emotions. Rowlands adds:

The problem is that responding to a failing marriage with nonemotional reasoning and solutions is likely to leave a marriage in a holding pattern with problems stored and resentment active whilst life moves on to the inevitable coming down to earth (children leave the nest, retirement, gravity!). Lives are lost in this way. (M. Rowlands, email exchange with author, 2017)

Rowlands believes that marriages, particularly marriages in stress, must be artfully and maturely negotiated in a way that recognizes some marital problems are immutable and must be accepted as such, while others can be renegotiated toward meeting a subjective standard of what's in the best interest of each individual spouse—and the relationship. Negotiating this calculus demands personal awareness, persistence, intelligence, and maturity. It also involves rejecting the sexist and outdated label of codependent in judging those women who make mature and informed decisions to stay.

According to Rowlands, there's a strong cultural approval of women who stay in relationships for "the sake of the children" but precious little for women who remain married to men who have socially stigmatized behaviors or have been accused of or actually been found guilty of misconducts:

There is a grudging kind of respect for the spouse who remains married for, say, the children, which differs markedly to the response to those who stay married to an addict or someone who suffers from a severe narcissistic or borderline personality disorder. In the second scenario, the corrosive and exhausting behavior is all too apparent to friends, family, and lawyers as the reason for the stasis. Inevitably, a recognition or label of "codependence" is given. (M. Rowlands, email exchange with author, 2017)

I'm confident that anyone reading this book has used the term *codependency* to describe themselves or others. Like "narcissism," the construct has become white noise in our modern lexicon.

It's also become banal and stigmatizing—especially to women.

While I'd like to think I'm skilled at containing my frustration when a female patient tells me, "I'm codependent and my husband is a narcissist," I still scrunch my toes in my shoes in response to her self-deprecating remarks. *According to whom?* I think to myself. *Dr. Phil, Wikipedia, or that chap who sat next to you on the subway?*

This isn't to say that the construct has no meaning. The insights and therapeutic model that came out of it are incredibly valuable. Melody Beattie's best-selling book *Codependent No More*, first published in 1986, remains a brilliant contribution to the field of addiction treatment and relational health. It's beautifully written and provides a road map to navigate diminishing relationships. It certainly holds a place of honor on my bookshelf, and I consider Beattie one of the most important voices in the field.

The term *codependency* emerged from the first edition of the Big Book of Alcoholics Anonymous, published in 1939. It referred to wives of alcoholics who were affected by their husbands' disease. Married to men who were "dependent" on alcohol, their relational dynamics subsumed an addictive quality. But unlike their husbands, who became addicted to an ingested substance, these women became addicted to feelings generated from providing caregiving at a level that diminished their well-being.

Over the decades, the application of this term has expanded exponentially to include anyone, in particular any woman who relies on other people for validation and acceptance (Johnson 2018). At the core of this reliance is caretaking and excessive responsibility for others (Haaken 1990). According to Scott Wetzler, PhD, at New York's Albert Einstein College of Medicine, "Codependent relationships signify a degree of unhealthy clinginess where one person doesn't have self-sufficiency or autonomy." He continues by adding, "One or both parties depend on their loved ones for fulfillment" (Sun n.d.).

Critics of the term, and feminist thinkers in particular, maintain that it penalizes women for assuming the sociocultural expectations of self-sacrifice and caregiving that have been thrust upon them in the first place. They maintain that the relating styles labeled *codependency* are not a manifestation of a disorder, but rather of robust adherence to clichéd feminine archetypes that involve a woman yielding to the power of a man (Hands and Dear 1994).

Over the last two decades, however, we've seen a slow but steady erosion of the male power monopoly. Some researchers suggest that the male chokehold on power has been diminished by women obtaining as much as (or is it as little as?) 20 percent of leadership roles in business, government, and the media. In the realm of business, this exceptional leadership has come from women like Indra Nooyi, formerly of PepsiCo; Abigail Johnson of Fidelity; and Meg Whitman, formerly of eBay. In the realm of politics, we've had strong leadership from Angela

Merkel in Germany to Janet Yellen in America. Many eyes are on Kamala Harris and Elizabeth Warren, senators from California and Massachusetts, as serious presidential contenders.

But the real watershed moment came in July 2016, when Gretchen Carlson stood up for herself and thousands of other women and challenged the conspiracy of silence in the power structure of media by calling out Roger Ailes for his reign of sexual harassment as the chairman and CEO of Fox News. Her bravery, coupled with her intelligence and strategy, led to an astonishing David-takes-down-Goliath moment. Finally, human beings who had been forced to endure decades of sexual terror by men who wielded elite power over them found a leader who inspired them to break through the glass wall of sexual exploitation. Carlson's suit was the tipping point that laid the groundwork for a purge of power mongers who had for centuries preyed upon other human beings to feed their narcissistic egos and animalistic sexual drives.

Just over a year later, the *New York Times* ran a series of articles on "the king of Hollywood," Harvey Weinstein, that brought down another glass wall (Chamberlain 2012). Within ten days of the article hitting the news cycle, King Weinstein had been not just dethroned, but also castrated. Then, like dominos, other powerful men who had been the subjects of not just whispers but settled lawsuits and industrywide understandings began to topple. These included the biggest names and highest earners in Hollywood and the media: Kevin Spacey, Matt Lauer, Bill O'Reilly, Charlie Rose, Louis C.K. Men who commanded extraordinary salaries and amassed enormous personal fortunes were summarily terminated and let go by their protectors. Women, united in Gretchen

Carlson's strength and courage, forced accountability, respect, and consequences into the male privilege paradigm. Finally, the age-old adage of "nice guys finish last" was being replaced with a new paradigm of karmic cause and effect. Sexual predators who operated in a culture of "open secrecy" experienced negative consequences for their actions. True, as I mentioned in chapter 4, there's an extraordinary amount of work that still needs to be done, but these actions mark a distinct beginning.

Some of these men's spouses stuck with their husbands. Others left. Bill Cosby's wife has stuck by his side through the multitude of accusations brought against him. Harvey Weinstein's wife left, as did Matt Lauer's (Telling 2018). The women who left have been, for the most part, applauded. The women who stayed, however, have been subjected to the same ridicule and disdain as Hillary Clinton.

Infidelity, known as extramarital sex or EMS in clinical and academic circles, is a polarizing topic. It's certainly not a new one. Infidelity, known by more inflammatory names like adultery, has been around for centuries and in some cultures is still used against women to justify brutal punishments and death. In the western world, cultures that consider themselves educated and advanced, it's still used to stigmatize women who make intelligent and mature decisions to stay in a marriage when their spouse has cheated. Typically, this stigmatization comes from labeling them *codependent*.

But it's sexist to automatically say a woman who remains married to a man who engages in EMS is codependent. In the time that I've worked in the realm of marriage and family therapy, I've found that women who engage in a complex and nuanced analysis to stay in or exit a marriage do not fit into the outdated and stigmatizing box of codependency. Rather than being toxically attached to their mate, these women choose to stay in their marriages for personal reasons that enhance their self-concept, self-esteem, and relational well-being.

One of the most memorable of these women is one I had the privilege of helping renegotiate the power dynamics of her twenty-seven-year marriage.

•

"Oh my God, Dr. Paul!" I was having a late and lazy lunch at my favorite Greek restaurant, Taverna Tony, at the Malibu Country Mart, when out of the corner of my eye I saw a former client rushing over to my table.

"So good to see you," she continued.

Her joy was infectious. I sprang from my chair and, in my enthusiasm, spilled a bottle of Pellegrino on my tablemate's lap. Fortunately, he was good-natured and laughed off my transgression. Plus, he was quite familiar with my all-too-common clumsiness. We had just spent two hours together out in the Pacific Ocean, where he was able to witness firsthand my inelegant moves on a surfboard. Spilling a bottle of water was nothing compared to the spills I took along the shoreline.

"Clare!" I met her with a warm embrace. Although more than five years had passed since we'd worked together, there was a warmth and familiarity between us that transcended time and distance. Like all of my patients, former and present, I internalized her on a deep level and recalled her often and fondly.

"This is amazing. I was just thinking of you. I heard you were spending time here in the 'Bu!" Clare continued to talk in a loud and enthusiastic voice while tables of nonplussed diners, realizing Dr. Paul was a nobody to them, attempted to get back to their pleasant salads and grilled salmon.

"Yes, I've got a place here, but I'm having a hard time settling in." I lowered my voice to a few decibels above a whisper hoping to encourage Clare to do the same. But talking about myself made me uncomfortable. I attempted to change the focus back to Clare. "But you? How are things?"

"Brilliant!" she exclaimed, flashing a beautifully imperfect set of teeth and waving her diamond-encrusted Franck Muller watch in the air. "I've never been happier."

"God bless." I began moving our conversation out of the patio and onto the sidewalk.

"Yes. God bless indeed."

Once in an appropriate range of privacy, I asked a question, the answer to which I was burning to know.

"And the family?"

"I assume you mean my marriage," Clare asserted pointedly. The years had only served to heighten her emotional intelligence and directness.

I chuckled sheepishly and kicked a stone on the curb. "Yes. That's exactly what I meant."

"It's working. He still has his mistress in New York. I . . . well . . . I kind of like her. She's a sweet girl. A bit lost, but . . . and I . . . well, I went back to school outside of Paris. I got a master's degree in luxury management, and I'm doing some consulting work with a few brands in Europe. I took a lovely flat in the Marais. Next time you're in Paris, give me a ring, and we'll go for a coffee and chocolate croissant."

"Wow, that's amazing. Well done, you." I began to feel

self-conscious standing on the curb in my flip-flops and faded Gap sweatshirt. "I'm happy for you; it's really great to see you."

"Yes, great to see you. And listen, thank you for guiding Ryan and me to a great place in our marriage. For that, I thank you."

"Well, the pleasure was—and actually still is—mine. I'm glad you're living a life that works for you and makes you happy."

I looked up to see tears forming in the corners of Clare's emerald eyes. As she wiped them away, I was struck by the simplicity of the wedding band she wore proudly on her left hand. It symbolized the strength of the institution of marriage as defined by Clare and Ryan. It wasn't a marriage that would work for everyone, or that incorporated unyielding and judgmental mandates, but it was a dynamic marriage that was working beautifully for them, and in the realm of a life that goes racing by too often without personal meaning and authorship, this was *un travail bien fait*—a job well done.

We departed in another warm embrace, and Clare thanked me once again. As I walked back into the restaurant, I recalled the trajectory of our work together, work that started one rainy Monday deep in the doldrums of a Manhattan March and work that began with a discussion of her handbag.

•

"Listen, my banker gave me an article that talks about your philosophy on infidelity in *Men's Health*. It was the one written by Mike Darling. You said that a guy's wife lashes out at her husband's cheating by spending too much money. I think you can help me and my wife" (Darling 2016).

I was taken aback.

I'd worked with Mike Darling quite a bit when he was a reporter at *Men's Health* and valued his journalistic integrity, but I doubted I'd said what Ryan quoted.

For starters, it felt manipulated.

I was curious how he came to that interpretation. I was also grasping to get more information about the man with whom I was speaking.

I attempted to slow him down and get some collateral information.

"Who's your banker?"

Ryan mentioned a name I'd never heard, but he attached it to a firm with which I had some connections. The firm only works with families that have an investable net worth of over $50 million and has a genuine interest in helping them navigate the destruction to family wealth and well-being caused by addictions and other mental health issues.

I hedged about the article. "I don't think that's exactly what I said, but I do contribute to *Men's Health* from time to time."

"Right, whatever." Ryan was eager to continue. "In any event, I think you're the perfect couples counselor for us. We've seen a few, and no one is able to get through to my wife."

Ding, ding, ding! Three alarms finally sounded off serially in my head.

The first marked Ryan's idolization of me based on a quote he read in a men's fitness magazine. There was a good possibility I was venturing into a relationship with a man who was facile with the narcissistic cycle of abuse that begins with an idolization, then moves into a period of devaluating those around him, and ultimately ends in a process of discarding.

The second alarm was related to the first and had to do with the fact that I would be the latest in a string of failed therapeutic engagements. True, I work in very niched space with highly sophisticated, demanding, and exceptionally intelligent patients, but my colleagues in New York are also highly competent clinicians. He would have had his pick of many of them. Typically, when a patient runs through clinicians, it's not the clinician's incompetency but rather the patient's narcissism that sends them out the door. The third alarm was the one that resonated most loudly. The gentleman was very up-front about his desire for me to manage his wife.

Certainly, this was not the first time I've encountered such an intention. The truth of the matter is that every couple and family I work with contains this dynamic. The setup is always the same. A family has what's called the identified patient. This is the person who is seen as "sick" and in dire need of change. If I declined every case where it existed, I'd never work. Nevertheless, I needed to pay attention to these alarms. They're important because they prompt me not to decline a case but rather to become aware of the clinical issues that we'll need to work through.

I was also intrigued that Ryan rang me to set up the appointment. Such a situation was an outlier in the realm of psychotherapeutic engagements. This is because Ryan was a man. In 90 percent of my relational cases, the mates who manifest the most feminine qualities make the initial contact. Typically, it's a woman, but in same-gender relationships, it's the partner who possesses the traits of nurturing and caregiving who ends up making the call.

This phenomenon is not one that's restricted to my practice

or limited to elite male populations. For decades, research has shown that men across the socioeconomic spectrum have a deeply entrenched cultural and personal resistance to seeking help for mental health issues. One study found that out of all outpatient mental health services, two out of three were delivered to women (Vessey and Howard 1993). This remains true in spite of the fact that men struggle with higher rates of depression, suicide, addictive disorders, and stress than women (Winerman 2005). The resistance of men to seeking treatment is due in large measure to the way they've been socialized and social norms that tell them emotions make them weak and are to be ignored and banished. Studies show that even when they are fully aware they are suffering, men still refuse to reach out for help, seeing it as a sign of weakness (Addis and Mahalik 2003).

I asked Ryan to describe the issues he wanted to discuss in therapy, but he punted.

"It's too complicated to go into on the phone."

It took only a few minutes after meeting the couple in my office to discover it was Ryan who was complicated.

"Where would you like me to sit?" Ryan paced around my office like a dog circling its tail, looking for the perfect place to settle. Clare stood patiently in the doorway, observing. It was obvious she had seen his act before.

Finally, I pointed to the sofa. "Why don't you take a seat there?"

Ryan looked at the sofa, then to one of the armchairs across the room. "That chair looks comfortable. I'll sit there. Clare, you sit in the one next to me."

I allowed them to get settled and took my seat on the sofa.

"Okay, then. I'll sit here on the sofa."

We exchanged pleasantries—did they have a hard time finding the office, wasn't the weather dreadful—before delving into the work.

To my surprise, it wasn't Ryan who kicked things off, but Clare.

"So thank you for seeing us, Dr. Paul. I'm sure you're busy."

Ryan interrupted her. "Well, he's not too busy to work!" It was clear he found his comment amusing, but his humor was lost on his wife. She glanced over to him to acknowledge that he spoke but immediately reassumed her relational leadership.

"I understand you're an expert in infidelity. I've read a number of your thoughts and strategies around this on the Dr. Oz website. I like your approach."

Ryan shifted in his seat, nervously tugging the starched white cuffs of his shirt out from under his navy cashmere sport coat.

"Thank you."

"So Ryan, my husband here, has a mistress. He's had a mistress off and on the last ten years of our marriage. A marriage that, I hasten to add, I've enjoyed and valued."

Ryan stopped fidgeting with his cuffs and began spinning the mother-of-pearl cuff links that held them in place.

I cast my glance in his direction. He looked up and stated with deep resolve, "Yes, true. This is all quite true," and then immediately returned to his spinning.

"Ryan has a hard time with this, but I need him to know I'm fine with it all."

Even though I knew what she was talking about, I wanted Clare to articulate clearly what "it all" entailed.

"What exactly is 'it all'?"

Clare nodded, acknowledging my intervention as one for absolute clarity.

"Well his affairs. His 'infidelity,' although I really dislike that word."

"Why do you dislike it?" I asked.

"Because it's so dirty. And it makes me look like a fool for staying in a marriage that I'm perfectly contented in."

Clare impressed me. She was smart and direct and had very sophisticated intuition. Like her name, she appeared to have exceptional clarity around a shadowy topic.

She turned her gaze over to Ryan and asked him directly, "Do you believe me?"

Ryan's "I do" was delivered with such tentativeness that he felt compelled to repeat it. "I do; I really do."

Clare shot me a skeptical look and retorted, "I don't think he gets it. In fact, he insists that I'm angry and that I act out in passive-aggressive ways."

I had to ask what she meant by the term. Whenever a patient uses a clinical term that's become jargon, I check in on their understanding of it. "What do you mean by *passive-aggressive*?"

Clare gave her response without missing a beat: "It's an indirect response to direct anger."

I'd never heard the construct of passive-aggression expressed so clearly.

"Yes, that's exactly what it is." I focused my attention on Ryan. "So, Ryan, it seems like we are spot-on with the definition of *passive-aggressive*. Can you give me some examples of what Clare's talking about?"

Ryan looked confused, so I tried to clarify.

"How does Clare express her anger?"

"Sure. Well, she sure can run up a credit card bill."

"Okay . . . and . . . well, to the extent you can't pay it off each month? Are you carrying a large balance?"

"No, not at all. It gets paid off each month. It's just that . . . well, the things she spends money on are . . . this sounds judgmental, but, well . . . they're silly indulgences."

Clare bristled but waited patiently for him to continue. It was obvious she'd heard this before. It was also obvious she was getting angry.

"Okay, like . . . ?" I asked, but apparently a bit too vaguely. "What do you mean specifically? What are these indulgences . . . the things Clare spends too much money on? Name one."

"Well, pocketbooks, for one thing. I mean she just paid what, like $3,000 for one."

The edges of Clare's calm, cool, and collected demeanor began to fray. "It's actually a handbag, and I paid $3,750 plus tax, which in New York City is 8.875 percent, so all in all, the bag was about $4,100."

Ryan looked dumbfounded. He too had heard all this before. They weren't covering any new ground yet in this session, but it was important for me to observe firsthand their relational dynamics.

Clare continued after a moment of silence.

"Ryan, let me ask you something. How much did we—not you but we—make last year?"

Ryan looked at me like a child who'd just been caught climbing into the cabinet to steal a cookie.

"A respectable amount."

Ryan's resistance to putting out a specific number didn't

surprise me. I was still a stranger to him and, as such, deemed unsafe. Even though money is one of the most powerful energetics in relationships, ultra-high net worth patients have deeply entrenched shame and guilt about discussing it in the psychotherapeutic frame. And their reluctance is often well placed. For starters, many clinicians haven't been trained to properly manage the power that emanates from extreme wealth. Second, patients are afraid that if they reveal their net worth with the clinician, they will be seen only for their wealth; and third, they've internalized the religious and spiritual view of people of wealth as unworthy recipients of salvation and enlightenment. These messages include those from Buddhism, wherein the Buddha had to renounce his wealth and nobility to obtain enlightenment. In the Bible, Mark 10:25 (NIV) warns that "it is easier for a camel to pass through the eye of a needle than for someone who is rich to enter the kingdom of God."

Clare met my need to ask Ryan for clarification.

"How much exactly is that respectable amount, my love?"

"I think we made just under $6 million last year."

"Actually, we made $6.75 million. Just slightly up from the $6.625 million we made the year before."

I knew where this conversation was going, but I needed to decide if I would take the lead or sit quietly, awaiting Clare to ably continue.

I decided to earn my keep and craft an intervention that would put things in perspective. I started, "So Ryan, you're concerned over a, let's just call it a $4,000 handbag . . ." but halfway through my statement, I succumbed to the seduction of wealth's sparkly trappings. "I'm sorry, Clare, I need to ask, what kind of bag did you get?"

"Oh, it's the Bottega Veneta Olimpia Knot shoulder bag," she announced proudly, lifting it up to show me.

I was impressed. It was a beautiful work of art, an example of craftsmanship that whispered class rather than shouting it through labels.

"When your own initials are enough." The brand's brilliant advertising slogan spontaneously rolled off my tongue.

While not the most clinically sophisticated response, it certainly was human and as such deepened my alliance with Clare but lessened it with Ryan.

Clare laughed.

Ryan looked confused.

I clarified for him: "It's the tagline for the brand. Sorry, Ryan. It's a beautiful bag, Clare."

I attempted to move back into my role as inquisitive therapist and establish at least a modicum of neutrality.

"And so the bag is something you can't afford? Is it putting a strain on your finances?"

I asked the question in a way that was a bit too biased. I was too committed in my view of Clare and Ryan's finances and too far on Clare's side of the argument.

Ryan shifted nervously in his seat. "Well, no. I guess we can afford it."

"We can afford it." Clare set the record straight.

But I also knew that the quantitative aspect of the bag—its price relative to their income and net worth—was just the veneer of the deeper issues that needed to be uncovered and addressed.

Yes, there was definitely anger in this relationship that was manifesting in corrosive ways, but the dynamics underlying it were complex and deeply entrenched. There was no way we could sort them out in the twenty minutes we had remaining in this session.

"So what is it about the bag that troubles you?" I attempted to start the excavation process and resume as best I could my position of therapeutic neutrality.

"It just feels . . . well, it feels excessive."

Brilliant! I thought to myself. *We've moved from the realm of numbers into the realm of feelings.*

I opened my mouth to validate Ryan's statement, but Clare interrupted. Her perception of Ryan's negative judgment fueled her anger.

"Excessive to what?"

Her response, however, shut Ryan down. He shifted his focus back to his cuff links.

Clare continued apace.

"You know, here's the deal. We spend hundreds of thousands of dollars—millions, actually—on things that you, my dear, insist we 'need.'"

The conflict between the couple was building. My job was to sit back and let it emerge.

"Like what?" Ryan asked defensively.

"Like the NetJets share at, what, $500,000 a year? Like the $120,000 Tesla with the ludicrous double engine you had to have . . . the real ludicrous thing is that it sits in the garage in LA collecting dust. How about your watch? You really 'need' a $45,000 Royal Oak. Shall I go on?"

Even though I suspected we both wanted her to stop, neither Ryan nor I moved to shut her down.

"How about the Ducati that hasn't run in, what, over a year?"

With the mention of the Ducati, both Ryan and I got the picture.

He returned his gaze to the cuff links. I cleared my throat for an intervention I hadn't yet formulated.

Clare was like a dog with a bone.

"And how about those $3,000 cuff links? And that tie, what is it . . . a $200 Hermès?"

Ryan looked up at me, frustrated.

It was time for me to intervene.

"Okay, I get it. Spending is an issue here. Look, you're certainly not alone. All couples have to navigate issues around money. Money is one of the most powerful and least discussed forces in a marriage. This is true in every socioeconomic class. But in ultra-high net worth families—and you guys are an ultra-high net worth family—it's not an issue of scarcity that stresses a relationship, but abundance."

My comment united Ryan and Clare, but not because they were stunned by the meaning in my statement. In fact, I'm not sure the distinction between scarcity and abundance registered with them at all. What immediately hooked their attention was the fact that I labeled them an "ultra-high net worth" family. Hearing themselves described as such sent the same tremor of anxiety through them as it did through Susan and Mark.

"Why do you say we're ultra-high net worth? We're not billionaires."

Ryan's statement made me pause. Even though I'm constantly negotiating this issue with patients in position of elite power, I always forget that people of wealth seldom view themselves as such. This is partially because notions of wealth are relative constructs and partially because we've been acculturated to attribute negative moral associations to people of wealth that include their being mean, selfish, entitled, greedy, narcissistic, dishonest, and not worthy of redemption.

I needed to clarify by moving my comment back into the realm of quantitative data.

"Okay, look, my understanding is that from a financial services industry standard, families with an investable net worth of over $30 million are considered ultra-high net worth" (Kenton 2018).

Clare and Ryan looked at one another, then back at me.

"No, you're right." Ryan confirmed my assertion.

"So in these cases, money and the approvals and disapprovals around how it's spent symbolize a deeper emotional issue that's connected to values. Typically, it's about control. But it can also be about discipline. Ryan, do you feel Clare is undisciplined?"

"Absolutely not. In fact, she's incredibly disciplined."

Clare regained her composure and sat eagerly awaiting Ryan's rationale.

"Well, then, do you feel out of control when Clare spends on something like a handbag?"

Ryan thought for a moment before responding.

"Maybe . . . I just don't get it."

I was impressed with the progress this couple was making in a short period of time.

"What don't you get, my question or the bag?" Even though I knew Mark was referring to the bag, the point we were making was important. I felt compelled to spend additional time on it.

"Oh, no, I get your question. My response has a disapproving quality to it, and there's an element of control there. I guess what I don't quite understand is why these pocket—I mean handbags—cost so much damn money."

Clare attempted to regain control of the conversation. "Because they are—"

Now it was time for me to put the brakes on Clare. "Let's allow Ryan to stick with this, shall we?"

Clare nodded in agreement.

"And you need to 'get it' because?"

"Well, I . . ." Ryan shrugged his shoulders and chucked. "I don't know, to be honest."

"Maybe because it's not yours to get." I threw out this option for both spouses to consider, and it sent shock waves throughout the room.

The three of us sat together quietly, considering the possibility, before I continued.

"Maybe it's simply a 'she' endeavor. If it makes her happy, and clearly it does, and it's not hurting you . . . then what's the big deal?"

Ryan's eyes lit up in a moment of clarity. It was clear he loved his wife and, at the core of his being, he wanted her to be happy.

"Well, now there's a concept. I guess I've never really considered that before."

Clare reached over and cradled his hand in hers. It was one of the magical moments in therapy when I'm humbled for the opportunity to work with human beings who have a capacity for love at a deep and meaningful level.

What I desperately wanted to say at the conclusion of this session was that it struck me as unfair that Clare allowed

Ryan his mistress but was being criticized by him for buying a handbag.

I withheld my observation.

At this stage of our engagement, it would be a crass, judgmental, and highly inappropriate statement. It would also taint our work by revealing to both Ryan and Clare that at least in round one of our working alliance, I was siding with Clare and eager to see the couple walk hand in hand off into the sunset.

While ultimately I'm able to allow relational outcomes to work themselves out, I usually start the process with a preconceived notion of "together" or "apart." My intuitive sense for this couple was that they would be better off together and that Clare was the partner who was more highly evolved in the realm of emotional and relational matters. I was also struck that even though there were some points of contention, there was a deep respect for each other, a genuine concern for the other's well-being, and absolutely no indication of emotional or physical abuse. When this is the case in a relationship, the prognosis for a joint stroll into the sunset is exceptionally good.

Yes, the marriage was "imperfect," but it held Ryan's extramarital affairs, Clare's intellectual curiosity, their professional ambition, and their *joie de vivre* with dignity and grace. In this regard, it was an arrangement that *enhanced* rather than diminished their collective and individual well-being. Like all marriages, it needed to be dusted off from time to time, but this relational housekeeping focused on building existing strengths and assisting the couple to reach higher levels of functioning.

Instead of constricting their relational expression, my task was to help them expand it. Central to this work was processing the elite power that existed in their marriage.

While the field of marriage and family therapy is quick to note that economic stressors are a leading cause of marital conflict, the therapeutic interventions offered are directed at economic scarcity and the powerlessness surrounding it (Dickler 2018). In contrast to these formulations, I focus on working in the abundance of power contained in elite marriages and crafting culturally competent interventions to address it and move the couple in a reparative direction.

One of the distinguishing cultural features of couples of elite power is their enhanced capacity to practice resilience and apply grit to work through their relational challenges and setbacks. By working in the context of these two traits, these couples don't simply resolve their differences but are able to move their relationship to a higher level of functioning.

The construct of resiliency is not new. Simply put, it's the ability to deal with stressors while maintaining a positive attitude, regulating emotions, and seeing the challenge as an opportunity to learn and improve (Dickler 2018). "Grit" is a similar construct that signifies a person's persistence in their pursuit of long-term goals (Duckworth et al. 2007). Instead of giving up in the wake of disappointments, setbacks, harsh criticism, and even cultural shame, people with grit are tenacious in their pursuit of their superordinate objectives (Duckworth and Gross 2014).

Not surprisingly, grit is a personality trait found to be more common among members of elite social classes than among lower ones. One study found that elevated grit, rather than elevated SAT scores, predicted student success at elite colleges (Duckworth et al. 2007). Another found that given equal levels of talent and intelligence, grit was the ultimate determiner of higher levels of success.

From a culturally sensitive point of view, Clare's decision to stay in a marriage with a husband who kept a mistress was a function of her resiliency and grit rather than a function of an assumed codependency. "Was I hurt when I learned about his mistress?" she asked. "Absolutely, but I also realized there was a lesson to be learned." The lesson Clare learned was that no one person can be or should be "the end-all be-all" for another person. "Look, Ryan and I operate on a different sexual frequency. When we were young I kept up, but to be honest, at this age, I'm more interested in wandering the alleys of the Marais looking for an exciting new designer than having sex—and Ryan completely supports me in my explorations. So why shouldn't I support him in his?"

Through an affirming lens of resiliency and grit, I was able to acknowledge Clare and Ryan as intelligent human beings with an abundance of resources and options at their disposal. On the basis of this shared understanding, I engaged them further in an intellectual inquiry around their nontraditional marital situation. Through this process, we discovered that while there were aspects of their relationship both disliked, in the context of their hierarchical goal of staying married to a partner they respected and loved, it made sense to *them,* both individually and as a couple. We also concluded that because Ryan's sexual relationship was consensual and took place with Clare's knowledge and approval, it wasn't an infidelity at all but rather an extension of their primary relationship. Is it an outcome that is appropriate for everyone? Probably not. They are unique people who have come together to form a unique couple.

6.

Flawless

Beauty's Siren Song

The madness of the eyes is the lure of the abyss.
Sirens lurk in the dark depths of the pupils
as they lurk at the bottom of the sea.

— JEAN LORRAIN, *MONSIEUR DE PHOCAS*

No, it can't be. I strained to see if the angelic woman hailing a cab on Hudson Street in Tribeca was really the supermodel I thought her to be. *Is it? Could it . . . impossible . . . she'd never take a taxi.*

I approached the woman cautiously as my heart raced recklessly. The crisp October air blowing off the Hudson River tousled her chestnut hair perfectly.

Moving closer, my suspicions were confirmed.

Oh my god. It's her. It's really her!

Dressed in green fatigues, a white T-shirt, and a brown suede jacket, the superlative Christy Turlington stepped, just like millions of other New Yorkers that late afternoon, into a yellow taxi while I was watching.

I can't believe she's taking a taxi!

In less than a second, the thrill of my celebrity sighting transmuted into indignation. *Why doesn't she have a driver? I mean, she's a GODDESS!* I thought as she slammed the rattling door shut.

And as her cab pulled away from the curb and joined the throng of traffic heading uptown, I laughed at my reactions and marveled at the extraordinary power of celebrity.

While Christy Turlington appeared to be managing its power quite well, I, on the other hand, wasn't. My training and expertise as one of the world's leading authorities on the treatment of celebrity patients left the room, ushered out by an irrational bouncer. The mere sight of a woman I'd known and admired only through photos, suddenly living and breathing right before me, hyper-activated my limbic system and stunted my rational thinking. Gone was the elevated Dr. Paul, an empathetic professional. In his stead appeared the primitive Paul, a grown man full of judgments, demands, and expectations. And this Paul had very clear expectations of what Christy Turlington should be and how she should behave.

This primitive Paul had abandoned what he'd learned from patients who taught him how the power inherent in physical beauty can damage a person's core and isolate them from the rest of humanity. For a moment, there on the busy sidewalk of Tribeca, Paul, the instinctively reactive human being, saw Ms. Turlington as a highly charged object rather than the human being she was.

Now let's pretend that my encounter with Turlington occurred not on a busy Manhattan sidewalk but rather in the privacy of my psychotherapeutic office uptown. To provide her with the cultural and clinical care she deserves, Dr. Paul must own and have a process to understand, manage, and utilize his reactions both outside and inside the therapeutic dyad. To remain blind to them, or to pretend they don't exist, would damage the integrity of the work by keeping the patient trapped in a bubble of isolation and placing me at risk for an ethical violation or clinical misstep.

Does this mean I need to grovel over beautiful patients and at the outset of our engagement immediately acknowledge them for their looks? No, it does not. What it means is that at some point during the process of therapeutic engagement, after I have a distinct clinical formulation for my intervention, I must put a name to the powerful energy that is with us in the room—and that has been defining the patient for the better part if not the entirety of his or her life.

Sometimes this happens in our first encounter. Sometimes it takes months before it can be acknowledged and discussed. An example of the former involved a phone conversation I was having with a potential new patient who was a celebrity of extraordinarily good looks.

I was winding my way through Chicago O'Hare airport, catching a flight back to Telluride, while we were discussing the possibility of working together on issues of substance abuse within his marriage. The entire time we were talking, I found myself passing newsstand after newsstand that had, on prominent display, a magazine with him shirtless on the cover. Even though I had never met this young man, I was so moved by the synchronicity of my sightings that I felt compelled to bring it up. "I have to stop you for a moment. I'm walking through O'Hare, and, well, I'm looking at a shirtless you on the cover of a magazine."

My comment was met with a startled moment of telepathic cringing and a deep sense of shame. "Oh Lord, yes . . . that . . . that unfortunate cover. My manager thought it would be great exposure. We're trying to get me more exposure as a romantic lead."

His repeated use of the word *exposure* wasn't lost on me.

"Well, maybe congratulations are in order, but I would think that the exposure also comes with a huge amount of vulnerability to you and your husband," I said. "It might also feel creepy to have millions of eyes seeing you on such an intimate level. I felt you cringe when I brought it up." I hoped my comment was received in the manner in which it was intended, a way to let him know I was capable of seeing beyond the sparkle of celebrity to the darkness that frequently resides inside.

Fortunately, it was.

The shame that had only moments before permeated our connection was replaced with the client's deep sigh of relief for being seen not as an object of strength and sexual virility, but rather as a vulnerable human being whose appearing shirtless before millions of lustful and envious eyes exposed him, his partner, and their relationship to a level of vulnerability unfathomable to 99.9 percent of the world's population.

His response, although simple, was incredibly revealing: "Wow, you get it."

What I got was that the "it" to which he was referring was actually himself, a person who, in his dogged pursuit of stardom, had lost sight of the fact that he's a fragile and vulnerable human being who is seen and treated like an inanimate receptacle of others' lust.

I also needed be mindful of and openly discuss my reactions to his physical beauty with members of my clinical support team. As we will see later in this chapter, human beings—regardless of their profession—perceive and process beauty on a primitive level.

Many addiction and mental health professionals whom I've

encountered over the course of my career, however, claim they are above these reactions. These are the folks who maintain that celebrities "don't affect them," or that they "don't even know who that person is." However, in lying to themselves and others, these professionals interact with celebrity patients in clinically destructive and culturally insensitive ways.

By claiming superiority to the phenomenon of elite power inherent in a manifestation of beauty, these professionals are disrespecting a central feature of the patient's identity and causing harm not just to the patient's well-being but to the field of mental health. Their position is akin to claiming to be "color blind" in working with patients of African descent or maintaining that a religious or sexual identity fundamental to a patient has no bearing on the transference and counter-transference that flows between the patient and the therapist. Regardless of how overt or covert these identities are, they manifest in the patient's life in a significant way. Such identities strongly influence how patients see themselves, how others see them, and how they are perceived by the world; as a result, they have a conscious and unconscious impact on their therapists.

Whatever features influence an individual's identity, they must be acknowledged and incorporated into the therapeutic process. If they're not, the therapist will be unable to establish a reparative alliance with the patient and will perpetuate the destructive relational patterns in the patient's life. While the field of mental and behavioral health has made significant progress in acknowledging that identity expressions such as race, sexual orientation, religion, profession, gender, age, and trauma significantly impact a patient—going so far as to develop identity-responsive care programs to address them—there are other identity contributors that demand consideration but are being ignored.

The elite power found in the celebrity construct of beauty is one such consideration.

Traditionally, if the construct of beauty is being addressed at all, it's within the context of the powerlessness and victimization that emanates from it. Feminist psychology is built on the diminished power women experience in their role or when they are treated as sex objects. This work is rich and an important foundation for my practice.

But there is another side of beauty that's seldom discussed.

This is the power of beauty to keep the human beings who manifest it isolated from meaningful relationships with themselves and others.

•

Human beings are always in transition. We move forward. We move back. We may feel like we're stagnating and stuck, but the current of life never ceases. Typically, we only remember the points of significant transformation, when the momentum of change accelerates, becomes more pronounced, crashes on the rocks, or pulls us out to sea.

My dive into the realm of psychology, first as a graduate student and later as an intern at a free clinic in Los Angeles, marked such a watershed moment. For this reason, the city and its surrounding environs hold a very special place in my heart.

People often refer to Los Angeles as the City of Angels. For many, it is. The weather's sublime. The people are creative. It's multicultural and sophisticated. There's a thriving arts scene, great restaurants, and beautiful people. But the city's treasures aren't evenly distributed. They're clumped on the side of town closest to the sea, west of La Brea Avenue up the coast and into Malibu. This is the part of the city people visualize when they think of LA.

But there's another side of the city that doesn't sparkle. This is the side where the gates are rusted in disappointment rather than gilded in dreams attained. It's the side that's rooted in disappointment, poverty, and pain. And it's on this side of Los Angeles where I learned my most valued lessons in the art of establishing a psychotherapeutic alliance with patients who are different from me.

•

"Are you really going to work there?" Dina, my best friend from graduate school, was shocked when she learned I was to begin my training at a free clinic in what was widely considered a rough-and-tumble part of town. Her question had nothing to do with the patient population I was going to treat, but rather with the fact that I, a buttoned-up former lawyer, didn't visually line up with the choice I was making.

While I'd like to say my choice of the free clinic was rooted in altruistic motivation, the truth of the matter was the clinic was not among the sites on which I'd initially focused my attention. The ones I'd originally wanted, it turned out, didn't want me. After being rejected by about a dozen "fancy" clinics, I started to panic and took to sharing my frustration with anyone who'd listen.

One of most generous among these listeners was a classmate, a "Dreamer" who'd emigrated from San Salvador and was pulling her family and herself up by her bootstraps. She was working at the clinic and enjoying her experience. She was also plugged in to the clinic's needs. "They'd love to have a man who speaks Spanish," she told me and generously gave me the number of the director. That afternoon I called the clinic. A week later, I had an interview, and the week after that, a gracious offer to join their team. But even though I got one of the most rewarding and impactful professional placements of my life, before starting at the clinic, I was feeling insecure and rattled by the process. My conversation with Dina only amplified my concerns.

While there were multiple ways I could have perceived Dina's question regarding my internship site, I chose the one that was the most critical.

"I'm a little offended, my Dina *jan*." (Dina and I had become so close that I'd begun to use with her the same Persian term of endearment she always used with me.) "So you think I'm not tough enough?"

Dina—a refugee from Iran who views herself as an outsider—has been one of my closest friends for decades. If anyone could tell me the truth in a way I could hear it, it was she. "No, Paul. It's just perhaps . . . you're too tough."

Me? Too tough? I was intrigued. I've always considered myself a softie.

The best thing about a dear friend is they can tell you the truth in a way you can hear it. I respected Dina and valued her opinion, but I needed her to explain.

"I'm confused. Help me out here."

"Well, for starters, my Paul, you're very white and privileged. And you don't exactly present like you're one of the people."

My confusion morphed into indignation. "Are you saying I'm arrogant?"

"Not to me. I mean, I adore you, but you can come across as a bit aloof."

"To whom?" I demanded to know.

"Well, to just about everyone who doesn't look or act like you . . . and even to a lot of those, you—well, my love—you're, well, *vous êtes l'élite*"—you are elite.

Dina knew my heart melted when she spoke to me in her perfect, formal French, but the music in her pronunciation didn't quell my indignation. It fueled it. Like most conversations of depth and value, this one was uncomfortable. Her sophisticated and cultured French failed to soften the blow.

Like the majority of the patients I would subsequently treat, at the time of our conversation, I didn't view myself as elite. My background, as I've noted, certainly was not of the manor born. At my core, I still view myself as the chubby boy I introduced you to earlier in this book: an out-of-place, serially uncomfortable, and often-bullied kid sporting "husky" jeans and trying to survive in a working-class neighborhood of Maryland.

Dina knew I was offended but didn't back down. I attempted to respond to her exquisite French with my hobbled pronunciation, "*S'il vous plaît expliquer, mon Dina jan.*" (Please explain, my dear Dina.)

In her inimitable style, she played her hand brilliantly. "My Paul-Paul, it's not a bad thing, it's just a thing. Don't forget you're there to learn. You'll take yourself into those relationships. And, well, you're not there to let them know you're fabulous. You are there to let them know that you are real."

My heart skipped a beat in hearing her declaration.

I still get goose bumps when I think of it today—and I think of it often.

It's sage advice that I've carried with me throughout the highs and lows of my career. *You are there to let them know you are real.*

At the time, the mere thought of *being* real plunged me into a sea of uncertainty. Dina's statement forced me to consider what being *real* at this transitional phase of my life actually meant. Was I a lawyer shod in Gucci loafers or a social worker wearing shoes from Payless? Was I still fat, was I smart, could I make a living as a therapist in a town that's overly saturated with them, and what did making a living even mean at this stage of my life?

But below the chatter of these superficial questions was the real issue that needed to be addressed: *Who was the human being I would bring into my psychotherapeutic encounters?* Before I could ever hope to help the patients I was called to serve get clarity around their issues, I would need to get clarity around mine.

On a deep level, I knew Dina was right. Connecting with the people I had the honor of working with meant that I'd need to connect with myself, a self who must acknowledge and transcend my deeply ingrained white, male privilege.

•

Meeting with a new patient always has been anxiety provoking. It was nearly paralyzing on a scorching Los Angeles morning when I saw my first patient at the Hollywood Sunset Free Clinic many years ago. The clinic catered to those in need—couples and families who were struggling to survive as low-income, uninsured human beings in an overwhelmingly expensive city. Many people who walked through its doors were refugees and immigrants, people who had risked their lives to provide a better one for their families. Because the clinic was in Los Angeles, it also attracted legions of struggling actors, models, writers, and other artists—hardworking people who were called by an unrelenting passion to follow their dreams and in the process were discarded by a mercenary culture. When I worked there, the clinic was barely hanging on, under-funded and overstressed by a community that desperately needed its services. I suspect the clinic's situation has not improved since then.

Chaotic chatter filled my mind as I left the therapists' work area at the clinic and headed toward the lobby to meet my new patient, a human being named Willow. *Will she and I connect? I wonder if it's still boiling hot outside? Am I smart enough to sort through that which overwhelms her? Willow is a lovely name. Can I tolerate that which she finds intolerable?* These were the questions that raced through my mind as I opened the door to meet her.

As I entered the lobby, I scanned the room. I spotted her in an instant. Willow attracted the eyes like a magnet pulls at scraps of metal.

When I mentioned her name, she sat erect in the tattered vinyl chair in which she'd been waiting. I'll never forget the look on her face as I walked across the lobby to greet her. I was expecting to see relief. Instead, I saw terror.

Like a statue carved out of marble, she stood perfectly still—only moving her intensely green eyes, which were frantically darting around the room. It was clear she wanted to escape or be saved.

I provided an opportunity for neither.

Nancy Etcoff, author of *Survival of the Prettiest,* describes the intense power of beauty as that which "ensnares hearts, captures minds, and stirs up emotional wildfires" (Etcoff 2000). Willow fit Etcoff's description perfectly. Even though the reception room where I met Willow was a drab mélange of harsh lighting, scuffed white walls, and mismatched furniture, she possessed an incendiary beauty.

Typically, when we think of celebrities or people who occupy positions of elite power, we think in terms of fame and fortune. But as we've discussed throughout this book, elite power manifests itself in a variety of ways, and beauty is one of them. Merely by virtue of their genetic coding, people can exist in the world in a different stratum of power that is defined by their beauty, and because of the power in their beauty, they are reduced to their features, stripped of their humanness, and reduced to objects.

Willow resided on this shelf, a human being defined and objectified by the external beauty of her physical presentation.

Eventually, I found my voice and cobbled together a sentence with purpose.

"It's nice to meet you, Willow. Why don't you come on back?"

Instead of eagerly rising from her seat, she sat like a corpse, rigor mortis setting in and bolting her to her seat. Her eyes, however, were very much alive. Bright and green and lit from within, they shone like beacons through a fog of fear, desperately scanning the room for a way out of the situation.

Wow, I thought, *I'm not the only one who's anxious. She's paralyzed by distress.* I shifted my thoughts to my stance and realized I'd assumed the aggressive perch of yet another privileged white male summoning a subordinate.

I took a substantial step backward and a deep breath in.

Willow welcomed the space.

Lord, Hokemeyer, you're freaking this girl out. My mind grasped an AA slogan: *Easy does it. If she doesn't want to come back, she doesn't have to.*

"No rush, no obligation," were the words I finally found to convey what I thought needed to be said to Willow. "When and if you want to come back to my office, just tell Mia, the receptionist, to find me. And, listen, if you'd prefer to speak with someone else, a woman perhaps, we can make that happen."

And by surrendering my control and demands on Willow, she surrendered her need to flee the situation.

On her own time, through her own resilience and grit, she found the courage to ascend from her seat and follow me down the stained and frayed carpet to the consulting rooms. I stood in the doorway of the one I'd chosen and allowed Willow to enter the room first.

"Sit wherever you like."

One tactic I learned early in my career is to give the patient the option of sitting in a seat of their choosing. It sends the message early on that they have a voice in their treatment.

Willow took a seat directly facing the door, a position of power. I interpreted it as a good sign. She had a keen intuitive aptitude. It was a valuable skill we could build on and add to.

"So, what brings you in today?"

My first attempt to establish rapport failed miserably. It

was too broad, too cliché, too overwhelming, too cold.

Willow's radiant eyes looked as if they would burst with sorrow. She tried to speak but choked on the words that she was trying to form.

I retreated and regrouped.

I thought perhaps I should leave the room and allow her the space, but didn't. I didn't want to overpower her, but I didn't want to abandon her, either.

"It's fine to just sit for a while. These first sessions are extremely difficult. Maybe we can just use this time to fill out the standard paperwork the clinic requires?"

Willow nodded in agreement.

For the next ten minutes we sat, ticking off boxes and filling in documents that would be filed away in a cold and dark basement. But the time was well spent. It allowed me to get some insight into her life's details.

I learned that she lived across the street. She was twenty-one and an actress who was making her living as a waitress. She was single, but dating. Her family lived in a working-class suburb of Detroit. Her parents were divorced. She'd lost touch with her dad. She had a strained relationship with her mother. The most telling of all was that she had no one to contact in the case of an emergency.

At the end of our task, I had the black-and-white details of her life, but I hungered for the color.

Being a novice and anxious to lift the heaviness that flattened the room, I regressed to my ill-fated attempt to control our session. I repeated my initial question, the question that had failed miserably before. "So, what brings you in today?"

Fortunately, Willow had more courage than I had clinical

acumen at that point and responded, "I live across the street."

"Oh right. Good, then. We're certainly convenient." Small talk. Banter. From the forms, I knew she lived across the street, but at least the wheels of conversation were unlocked and had started spinning. It didn't matter what she said. The important bit was that she was engaged.

"Yes," she agreed.

I grasped for things to say, any form of idiotic conversation. "Do you like the neighborhood?"

"It's fine."

"How's your career going?"

"It's not."

"Rough business. Tough town." My response was a feeble attempt to empathize with the exhaustion that comes from chasing after a camera that's always pointed in another's direction.

Willow nodded but continued staring into her lap. The clenched fists nestled there seemed to ground her. Although in the entire time we'd been together we hadn't made direct eye contact, her body radiated the rawness of emotional pain that has its origins in trauma. I sensed that while I needed to proceed gently, I also needed to proceed.

While I thought my comment was feeble, I sensed that it brought her sadness into sharper focus. I thought of repeating it, of trying to move closer to the pain. But instead of reiterating the words, I articulated them as I felt them ten years earlier as a struggling and poor young man who'd recently moved to LA and experienced the humiliating rejection of someone I loved.

"It's really tough."

Finally, Willow looked up at me, drew in a deep breath, and started sobbing. Those eyes that could captivate the world finally began to release some of their sorrows.

Over the next three months, I learned the details of Willow's life. Dark moments were shared sporadically. Willow would alight on a painful truth, then fly back into the realm of her ordinary existence. We'd begin by discussing the mundane details of her life—her ineffective agent, the demanding customers she waited on, a funny movie she'd watched. But interspersed throughout these conversations were revelations about the darkness that beleaguered her life.

When she was seven, the fifteen-year-old boy who lived across the street sexually abused her. Her parents ignored her cries for help. To make matters worse, from that point on, Willow was looked at with scorn by her parents and neighbors, who all accused her of being too "seductive."

"My mother called me a little whore and condemned me to damnation. My stepfather looked at me with a little disgust and a lot of lust. All the mothers in our neighborhood gossiped that I was a tramp."

What she took from this and other experiences was that her voice didn't matter, that men were in charge, and that she was powerless to change things. Willow learned that she was helpless to fight off male domination and abuse, and so she surrendered to it.

As she continued to mature, she learned that while her beauty submitted her to male domination, there was also a power in it that could be used in her favor. "My history teacher in ninth grade came on to me. I told him if he didn't give me an A, I'd tell my brother that he'd hit on me, and my brother's friends would beat the hell out of him. I got the A, and he never hassled me again."

Eventually, she felt comfortable enough to discuss her physical body in our sessions.

"I came to blossom very young. I started my period when I was twelve. Kind of freaked me out."

Instead of being loving and supportive, her mother accused her of being sexual. "She said I had to be blowing the boys in the neighborhood to have started my period at that age."

I also learned that both her father and stepfather were creeps, constantly getting drunk and cheating on her mother.

Eventually, Willow realized that she could get out of Detroit and away from her family by relying on her beauty.

"I went to New York City when I was fifteen as part of a cheerleading competition and, well, it was a new world. Everyone was so attractive and nice. I got scouted by a modeling agency."

At sixteen, she dropped out of high school and started traveling around the country as a model. Her parents took the money.

"I guess I made decent money. My dad bought a Mercedes, and my mom had closets full of Louis Vuitton handbags. I never saw a dime."

At nineteen, she'd had enough and moved out to Los Angeles to try her hand at acting. At twenty, things weren't going very well, and she started noticing the clinic across the street.

"I've walked by this place a million times. Then about a month ago, I realized it was a mental health clinic. Eventually, I got up the courage to call and schedule an appointment."

She scheduled about three appointments, only to cancel them all. Eventually, she made her way in. I admired her courage and was glad she channeled it in a reparative direction.

In discussing the case with my supervisor, a seasoned and brilliant clinician named Susan, who left this earth far too soon after a courageous battle with breast cancer, it was called to my attention that I kept referring to Willow's beauty.

"Paul, that's about the sixth time you mentioned how beautiful she is. Have you addressed it with her?"

I responded defensively. The thought of discussing it directly terrified me. I feigned ignorance. "What exactly is 'it'?"

Susan, like my friend Dina, had no fear of being direct. "Her beauty."

"Well, no. It's inappropriate." I was guarded and defensive, a sign that an important issue needed resolution.

Susan chuckled. "What's inappropriate is the presence of something so large in the room that's not being addressed. You need to bring it up in a way that doesn't objectify her or make either one of you feel slimy. Men have responded to her that way her entire life. Give her a new experience."

I was confused. "What exactly would that look like?"

Susan responded wisely, "I don't know, Mr. Lawyer. Wait and see. Figure it out. Gently question our witness."

I considered Susan's advice and waited.

During our seventh session, I felt it was time to address her beauty directly.

"When did you understand the enormity of your beauty?"

Willow jerked upright in her seat. My comment was electric. She stuttered, not knowing what to say.

"I . . . I . . . well, I—"

I cut her off, perhaps too soon, perhaps not. There's a great deal of gray space in therapy when you take a risk and say something that could invoke a negative reaction in a patient.

I got nervous that my comment might scare Willow away, but I dove into it more deeply.

"You know you possess an exceptional beauty. We've talked about it indirectly, including how men are attracted to you in frequently destructive ways, and how other women resent it and act in hostile ways toward you. There was your mother, for instance, and women customers who stiff you or leave shitty tips. Or how you used it to escape . . ."

When nervous, I blabber. But I caught myself, hoping I hadn't overwhelmed Willow. I forced myself to stop talking long enough to allow her the space to absorb my comments.

Willow retreated back into herself to evaluate my comments for their safety. Her retreat was a good sign. In it, she could tap into her strength and resilience.

I waited and resisted my urge to take my comments back, to apologize for saying them. To do so would be to assume the role other men had played in her life, men who viewed her as weak, an object incapable of autonomous thoughts, feelings, and actions.

As Susan so wisely advised, my job as her therapist—specifically as a therapist who is male—was to provide Willow with a different relational experience, one that would embolden her and move her in a reparative direction. I was hoping my directness regarding her beauty would start us on this journey. But in hoping, I'd also taken a risk that my comment would send Willow running away.

Fortunately, it didn't.

In her own time, Willow looked up.

The muddied sorrow in her eyes was replaced with the sparkle of strength.

"You know, you're absolutely right," she said. "No one has ever said it that directly. There's always this thing that people see before they see me. As much as I feel guilty saying it, there are times—a lot of times, actually—when people seem to see me and hate me. Really hate me because of how I look. Always have . . . probably always will. It's time I get a handle on that and stop abusing myself and being abused by others for it."

And with this honest acknowledgment, our true journey began. Willow finally found her voice to admit truths that, while real, held the potential to be viewed as unflattering. "I never talk about my looks because, well, I don't really feel attractive, and if I do talk about it or complain about it, people will think I'm boasting or ungrateful."

I hoped I could help her understand the work we were doing by placing it in a new perspective. "That's admirable. But here, the work we are doing in this room for an hour a week exists independent of that world out there." Willow looked up at me expectantly, so I continued. "The point of this room is to provide a container that we open at the top of the hour, spread around bits of you during the hour, then repack and close up again at the end of our hour."

And for the next several weeks, we did just that. We unpacked. We explored and we repackaged.

Eventually, Willow felt safe enough to talk about her beauty in the fullness of its expression, an expression that included a healthier relationship to humility rather than hubris. She acknowledged there were aspects of her appearance she appreciated, but there were also bits that caused her distress. The result of her integration was that she could begin to see herself as a multidimensional, dynamic human being who was not controlled by the objectification of others. Three months into treatment, Willow shared an experience she'd had with a male customer who told her with a wink that she'd get a "substantial tip" if she came over to his apartment after work that night. "Instead of feeling powerless and tongue-tied, I told him straight up that wasn't going to happen," she said.

Six months into treatment, Willow began to acknowledge and appreciate her intelligence. At first, I acknowledged her capacity to get herself out of situations that didn't suit her, but she rebuffed my observations. Eventually, she started to integrate my comments into her self-concept. "You're the first man who ever told me I was smart," she said.

Four months later, I walked Willow through the GED process and helped her apply for nursing school at UCLA. She was accepted with nearly a full scholarship and embraced the work with gusto.

When I left Los Angeles for New York City to work on my PhD several months later, Willow was excelling in the nursing program and had taken a break from dating. Five years later, I got a text message from Willow. "Hey Dr. Paul. I hope you get this. I just want to let you know I'm starting medical school in the fall!!!!!!!! I'm incredibly grateful for your encouragement and helping me to see myself in a different light." I desperately wanted to write Willow back and say, "Oh no, it's me who has a huge debt of gratitude to you for helping me understand the darkness that accompanies beauty." But I didn't. I simply responded "#Brilliant! #Grateful! #Proud!"

•

While the pain of beauty that Etcoff refers to in her work relates to the impact that beauty's force has on the observer, it doesn't capture its pernicious force on the observed. Many men and women like Willow are confronted with the fire of their beauty before they even understand its heat. Some never develop adequate insulation.

Others, like Willow, do. Those who fall into the class of the "do" diversify their psychic portfolio by developing other parts of themselves. For Willow and Marcelo, the young client from Brazil I introduced earlier, this meant working toward a distinct professional identity. For the young, shirtless actor referred to earlier, it meant investing emotional capital into his marriage and having children.

For most people, Willow's need to move *away* from her beauty in order to find a healthier and happier way of being in the world is difficult to comprehend. Millions of men and women spend hours slaving away at the gym, starving themselves, undergoing painful and expensive surgical procedures, and spending billions of dollars on cosmetics and wardrobes to make themselves *more* attractive.

Therefore, it's difficult for us to develop empathy for the pernicious side of beauty. Typically, when we think of beauty, we only see the promises of relational nirvana that is sold to us by commercial interests.

And there are plenty of promises being sold.

For starters, beauty is huge business. In 2015 in the UK alone, the things people turn to to make them look and feel beautiful were the foundation of a £17 billion a year industry (Raconteur 2015). In America, we spend about three times that amount (Statista 2017). This results in legions of commercial interests dictating impossible standards of beauty to both women and men. In addition, men and women who sell their beauty get paid astronomical sums of money. According to *USA Today*, Gisele Bündchen earned around $30.5 million in 2016 (Kerr-Dineen 2016). And while the bulk of his net worth comes from his athletic prowess, her equally beautiful husband, Tom Brady, earned approximately $44 million that very same year from his salary and celebrity endorsements.

And then there are the empirically proven social and economic benefits of being attractive. Numerous studies have shown that attractive people (both men and women) are judged to be more intelligent and better in bed; they earn more and are more likely to marry (*Economist* 2003).

But there's also a darkness in beauty's bright light, and it's a side that needs to be acknowledged, honored, and managed. This is especially true with middle-aged women and men such as Sally, Luke, and Mark, who desperately cling to an outdated vision of their beauty.

•

"I'm an actress," Gloria announced with exaggerated pride three minutes into our first session.

I made a mental note of her comment and tucked it away. "Oh, okay," I responded.

I sensed Gloria wanted more of an affirmation of her celebrity identity, but I resisted giving it to her. I'd forgotten our session was not about me.

I retreated to the notes I'd made during our initial conversation, when Gloria called to set up the appointment. "So," I said, "you are looking to get some help on improving the relationship with your son, who you say is difficult."

"He *is* difficult! You say that like it's not true." Gloria's rapid-fire reaction and its attendant defensiveness startled me. It also indicated I was dealing with a hypersensitive person who quite possibly also presented with borderline personality disorder. I needed to retreat and tread lightly on her eggshells.

"Oh, I'm sorry to give you that impression. I'm sure it's true."

"It certainly is," she responded. Without pausing, she moved back to the identity for which she wanted to be seen. "I'm an actress, and I get a lot of calls for auditions and bookings."

For the second time in less than a minute, Gloria had told me she was an actress.

Her comments were fly balls that I was unable to properly focus on catching. I felt myself standing out in left field, alone and frustrated.

I wanted to ask, "I'm sorry, have I seen you in anything?" but I didn't. Such a response would have been insulting and divisive. My goal at this stage of our engagement was to move myself into her world instead of pushing her out of mine.

I struggled to hold my tongue and figure out an appropriate intervention.

I knew my feelings were important, but I wasn't sure what to do with them—until I did. *Just surrender to it, Hokemeyer,* was the intuitive thought that finally emerged. *See her as she wants to be seen.*

"Oh yes, well, being an actress and," I hastened to add, "a successful actress at that, is incredibly demanding. I do see the issue here."

"What exactly do you see, Dr. Paul?"

I once again found myself alone, but instead of being out

in left field, I found myself up at bat, under pressure from the fastballs Gloria was launching in my direction.

I resisted the urge to swing thoughtlessly and instead focused on Gloria's physical presentation.

While I suspected there were some aspects of Gloria that she had permitted to age without surgical or chemical interventions, none were visible. Her hair, a blond patina that was dry and brittle, was heavily laden with extensions. A pair of oversize Chanel medallion earrings stretched the holes in her lobes into wizard's sleeves that wobbled when she spoke. A ribbed black cashmere turtleneck speckled with cat fur clung to augmented breasts and retreated from a pair of leather tights as she shifted in her seat. Her face was pulled tight, to the point of rendering her expressionless. Her skin looked burned from what I had to imagine was some sort of laser procedure. I wondered if what looked like intense outward pain mirrored the pain of her internal experience.

I tried to focus my thoughts on what it would feel like to live behind all that artifice, but I struggled to find compassion. Finally, I responded, "I see a hardworking and successful woman who is frustrated that the people in her life, people who don't—I don't know; help me out here—do they not appreciate you? Maybe they disappoint you?" I wanted to put Gloria back on the pitcher's mound and allow her the opportunity to throw out another pitch—a pitch that I could hopefully get on base with.

Gloria relaxed her defensive posture.

"That's pretty good."

I let out a sigh of relief, learning that I'd finally moved our relationship into the playing field.

"So what's good in what I just said?"

"You were right. It's disappointment."

"Disappointment that they don't appreciate you?"

"Well, it's my son, really. My daughter I don't have a problem with."

"Tell me about your son. He's a big entertainment lawyer, right?" As soon as my comment left my lips, I could see that I'd sent an electric current up Gloria's spine.

Gloria's eyes radiated fire as she barked, "Why are we talking about my son?"

I stuttered. "I . . . well . . . I . . ."

"Are you obsessed with my son?"

I was starting to feel trapped, panicky, and defensive. Fortunately, I knew the way out of our dynamic was through the truth.

"Only to the extent that I know he's paying for your treatment. You put me in contact with his secretary to arrange for the billing."

Gloria huffed and reached down for her Louis Vuitton bag. Its signature LVs were embellished by the artwork of a famous contemporary artist. In stark contrast to what I'd noted with Clare's discreetly labeled bag, the thought that lingered for me about Gloria's was *When a countless number of initials are not enough.*

Gloria waved her right hand dismissively in my direction. I saw it as a sign to redirect our conversation.

"He frustrates you?" I asked with as much confidence as I could muster.

My question resonated with her and brought her back into the game.

"Everything is about him. Babysit my kids. Listen to me brag on and on about my stable of A-list clients. Isn't my wife gorgeous? It's sickening."

"I should think." I was finally able to calibrate myself in Gloria's pinching stilettos. "Sounds like he's a bit of a narcissist."

"A bit? He's a textbook example of a narcissist."

The psychological term *projection* ran through my head. I kept it in there.

"Yes, that's difficult. I see why you're frustrated." My use of the word *see* to describe her irritation was intentional. It was obvious that Gloria, like Luke, the decorator we met in chapter 3, had developed her identity through external validation; like Luke, she lived in a state of constant disappointment and self-flagellation over never quite hitting an unattainable mark. My job as her therapist would be to teach her a different, richer way to express the fullness of her being.

But providing a frame that enabled Gloria to expand her view of herself and others would be difficult work that would take time, courage, and trust. Unlike a physical procedure such as a breast or lip augmentation, something that's done *to* a person to freeze him or her in a past moment of time, our work would involve allowing Gloria to evolve toward the future. It would require her to accept parts of herself she'd been told were unattractive and to accept that the industry of beauty is built on unhealthy, unrealistic, and profit-driven standards, standards that are impossible for human beings to meet. But before we could begin cobbling this frame, I needed to be present in a way that enabled her to feel safe.

Unfortunately, Gloria and I never made it to the next stage of our relationship. As I've mentioned previously, initial patient contacts don't always turn into working alliances. Perhaps it was my stumbling on her ego. Or, perhaps, in spite of my best attempts to cover it up, Gloria perceived the sorrow I felt when I realized the extent to which she had manipulated her physical form. Although I'm reluctant to admit it, perhaps Gloria would have been better off with a female therapist her own age. With a woman, she may have felt less judged, less competitive, less driven to displace the hostility she held toward her son onto me. Regardless of the cause, Gloria never returned for our second session. She didn't cancel; she just didn't show up. In doing so, she made a preemptive strike and rejected me before her fears that I, like her son, would discard her could be realized.

When I think of Gloria, and I think of her often, I do so with regret. While I try to move through my remorse over letting her down, it still haunts me. It's also increased my resolve to do a better job in holding the fragility of a soul who's terrified to emerge from behind a steel door of cosmetic manipulation.

•

Beauty resides in the eye of the beholder, but how we perceive it also sears itself on the souls of the observed and the desperate to be seen. Such was the case with the human beings you've met in this chapter and throughout this book. For Willow, beauty was a feature of her being that she was ill equipped to manage. For Luke, Jonathan, Brenda, and Lionel, the acquisition of people as beautiful objects for sexual domination left them feeling diminished, empty, and tarnished. For Gloria, and the millions of other men and women who chase an unattainable ideal of beauty sold to them by commercial interests, beauty is a siren song that compulsively pulls them toward self- and relational destruction.

While the power inherent in beauty will not soon fade away, its destructive pull over us can be diminished. By anchoring ourselves in a harbor of interpersonal relationships based on mutual respect rather than objectifying lust, we can fend off the dehumanization that occurs in beauty's stirrings.

7.

Opulent

Luxury Rehab and the Dynamics of Treatment

No human being is ever beyond redemption. The possibility of renewal exists so long as life exists.

—GABOR MATÉ

Sidecar at P.J. Clarke's in Midtown Manhattan is one of my favorite restaurants at which to meet colleagues for lunch. For starters, it's slightly off the beaten track. There's a side door on East Fifty-Fifth Street that leads you upstairs to a restaurant that feels like a private club. They serve delicious fries tossed with garlic butter and fish and chips with a chunky tartar sauce that rivals anything I've eaten in London. It's convenient to my office, and if you get there at an unfashionably early hour, it's quiet by Manhattan standards.

Over the past few years, I've dined there with some of the mental health and addiction treatment fields' brightest lights—clinicians, interventionists, case managers, entrepreneurs, and sober companions. These relationships are important to my work. As a licensed marriage and family therapist, a significant part of my clinical practice involves identifying and treating addictive disorders. Early in my training, I found the incidence of addictive disorders in the context of relational challenges to be upward of 50 percent. Nearly two decades later, I'd say it is higher. Nearly 75 percent of the time, when a couple or family comes to me for help, it's because one member in it has an unhealthy dependency on a substance or is manifesting some sort of compulsive, destructive behavior. Accordingly, understanding addictions and having a robust network of ethical and effective colleagues to whom I can look for guidance and help is an essential part of my practice. It's also important that I constantly educate myself on the most up-to-date addiction treatment modalities and stay apprised of the latest developments and staff changes in the rapidly changing field of residential and outpatient addiction treatment.

As you can imagine, marketing representatives from these centers frequently approach me looking to fill their beds. They view my patient population as one that can provide them what is known in the field as "private-pay" patients. In contrast to patients who need to use their insurance, private-pay patients are those who are able to pay cash for a month, several months, or even years of treatment. In a field that is oversaturated with treatment beds and centers, private-pay patients are a lifeline for many treatment programs.

Unfortunately, in order to keep their doors open and fill the surplus of beds that have flooded the market, some of these programs are looking to maximize profits rather than provide culturally competent and clinically effective care to their patient populations. Typically, these programs are sited on gorgeous mountaintops or on cliffs overlooking a crashing sea. They are rich in amenities but lacking in clinical substance. In the words of my British colleague Adrianna Irvine, these facilities are "all fur coat but no knickers." This isn't to say that amenities aren't important—as you'll see later in this chapter, they are, but only if they're provided as part of a clinical rather than a marketing formulation.

Central to a program's effectiveness is the ability of the professionals working within its buildings to provide a culturally relevant frame for the patients who have found the courage to enter treatment and gently but firmly move them in a reparative direction. For this reason, I'll only refer a patient I'm working with out to an addiction treatment center if I personally know their administrative and clinical staff and intuitively feel they see their patients as human beings worthy of respect rather than profit centers capable of paying inflated fees. The same standard applies to the individual professionals to whom I refer patients. These are typically professionals who have devoted their lives to addiction treatment because they, or a loved one, struggled with the demonic forces of the disease and have professionalized their calling by pursuing higher education and training to bring professional integrity and heightened ethical standards to their personal passion.

But over the last few years, I've witnessed a dramatic change in the field. Fueled by explosive profits, the "luxury" and "executive" addiction treatment centers have been saturated by MBAs and venture capitalists who see addiction treatment as an industry rather than a calling. These savvy businesspeople seek to maximize return on institutional investment (ROI) instead of return on patient well-being (ROW).

•

As is typical when I'm working in Manhattan, I'm running late and feeling stressed out. Such was the case on a glorious spring day in May as I hurried from my office to Sidecar. The patient I had just seen, a fifty-three-year-old woman, ended her session in tears. The night before, her husband of more than thirty years had relapsed into his alcoholism, and she was exhausted from a sleepless night and two decades of worry. We spent an extra fifteen minutes sorting out a plan to address her distress and allow her some time to put herself together. While necessary, our extra time was going to make me at least twenty-five minutes late for my lunch at Sidecar with a Wall Street executive named Jack. As I packed up my bag to race out the door, I hurried off an email to Jack's assistant, alerting him to my delayed arrival.

Neither the thought of garlic fries nor the flower boxes that lined Second Avenue with their bursts of white tulips and purple hyacinth soothed the agitation I felt over being late. Like the squeaking E train that snakes its way through Manhattan, I huffed and puffed my way through the throngs of pedestrians meandering in front of me, all savoring the glory of the day.

Finally, I reached my destination.

Throwing open the door, I raced, two steps at a time, up to the dining-room floor. When I reached the hostess stand, I was not just out of breath but also sweating profusely. "Oh, hi, Dr. Hokemeyer," the hostess greeted me warmly. "Your party is already seated." As she walked me over to the table, as much as I tried to collect myself, I couldn't. Instead, I approached the table with an unpleasant disposition.

The thirty-something man frantically typing into his smartphone arose to greet me.

"Jack? I'm really sorry I'm really late," I blurted out, looking like I'd just spent the night in a truck-stop toilet.

"Yes," he responded condescendingly.

"I reached out to your assistant, because I don't have your direct number." I was feeling insecure, and it bubbled up as contrition.

Instead of responding, he gestured for me to sit down and snapped his fingers for a waiter.

Did he really just snap his fingers? I asked myself.

He did.

And not getting anyone's attention, he snapped his fingers again.

This time he enhanced the snapping with a bellow, "Waiter, can we get a waiter over here?"

I took my seat and observed with a tinge of envy my lunch mate's presentation. While I was disheveled and sweating, he was a model of perfection. Strikingly handsome in an athletic, lacrosse player sort of way, he wore his salt-and-pepper hair short and, at midday, sported a five o'clock shadow. But it was the symmetry of his face that really captured my attention. Solid, strong, masculine, his face formed a perfect triangle with two violet blue eyes peering outward and a chin with a cleft so deep you could slide your Mastercard through it.

He stuck out his hand aggressively and shook mine with a Samson-esque force.

"Thank you for making the time to meet with me. I know you've got an incredibly busy schedule." His words came out like a wooden rose, perfect in form, but lacking authenticity.

"Yes, of course. I apologize for being late. I had a patient run over . . ."

He leaned in toward me. "I'm sorry, I didn't get that."

My voice was dry, and I was anxious. It's a recipe for

inaudible speech. I repeated myself, focusing on my articulation. But my agitation grew over not being heard.

In the middle of my redelivery, our server appeared.

"Do you know what you want?" she asked.

I did. "Fish and chips."

Jack ordered a grilled chicken Cobb—"dressing on the side, hold the blue cheese and bacon."

I admired his discipline. No wonder he looked like the models of perfection that grace the covers of men's fitness magazines.

After the server left, Jack continued. "So, I understand you've captured the market for rich patients."

I was stunned by his characterization of my work.

"Captured? I . . . well . . . I'm not sure I'd put it that way."

Jack cocked his head. The light from Fifty-Fifth Street illuminated his deep violet eyes, making him look like the love child of Elizabeth Taylor and George Clooney.

"But I've been told you are the go-to guy for successful luxury treatment programs. My firm is looking to invest in the space."

I knew who he was and why he had contacted me. I willingly accepted his invitation to meet. Seldom do I turn down the opportunity to talk about the treatment space referred to by a number of descriptors including *luxury, high end,* and *executive.* But even though I was a willing and eager participant in our meeting, my agitation morphed into anger. "Well, I'm sure you are. Lots of people are."

"You're the brains behind some of the leading luxury programs being set up around the world."

I tried to respond coolly, but I also needed to clarify my role in the treatment space and reel in his expectations of what I could bring to our meeting. "I have been and am part of a team that uses my research for the clinical formulations that are used in these programs. And just so you know, we don't 'capture' anyone. We provide a culturally relevant space for human beings to heal."

Cultural relevancy and the notion of "healing" as a deliverable seemed to bore him. "What are your margins?" he asked.

The temperature on my indignation rose. "My margins? Our margins are exceptional in terms of the care we provide to individuals and families who look to us for a reparative experience through a culturally relevant and clinically excellent frame . . . these come in the form of qualitative experiences, things like better intimacy, self-esteem, peace of mind. My focus is on the families and patients, not the investors."

Apparently, I wasn't the only one getting annoyed. Frustration washed over Jack's face. He began fidgeting with his Rolex.

I used the break in our conversation to regain some control over my emotions. "So let me ask you. You're a smart guy looking to invest in the luxury addiction treatment space. Right?"

"Yeah, that's right."

"So what are you investing in?"

Jack's violet eyes glossed over. I waited for his answer.

"Treatment. The best treatment money can buy."

I scrunched my toes in my shoes.

"Okay, so let's start with the first. What exactly is treatment?"

Jack suddenly became introspective and silent. I allowed him all the time he needed to think. Unfortunately, no amount of time would permit him to articulate a concept he didn't fully understand.

He punted and pulled out a glossy folder from a high-priced briefcase.

"So let me show you what I'm thinking."

He shoved the folder in my direction. On its cover was a brick Georgian mansion set deep behind a set of gates. From inside the folder, Jack produced a leaflet depicting a rich middle-aged white couple hugging in marital bliss. Another leaflet sported a handsome salt-and-pepper-haired man sitting in a private jet talking on a smartphone. "We're going to let the clients keep their cell phones throughout the course of treatment," he boasted.

"Regardless of the presenting issues?" I asked.

Jack ignored my question and prattled on. "We'll also allow them to attend important events, like their child's wedding or an important business meeting."

I was getting bored with our conversation. Jack wasn't showing me anything I'd not seen many times before. I tried to liven up our interaction. In a tone more suited to a comedic roast than a professional lunch, I pointed to the man sitting in the private jet and asked, "Is this you?"

Jack seemed more insulted than amused. He indicated it wasn't.

"Certainly could be," I responded.

Just then we were interrupted by the delivery of Jack's antioxidants and my cholesterol. But Jack had more doves to pull out of his hat. "Here . . . this is our clinical schedule."

I quickly scanned the list: meditation, yoga, group and individual therapy. Nothing new. Nothing I'd not seen before.

"What are you going to charge for this . . . this mélange of amenities?" I wanted to see if Jack caught my catty intonation, but he didn't.

"Eighty-two thousand and five hundred dollars a month,"

he said proudly.

Finally, I'd had enough. "Look. Your marketing materials are beautiful. Really well done."

Jack drank in my compliments like a new sponge being introduced to water.

"But there's nothing new here. There's nothing to distinguish your program from the hundreds of others out there competing for these patients. How are you different?"

"Different from what?"

"Different from every other treatment program that has the exact same amenities-based treatment . . . and elevated fees."

Jack aggressively stabbed a cherry tomato. "We're the best. We provide the highest level of care."

"How?"

The temperature in the room seemed to rise by fifty degrees. Now it was Jack's turn to sweat. Beads of perspiration formed on his well-moisturized and perhaps Botoxed brow. I decided to retreat and rephrased my question. "Okay, let's back up. What are you selling?"

"Treatment."

"Exactly. But what is treatment? What's the one-line elevator pitch?"

Finally, Jack gave up. "I guess I don't know."

I was relieved by his surrender.

"So can I give you my four-word definition?"

"Please."

"Treatment is a frame."

Jack looked at me expectantly. It was clear he wanted more, so I continued.

"It's a frame where individuals come to address and heal

from the destruction that results from personality, mental health, relational, and addictive disorders, as well as physical ailments."

"Okay." Jack was with me.

"We have a person who is operating in a system that is framed by destruction. We take them out of that system and create a new one that is framed by reparation."

Jack pointed to the glossy brochures, "But that's what this is."

"To an extent, you're right. This gloss, this glitter, this upholstery is what we call ego syntonic. It enables people of wealth to identify in as opposed to identify out. But simply catching a fish in a sparkly net isn't treatment. You've got to get the fish out of the net and teach it how to thrive in a new environment, an environment that for a while will leave them gasping and thrashing around. It's a tall order."

Jack pushed his salad away. I looked down at my plate of grease and felt queasy. I soldiered through my nausea and continued.

"The problem is everyone is only concerned with catching the fish, and I hope you know, the sea is suffering from overfishing. There just aren't enough heads to fill the number of beds that are coming into the market. And as a result, everyone is getting hysterical, frantically searching for heads while not paying attention to the needs of the people who actually fill them."

To Jack's credit, he took the news I was delivering in good stride.

"I see."

"I hope so. I also hope you realize there's an opportunity to do something significant for a distinctly defined group of human beings who have distinct cultural markers and very complex clinical needs. This isn't about producing instant coffee and demanding a premium price because you put it in a fancy container. It's about making artisan espresso, a cup at a time, by a trained and highly skilled barista."

Just then the server appeared to remove our half-eaten lunches. "Coffee?" she innocently asked. Jack and I looked at each other and laughed. Jack ordered a double espresso. I ordered a chamomile tea.

•

In his best-selling book *In the Realm of Hungry Ghosts*, Gabor Maté described addiction as a phenomenon wherein the people who suffer "constantly seek something outside [themselves] to curb an insatiable yearning for relief or fulfillment. The aching emptiness is perpetual because the substances, objects, or pursuits [they] hope will soothe it are not what [they] really need" (Maté 2010). While Dr. Maté made these observations through his work with human beings who live in states of diminished social and economic power in Vancouver's drug ghetto, his observations are equally relevant to human beings like the ones you've met throughout this book, women and men who live in states of enhanced power behind gates in Beverly Hills or up in the penthouses that tower over Park Avenue. Although these people may live in the world's safest neighborhoods, drive the safest cars, and eat the safest organic foods, they still ache from a hunger that tells them they are inadequate and flawed, unlovely and unlovable. What these people need, like the patients Dr. Maté treated, is to be seen and heard as a person of value rather than an object of desire or disdain.

But seeing and hearing a person in a way that produces a curative response requires a relationship that pierces their external presentations in a way that reveals their internal realities. In this regard, my work with elite patients in the realm of substance use disorders is strikingly similar to that of Dr. Maté. In both of our patient populations, guilt and shame keep the human beings who suffer under the weight of addiction trapped in cages of isolation and despair. While Dr. Maté's patients feel guilt and are shamed for having so little, my patients feel guilt and are shamed for having too much.

As you've learned throughout this book, power, property, and prestige are often thin veneers that cover deeply buried and malignant feelings of inadequacy, disquiet, and discomfort. Elite patients' feelings are intensified by the shame projected on them from the world in which they live for "failing" to use their power to avoid—and to cure—the intangible ache that tortures them from within.

In the realm of addictive disorders, these patients experience guilt and shame not only in response to the larger communities in which they live, but also in the very rooms that promise them community and relief from the isolation of their disease. In contrast to my patients who live squarely within the socioeconomic bell curve of the middle class, those who live at the economic and power extremes of abundance often internalize enormous shame through the Twelve Step program's use of gratitude as a tool to help them abstain from their destructive use and behaviors. What these people hear when they first walk in the door of these programs is akin to the legacy of the Buddha and Mark 10:25, that to find "the cure" they must relinquish all their power and renounce their wealth, else salvation will elude them. This result is not just sad and unfortunate; it often leads to a tragic ending.

Before these patients can get to a place of gratitude, they must spend time exploring how their wealth and power manifest in their lives and their relationships. They must come to understand how some features of their being have enabled them to survive while others have diminished their existence. In short, they must cultivate the first-rate intelligence that we discussed at the outset of this book, which is the ability to hold two opposing ideas in the mind at the same time while moving to a higher level of functioning.

Individual psychotherapy is incredibly valuable in addressing most chronic mental health and personality disorders, but when an acute and life-threatening addictive disorder is involved, one-on-one talk therapy is typically not enough. This is because addiction causes significant deficits in a person's "learning, memory, and reason" (Gould 2010). These deficits cloud the judgments of the afflicted and make them highly susceptible to external triggers that pull them back into their pathological use. More effective recovery interventions come from providing patients with a safe and contained frame filled with a community of their peers, other human beings with whom they can see bits of themselves and feel safe enough to share their vulnerabilities.

This isn't to say I don't believe in the Twelve Steps as an effective treatment modality. I do. In fact, in my experience, the Twelve Steps are highly successful and provide women and men of all backgrounds with a path to meaning, purpose, and health in all spheres of their lives. What I do mean to say is that some people, because of the rarefied and unique positions they hold in the world, have very real and very valid challenges in making a curative connection to people outside of their identity in the initial stages of healing in the rooms of Twelve Step recovery.

In addition, while the Twelve Steps and the message of gratitude contained within them are miraculous in healing the wounds of addiction and opening the door for people to address their underlying personality and mood disorders, they were never intended to stop the suicidal ideation of a mother who lost her son to a heroin overdose, or a father whose acute anxiety prevents him from leaving the house, or a husband whose malignant narcissism has destroyed his relationship with his wife and children. These people need more than the Twelve Steps; they need a safe, contained, and structured program to stabilize their bodies, rewire the neurological networks in their brains, and reconnect with their spirits. This heightened level of highly individualized care is what residential treatment should provide.

In the same way that treatment programs have evolved to recognize the distinctive needs of patients with specific identities in terms of age, gender, religion, race, and sexual orientation, so too must patients of elite power be treated in a frame that clinically addresses their uniqueness in the world. Central to this work is providing them a safe space where they can come forward with the fullness of their being and process the challenges inherent in it. At every level of the organization in the treatment center—from the corporate suites to the therapist suites to the housekeeping staff—the professionals working in these programs must have the capacity to see past the veneer of these patients' culturally celebrated features to *feel* the fragility of their humanness.

As I explained to my hale and hearty but culturally insensitive lunch mate, Jack, in the realm of addiction treatment, we call these culturally designed programs *ego syntonic*. This means they provide a treatment environment the patient will identify into rather than fight to escape. Anyone who has worked in the field of residential treatment knows that for at least the first two weeks of treatment, the patient is desperately searching for ways to identify out.

"These people are not like me," "I wasn't that bad," and "this place sucks" are the common refrains of newly admitted patients into residential treatment programs. Such refrains take on different timbres depending on the person's identity. A male Orthodox Jew will have different identity concerns than a transgender person or a woman. In the same vein, we must be aware of the pitch of patients whose identities are manifested through an elite power construct and create a frame to hold them while they assimilate their three distinct cultural markers into their radically different and terrifying new reality. These markers consist of

- isolation
- suspiciousness of outsiders
- hyper-agency

But as it's been historically delivered, the very essence of residential treatment is in direct opposition to these markers. As it relates to the first, at the heart of residential treatment's effectiveness is its value in taking patients out of a destructive environment and providing a safe and contained space where they can interact with others in a curative dynamic. In clinical speak, we refer to this as the psychosocial aspect of treatment. While we empirically know that the peer-to-peer interactions that occur in treatment are highly effective, for a person who has spent decades of their life in an elite bubble of isolation, the prospect of joining a community of strangers is repellent, terrifying, and often a deal breaker.

The first question I get from elite patients with whom I'm discussing residential treatment as an option is "Do they have private rooms?" A follow-up declaration of "There's no way I'm sharing a room" is always made. While in theory it *could* be good for them to share a room with a stranger, in reality it's culturally insensitive to force such an intimate living arrangement down an elite patient's throat, especially in the initial stages of the treatment process.

Assuming elite patients can get past the host of negative reactions to having to live with a group of strangers and agree to enter into a structured treatment program, these patients are then expected to trust their deepest, darkest secrets; their most triggering traumatic memories; and the vulnerability that underlies their personality presentations with a clinical team who most certainly is going to come from outside their social class. While some patients may actively vocalize their skepticism of these treating professionals' abilities—"Are you kidding me, some social worker is going to tell me how to live my life?"—most will express it by testing the trustworthiness and integrity of the team.

Unfortunately, many of these programs and professionals fail the tests they are given.

In the time that I've been working in the luxury treatment space, I've witnessed too many culturally blind, clinically incompetent, and downright unethical treatment teams being manipulated into traps set by highly sophisticated and incredibly intuitive patients. One patient, an heiress who suffered from one of the most severe borderline personality presentations I've ever worked with, seduced her poorly paid—and poorly trained—clinician into a sexual affair. In so doing, she justified her claims that the treatment center was only interested in her for her money and not worthy of her trust. In discussing the experience with me several months later, she stated, "He was dying to get out of [insert small town] and thought I was going to be his ticket to the bright lights and big city. I showed him . . ."

In addition, tales abound of wealthy patients offering expensive gifts and even cash payouts to treatment center employees to manipulate them into outcomes: "Convince my wife not to divorce me," "Get my kid into Harvard," and the most common and least expressly stated, "Allow me to just slide through this program." Over the years, I've personally seen and heard of patients offering staff members and programs "rewards" including a $100,000 cash payment to fend off an expensive divorce proceeding, an Audi S4 because "you saved my life," a million-dollar donation to a treatment center's charity arm for "fixing" a child, and countless other "tokens" of appreciation, including a personalized painting from a famous artist, a Louis Vuitton suit, Montblanc pens, and tickets to the Oscars.

In no uncertain terms, these gifts are not to be accepted, but rather graciously declined and brought immediately to the clinical team's attention. Once framed in the context of a *clinical issue,* the patient's offering must be processed with the patient in a clinical frame that addresses the relational and personality dynamics at play. These dynamics include the objectification of both the patient and the professional, as well as the use of money to manipulate and convey love.

The third cultural marker of elite patient populations that conflicts with the traditional approach to residential addiction treatment relates to the construct of hyper-agency and an elite patient's mastery in manipulating his or her life to avoid any discomfort. But residential treatment, with its detox process, interpersonal challenges, and requirement that the patient surrender his or her control and will to myriad administrative rules is an experience steeped in discomfort. And herein lies the greatest challenge to effective clinical engagement with elite patients. These individuals have spent their whole lives in a race away from emotional and physical distress. As they accumulated more wealth, more power, or more fame, their ability to exert their control over their lives to avoid any discomfort grew exponentially. Now they are forced, in most cases against their will and through infantilizing tactics, to go into a controlled, monitored system where they will need to follow rules instead of making them and in all likelihood will be asked to admit powerlessness and defeat.

That these human beings even consider residential treatment as an option is an act of pure grace. That they enter into it is an act of extraordinary bravery, and that they stay long enough to engage in the treatment process results from a combination of art and science on the part of the treatment professionals.

Even if you don't lose patients by having them physically leave treatment, there's a strong probability you'll lose them emotionally. At the beginning of this book, we addressed the questions so commonly and publicly asked when a person of elite power is at a point of emotional crisis: *Why can no one help? Why can't she help herself? Why doesn't treatment help?* The answers are found in the mental health and treatment field's failure to accept that these human beings have very specialized cultural needs that must be specifically addressed through distinct clinical formulations. The field of addiction treatment has figured out that luxury amenities appeal to elite patients, but with very few exceptions, they've failed to develop culturally effective programs within the luxury space to emotionally connect with the human beings who, to borrow a word from my handsome colleague Jack, they've "captured" through their sophisticated marketing efforts. Unfortunately, if an emotional connection is not made, patients will remain in the program long enough to comply with the demands placed on them, but in a superficially compliant way. In other words, they will be there because they have to be, not because they want to be. As masters of manipulation, they'll say exactly what you want to hear—"I'm willing to do what it takes," "I'm powerless over my disease," "AA is such a great program"—while counting the hours to their liberation from your program's grasp. Yes, you may succeed in externally motivating them to enter and stay in treatment by hard-line tactics, but in so doing, you'll have set up a dynamic where they will need to retaliate against you by sabotaging their recovery.

Short-term recovery can be based on external leverage, but long-term recovery and wellness require the patient's motivation to come from within. Ideally, patients enter treatment internally motivated. They're sick and tired of being sick and tired. They're beaten down and have had enough. But in my work with elite patient populations, while a spark of internal motivation may exist, it doesn't burn intensely enough to push them through their resistance to the features of the programs that are in direct opposition to their cultural markers, which I've discussed in this chapter.

In nearly 90 percent of the cases where I'm involved in getting an elite patient into treatment, his or her motivation comes from some external source. The patient is caught in an unsavory act and shamed into submission. "You did X, now do Y, or Z will happen." In polite clinical terms, we refer to this as leverage. In Dr. Paul speak, I call it coercion that borders on bullying (Urbanoski 2010).

Getting people into treatment through coercive methods is a waste of money, goodwill, and emotional energy. In short, it's highly ineffective and can be damaging to the patient and the patient's family.

One study published in the *International Journal of Drug Policy* found that forcing patients into treatment was ineffective—or worse—in approximately 90 percent of the cases studied (Werb et al. 2016). This data is consistent with my clinical experience.

Examples of coercive and bullying interventions I've witnessed among my elite patients have included these threats:

- Go to treatment or I'll divorce you.
- Go to treatment or I'll take away the kids.
- Go to treatment or I'll cut off your trust fund.
- Go to treatment or I'll stop representing you.
- Go to treatment or I'll terminate our business relationship.
- Go to treatment or I'll tell your parents, the kids,

the neighbors, your business partners, etc. what a mess you are.

- Go to treatment or I'll lock you out of your house(s).
- Go to treatment or I'll sue you.
- Go to treatment or I'll send this drunken video of you to the press.

For people who live in the world in positions of elite power, the shaming that comes from these coercive interventions doesn't just diminish their chances of therapeutic success, but it also invites retaliation. They may comply in the short run with your coercive tactics, but in the long run, they'll prove you wrong and react against you by escalating their destructive behaviors.

The more effective interventions for people who exist in positions of elite power are grounded in what's known as Self-Determination Theory (SDT) (Urbanoski 2010). When utilized as a motivational tactic, SDT engages with a patient's fundamental tendency to act in healthy ways rather than causing them to act out through anger and retaliation. So rather than shaming a person into treatment, an intervention based in SDT will build on a person's competence and autonomy to internally motivate them toward physical health and relational well-being (Ryan and Deci 2000). Typically, I start my SDT interventions by focusing on patients' external successes in the world. Once we've articulated the features that have enabled them to realize their external accomplishments, I engage them in a conversation to explore how they can utilize these same qualities to achieve success in their emotional, physical, and relational realms. We need only think back on my intervention with Mark, when I explained to him that if he devoted a fraction of the energy he spent on his productions on his marriage, he would win an Oscar at home. I use the same approach with a person suffering from an addictive disorder: "Let's talk about the courage, focus, and discipline it took to build your company. Which of these can we channel to get you back to optimal cognitive and relational functioning?"

According to Maia Szalavitz, author of *Unbroken Brain: A Revolutionary New Way of Understanding Addiction*, research shows over and over that empathy, kindness, respect and support work better than force, brutality, humiliation, and shame (Szalavitz 2012). As an approach, SDT provides a supportive, constructive approach and discourages the opposite. It allows elite patients a clear and distinct voice in the ifs, hows, whens, and wheres of their treatment and treats them like the high-functioning adults we want them to become, rather than fortifying their destructive and adolescent behaviors.

Too often, however, allowing patients a voice in their treatment invokes hostility toward them from their support system. "Sure, he gets to go off to some country club, while I'm stuck back here in the city with the kids, trying to manage his destruction" is the frequent refrain of a spouse or family member when the patient finds a program that's located on a sunny shore or tucked into a rugged desert landscape. In their mind, these programs reward rather than punish, and for all the destruction caused by the patient, some sort of punishment is in order.

Punishment, like coercion, heightens individual and relational destruction. This is why the most effective treatment programs involve family members as fellow patients in the treatment process. These individuals have had to manage disappointment, shame, guilt, powerlessness, and a battery of other caustic dynamics. They don't carry the most obvious symptoms of the disease, but they're very much infected.

Most programs, however, only involve family members as strong-arm agents to keep patients in treatment or engage them in what are known as psychoeducational sessions. In these limited engagements, the family learns about the disease of addiction as a student didactically learns French. They get an understanding of the disease but not the culture or their place in it. Unfortunately, these sessions further pathologize the person in treatment and keep the entire system trapped in its destructive dynamics.

An additional element of successful elite treatment involves assisting the patient to assimilate into the psychosocial community of their peers, fellow travelers on their recovery journey. At the breakfast table, on the deck outside, or during one of the patient outings, the patients share their experiences with the disease of addiction, their thoughts about the program, and the recovery process.

And it's this bit, connecting to a group of one's peers, which has been empirically proven to be the most impactful element of residential treatment. According to the Center for Substance Abuse Treatment, "The effectiveness of group therapy in the treatment of substance abuse also can be attributed to the nature of addiction and several factors associated with it, including (but not limited to) depression, anxiety, isolation, denial, shame, temporary cognitive impairment, and character pathology (personality disorder, structural deficits, or an uncohesive sense of self)" (Center for Substance Abuse

Treatment 2005). This finding confirms what we instinctually know: that human beings are relational creatures who, when faced with an outside foe, organize in tribal hierarchies. As these tribal hierarchies relate to the treatment of substance use disorders, studies have found a host of therapeutic benefits to a peer-to-peer group treatment component including

- providing positive peer support to tweak personality presentations
- reducing the isolation from which patients suffer
- enabling members to witness the recovery of their peers
- providing coping skills by allowing patients to see how others deal with similar problems
- imparting useful information to patients new to recovery
- providing insights into managing recovery in a similar identity presentation
- learning or relearning skills to cope with life on life's terms
- confronting members about their harmful behaviors and personality presentations
- instilling hope, a feeling that "if my peers can make it, I can too" (Center for Substance Abuse Treatment 2005)

But these tribal connections don't happen immediately or even in the first week of treatment. They require patience, time, and tact. They also require clinical savvy in the treatment team to get the patient settled into the community in the first seventy-two hours of their arrival. Unfortunately, too few luxury programs have trained their staff to properly handle the unique cultural needs of the elite patients to whom they've successfully marketed their services.

•

Several years ago, the husband of a former patient of mine hired an expensive case management service to intervene on his wife. The patient, a sixty-two-year-old woman I'd not seen for three years, called me frantically from her mobile phone in the lobby of her husband's attorney's office. "Thank God you picked up. This is Antonia; we worked together a few years back. You're not going to believe this, Dr. Paul, but my husband is insisting I go to treatment." Instead of allowing her dignity in the process by going home and properly packing for her journey, the case manager convinced the husband to force her to go directly from the lawyer's office to a $75,000-a-month facility the case management company had chosen. "He has the divorce papers drawn up. I signed a prenup, and I get basically nothing in it. The jet is waiting for me at Teterboro, and my bags are packed." Left with no real options, she complied with her husband's demands and flew off to the treatment facility, terrified, angry, and humiliated.

Once checked into her suite, Antonia, a former model, realized that in her husband's haste he'd failed to pack what she considered a "critical" skin cream she had custom-made for her in Switzerland. For her, this was the last straw, a straw that caused her to devolve into a state of hysteria. She demanded that "someone, anyone," go to her apartment, find the cream, and overnight it to her for a morning delivery. Absent such delivery, she'd be "checking herself out."

The clinical assistant (CA) assigned to her by the treatment facility was a young man I subsequently learned was an undergraduate student making $14 an hour. He called me just before midnight to see if I could settle her down.

"Dr. Hock . . . Hock . . . meir?"

"Hoke-a-meyer. It's Hoke-a-meyer, but Dr. Paul is fine; actually, Paul works well too."

"Okay, Dr. Paul, I'm working with your patient, and we have a bit of a problem here."

"What's the problem?"

"Well, she's being difficult."

"How so?"

"She's making unreasonable demands."

"Unreasonable to whom?" I waited for his response, knowing the answer before he spoke it.

"Well, to the staff," he replied.

"You'll need to explain."

"She's having a meltdown over some cream."

"Cream? For her coffee? Her pie? You'll need to do a better job of explaining."

"I guess whoever packed her bags forgot to include her face cream."

I was insulted by the dismissiveness in his voice but remained silent, allowing him to continue. "I mean it's just skin cream. We can go to the Rite Aid or, heck, even Saks in the morning and get her some."

I took a deep breath before responding, "That's completely unacceptable." I attempted to cloak my outrage in a tone of authority, but failed miserably.

There was no reply on the other end of the line.

"Are you operating a prison or a treatment facility?" I was upset and annoyed. When I'm in that state, I tend toward the dramatic.

"I'm not sure what you mean?" the CA's tone was becoming more frazzled with every clarification he tried to make. It was clear he'd expected me to side with him rather than with my patient.

"Why are you punishing her?" I asked again, with a flair for the dramatic.

The CA began to stutter. "I . . . we . . . well . . . we're not punishing her."

"She certainly thinks you are."

To the CA's credit, he stopped to consider my assertion.

"But her primary [therapist] thinks her vanity is an issue that we need to clinically address."

The hairs stood on the back of my neck. I paused before responding lest I'd devolve into a hysterical fit of my own.

"Perhaps a month from now . . . but in the first few hours of her landing? Shouldn't you be getting her settled before you start poking around her personality presentation?"

I took his silence as license to continue.

"Okay, here's the deal . . . the clinical deal. It's not about the skin cream. It's about her connection to the fragments of dignity she has remaining. She's been judged for her appearance her entire life. Being seen as beautiful is her primary identity . . . an identity, I hasten to add, she's terrified of losing. So it's not just skin cream, it's her oxygen. She needs it to breathe."

His silence continued.

"Do you get it?" I asked, skeptical but optimistic.

"Uh, yeah. I get it," he sheepishly replied.

"I hope so, because if you don't, you're going to lose a woman who's just suffered a major humiliation by her husband, a team of strangers who were hired by her husband, and now your staff, who, again, I assume is being paid by whom?" I knew the question was rhetorical, so I continued through it. "How are you going to distinguish yourself from the rest of these hired guns?"

"Umm . . ."

"Get her the skin cream and let her know—immediately—that it's coming. And for God's sake, treat her with some respect. She's terrified right now and deserves to be treated better. And have her primary call me first thing in the morning."

The next morning my phone rang at 9:00 sharp with a private number. I was impressed that the clinician was on top of the case.

"Hello, this is Dr. Hokemeyer."

The voice on the end of the other line was superficially contrite, but deeply resentful.

"Yes, hello, this is Marsha Smith. I'm going to be Antonia's primary therapist. I understand you wanted me to call you?"

Anger began to well up inside me again. "I did."

"How can I help you?" she asked.

I looked at the time and date on my phone to ensure I wasn't in some twilight zone, dreaming I was having this conversation.

"How can you help . . . me?" I parroted back her question, hoping she would hear the mockery in it. She didn't. Indignation greeted me on the other end of the line. I mirrored it back. "Shouldn't you be asking me how you can help your patient?"

Again, silent annoyance.

So I continued. "I got a call at midnight last night from your clinical assistant. Apparently your team was unable to contain the patient and got into a pissing match with her." The call wasn't going well. Admittedly, I was angry at the program and taking it out on the clinician.

Still more silence.

So I asked, "Perhaps you can explain to me the clinical formulation behind your decision to challenge the patient's need for face cream."

Now it was my turn to be silent.

Finally, Marsha spoke, "Well, the case manager said she's very entitled and vain. We need to address her narcissism."

Her comments pierced my ears like an ambulance heading up Lexington Avenue, loud and painful.

"Let me get this right: the case manager? A firm who was hired at great expense by an angry and, from what I can tell, vindictive husband to carry out a task?"

"I'm not sure I'd characterize it that way."

"How would you characterize it?"

"Well, the husband did an intervention on her. I guess she was a real mess. We work with this case manager service a lot."

"And you've met with the patient, I assume?"

Silence.

"So you've not yet met with the patient?"

"We have a session at 1:00 this afternoon."

At that point, there was so much to say, I wasn't sure where to start. "I'm sorry, but I'm . . . well . . . I've lost the plot here. Let me repeat my question. So the clinical formulation for this intervention and strategy is based on a diagnosis of narcissism from the husband to the case manager whom he's employing . . . and you're just rubber stamping this diagnosis . . . and addressing—well, if in fact it's an accurate diagnosis—a personality trait that's deeply embedded in Antonia's psyche in, what, the first hour of her arrival into a completely foreign and, from what I can tell, hostile environment?" I tried with all my will to avoid adding, "And for this, you're charging, what, $100,000 a month?" but I failed.

"We're not that much." Of course, the clinician chose the easiest point of pushback, the fees that were being exchanged.

"Oh, please forgive me. What are you charging?"

"I don't handle that part of the relationship. That's all negotiated by our business office, but I know we're not a hundred grand."

"I find it very hard to believe you don't know what your fees are, but let's move past that. I assume you do handle the clinical part of the relationship?"

Marsha hesitated, but finally conceded, "Yes, that's right. I'll be her primary therapist."

"And so I assume you're familiar with the work of Professor Alison Fragale?"

"I'm not."

"I suggest you read it, because it's highly relevant to the patients with whom you work. Her work explores the relationship between power and status" (Fragale, Overbeck, and Neale 2011). I visualized Marsha nervously shifting in her seat, examining her nails for imperfections in their lacquer. I continued: "Dr. Fragale found that to successfully exert power over someone, you need to have status, which in essence means exerting your power with respect . . . allowing them dignity. If you exert power without status, you're going to get a kickback."

Silence. Shifting. Nail examining.

"We see this play out in cases where parents and spouses cut off loved ones from their money to get them into treatment. The patient complies in a superficial way, but once they are out, they reclaim their power through a major 'F-you' to the family. I'm afraid that's been the setup here."

"I see." To Marsha's credit, she seemed willing to hear what I was saying.

"With patients like Antonia—patients who are used to getting their way because of their money and social status—it's a dynamic that needs to be addressed from the moment the case is being teed up."

I thought I heard Marsha sigh and surrender into the concept I was attempting to deliver. I too began to surrender my pride, ego, and anger.

"Okay, I see what you're getting at," she finally allowed.

I decided to quit while we were ahead. I didn't need to drive my point home any further.

"Great. She's an extraordinary human being. You'll enjoy working with her once she gets her sea legs. Where are we with the skin cream?"

"I'll need to double check."

"Thank you. In the scheme of things, it seems really trivial, but to Antonia it's a point she needs to win to feel respected. We have to pick and choose our battles, and I'd strongly suggest we let her win this one. It will make all the difference to her long-term care and the success of your program."

Marsha appreciated the guidance and found her sense of humor. "Okay, I get it. Hell, maybe I'll order a tube for me. Given the stress of this work, I could use some miracle potions."

Relational dynamics, self-perceptions, cultural characteristics, and treatment center motivations: these are factors that must be acknowledged and addressed by professionals working with patients of elite power in the realm of addiction treatment. The financially aspirational entities struggling to find private-pay patients in an overly saturated market infrequently provide the specialized skill and care required to effectively treat the patients who actually make it in their door. This failure results from untrained and culturally destructive therapists and employees viewing these human beings as either profit centers or objects of desire or disdain. To avoid viewing these patients as profit centers and causing further damage to their well-being, "luxury," "executive," and "high-end" treatment programs must deliver specialized care that meets their patients in the reality of the *patients'* world rather than in the financial insecurities, cultural prejudices, and narcissistic aspirations of the treatment programs themselves. If these entities are charging elevated fees to treat these human beings, they must deliver elevated care to repair them.

8.

Connected

A New Standard of Compassion and Healing

The unexamined life is not worth living.
— SOCRATES

Stories abound about professionals working with powerful patients. They're fascinating. They're interesting. But shared for the purpose of sensationalizing the patients' plight or objectifying them for money, they are damaging to the teller, the told, and, of course, the object of the conversation. The point of this book is to utilize the challenges I've faced as a clinician struggling to make reparative connections with individuals who live in the world in positions of elite power to advance the field of mental health while helping human beings who exist at all levels of the socioeconomic spectrum live richer, happier, more authentic lives. *It's a narrative of becoming rather than being.*

In my own evolution, I've had to work through my own issues around money, power, and success. I've had to walk through my fears and insecurities, anger and resentments, and I've had to utilize mindfulness techniques and cultivate interpersonal relationships to repair the damage to my psyche and enrich my being in the world. In this process, I've learned that while my decades of academic learning and formal training are valuable, my most valuable diagnostic and curative tool is the dynamic being of me.

A week before Christmas last year, I was discussing this point with a group of treatment professionals intent on designing a "world class" family program with the most earnest of intentions. They wanted to create one set of instruments to identify relational issues to be addressed at the beginning of treatment and another to measure results at the end. "What instruments do you recommend for an intake?" they asked, convinced that I had files full of devices to locate a patient's issues with surgical precision. In response, I just pointed to my charcoal gray turtleneck sweater. "You're looking at it," I responded.

My colleagues nervously glanced at one other. It was not my sartorial choice on that cold December day that confused them, but rather my lack of standardized tools. I felt compelled to explain. "I try to avoid using documents at an initial session. I find they get in the way of my ability to feel the patient's pain and hear what their soul needs to convey." Thinking back on my work with Willow, I felt the need to defend myself further. "Occasionally, forms can ground the patient if he or she is spinning in an anxiety cyclone, but most of the time, they only serve to manage the clinician's anxiety and keep the patient and the clinician separated."

The director of the program, a recent graduate from an Ivy League PhD program, was unsatisfied with my answer. "But we want to provide our patients tracks—"

"Like for trains pulling out of a station," I added sardonically.

Not wanting to be labeled an arrogant prick, I drew in a breath and advised myself to allow her to continue.

"Well, no . . . like a trauma track or an infidelity track for couples," the incredibly bright PhD replied.

I realized that we were talking about apples and oranges. I was thinking in terms of individual, long-term psychotherapy to address chronic conditions, while my colleagues were focused on short-term residential care for acute ones.

"Oh, right," I responded. "Yes, of course. I see how these measures are important in an institutionalized setting, but I'm basically a country doctor. I'm very light on forms."

"Well, how do you know what to treat?" another bright-eyed and enthusiastic colleague asked. It was a great question and one I stopped to consider before responding.

"It comes out from what the patient says . . . or doesn't say. Where they sit, how they sit. It comes from how I feel. Am I sad? Do I get hyper-activated in their presence? Am I exhausted when they leave? Do I feel bored during the session? Does the time fly by or tick by incessantly? Forms can't measure this data, but I—well no, not I actually—the being of me can."

My colleague was intrigued, but still confused. "Can you explain?"

I took a few moments to reflect and distill my thoughts before responding. "I hope so. The *I* that I referred to and retreated from is a noun, isn't it? It's a fixed entity, like a form. The *being* of me is a verb. It's an active, dynamic construct. It has to live and breathe. It has to get knocked around and tolerate discomfort and ambiguity."

The heads around the room bobbed up and down in agreement. I heard a sigh from an intern sitting to my right.

I looked over and asked her directly, "Was that a sigh of relief or a gasp of terror?"

Finally, my colleagues laughed and relaxed into the knowledge that creating a reparative psychotherapeutic alliance with powerful patients is an art that requires a great deal of practice and a large measure of innate talent—talent that, I hasten to add, is not found in every professional who wants it.

Not all treatment professionals are able to push through the arduous process of establishing a working alliance with powerful patients. These otherwise intelligent professionals are unable to challenge their conscious and unconscious prejudices against a group of people they simultaneously idolize and disdain. They remain trapped in a stagnant pool of inaccurate perceptions that have been ingrained in them by their families, their communities, their religions, and the world around them.

The energy it takes to shift out of decades of socially and culturally entrenched thoughts and feelings toward patients of elite power is difficult to muster. In contrast to patients whose identity manifests through positions of diminished power—patients who idolize treating professionals as sage authorities—patients of elite power are labeled as difficult. They frequently come across as angry, defensive, resistant, and manipulative (Hull and Broquet 2007). They challenge our credentials and our clinical interventions, and they keep us at arm's length. Professionals untrained to work in this dynamic feel threatened and insecure and act out on the conscious and unconscious levels of their being to equalize these power dynamics. They objectify these patients as ATMs ("Oh, he just sold his company for $50 million; I'll charge him twice my standard fee"). They use them as fodder to feed their narcissist egos ("Yes, that was _____ you saw sitting in my waiting room"), and they act out with punitive and shaming interventions ("If your daughter won't stop shooting heroin, you'll need to cut her off").

For these reasons, in my experience, the most effective colleagues, clinicians, and treatment professionals who work with wealthy or celebrity patients have small practices and a network of trusted colleagues to whom we can reach out to help us process the raft of negative and hostile reactions these patients invoke. Just as we expect our patients to work hard, form a network of self-care, and challenge themselves to grow, we must do the same. We also must stick around while our patients test our commitment to their well-being and our capacity to hold the enormity of their pain.

Most recently, I discussed with a colleague the frustration he was experiencing in what he felt was a failure to establish a working alliance with a powerful patient who was constantly canceling appointments due to her life of perpetual motion. In discussing the nomadic nature of his patient's life, my colleague had a breakthrough that he shared: "I realized over time that to apply a linear, logical paradigm to her life was just leading to my frustration and putting stress on the integrity of our relationship. Now, when I get frustrated—disappointed, really—that she chooses a trip to Paris over a session with me or runs down to Miami to check on her compound, I think in terms of expansion. Her life—like her personality—is expansive. When I put it in that frame, I'm able to formulate my treatment plan accordingly."

I was inspired by another colleague who readily owned

her feelings of resentment toward her jet-set clientele: "I find myself begrudging my patients for the fact that, while I'm tied to this chair, sitting in this office eight hours a day, sometimes six days a week, still paying off student loans, my rich-and-famous clients are out living a very glamorous life, jetting all over the world. I need to be careful and have a place to put these feelings, or they will infect my relationship with them." She's absolutely right.

The challenge faced by treating professionals who work with patients of elite power is large and can be articulated as follows: Human beings in the throes of relational, mental health, and addictive disorders need help. How can we help them when they are culturally oriented to identify out of the traditional treatment paradigm and to be suspicious of our motives and when they have the power to orient their world to avoid consequences and discomfort?

The answer to this challenge is easy to articulate but nuanced in its application:

> *We must create treatment frames that are wide enough to hold these individuals in the uniqueness of their identity while facilitating a relational connection that moves them in a reparative direction.*

Instead of getting into power struggles with patients of elite power—struggles the patient *will* win—clinicians must formulate a treatment strategy that contains the following three elements:

- a firm and collaborative psychotherapeutic frame that is influenced by feminist psychology
- an intellectual engagement

- a reparative therapeutic alliance that is grounded in a humanistic embrace

Let's start with the first. Through my clinical experience and academic research, I've found that creating a culturally relevant frame is best accomplished through interventions that are informed by fundamental tenets of feminist psychology. Unlike clinical formulations such as psychodynamic theory that focus on the internal drives of the individual as an isolated entity, feminist psychology actively considers the external social and political structures that perpetuate individual and relational distress and suboptimal functioning. It looks at the person in the context of his or her life. Through this lens, reparative change comes through assisting patients to understand their being in relation to the dynamic world in which they live and to develop healthy strategies to respond to these external forces; the most relevant and impactful of these forces are the unequal dynamics that thrive in human hierarchies.

In contrast to traditional feminist practitioners who see the *lack* of power as the root of their patients' struggles, my brand of psychotherapy helps my patients see their struggles as products of their *excessive* power. In this regard, the *quantitative* analysis is different. While traditional feminist theory focuses on a deficiency of power, my expanded version focuses on its abundance. In both cases, power and the ways it has manifested in the patient's psyche and relationships and in the world in which he or she lives have influenced their physical, relational, and emotional well-being. Accordingly, it must be intellectually understood and channeled in a curative and reparative direction through a new relational dynamic. And while all of this may sound elevated and complex, in practice it's simplistic: The patient intellectually articulates and explores his or her abundance of power and then intentionally and strategically tweaks its impact on his or her interpersonal relationships.

In the context of individual psychotherapy, this new relational dynamic originates in the psychotherapeutic dyad—the relationship between therapist and patient. To assist patients in managing their power toward a constructive and productive end, a professional working through my therapeutic lens will assume the role of a collaborator rather than an expert with superior knowledge. But simply collaborating with an elite patient is not enough, which brings me to my second point. The goal of the work is not to pander to the patient or to become complicit with their patterns of destruction, seduction, and manipulation, but rather to artfully challenge patients as they move in a reparative direction. To do this, the therapist appeals to the patient's cognition through a clinical technique based on Socratic inquiry. What does that mean? Allow me to explain.

While most of us are aware of the use of the Socratic method of inquiry in the realm of legal training, few realize how committed Socrates was to personal growth and how applicable his teachings are to people who live with or yearn for power and external markers of success. Socrates was considered the wisest man in Greece, not for what he knew, but rather for his claim that he knew nothing. From this place of not knowing, he would guide his students through a series of questions designed to identify their false, inconsistent, and defeating beliefs. Personal well-being, according to Socrates, resulted from self-development rather than the acquisition of material things. Socrates encouraged his students to develop intimate connections with other people and to be constantly improving themselves and the world in which they lived.

I've found the Socratic method has a strong resonance to the elite patients and families I treat. As this relates to my clinical technique, I engage patients in a slow and considered process to reveal their understanding of their situation rather than presenting it in prepackaged terms like *narcissist, alcoholic,* or *codependent.* An example of a Socratic case formulation from my clinical practice involved my work with a female financial executive whose husband caught her in a sexual affair with a colleague at the Swiss bank where she was a senior partner. The woman had attained enormous professional success in the male-dominated and misogynistic world of private banking by becoming, in her words, one of the boys. In the first two months of our engagement, I worked diligently to practice a state of Socratic "non-knowingness" and deep curiosity around the beliefs she internalized during her developmental path and subsequently brought into her contemporary life. Together we explored what the construct of "success" meant in her Irish Catholic family of origin, the prestigious and highly competitive community where she lived, and the international banking system that she masterfully navigated to attain her elite status. Once we established this baseline, we began exploring it in relation to her evolution into a middle-aged woman who was married to a man she loved and respected, but who was afraid of "losing her light" and who felt entitled to keep a lover. In this process, we constructed a balance sheet of her assets and liabilities. Armed with this data, we then created a highly personalized frame where she could move emotionally, intellectually, and physically through her fears and into a higher, more rewarding state of being.

In my experience, the women, men, and families who live with an elite identity appreciate how this cerebral engagement honors how they operate in the world as intelligent and successful people. Elite patients who present to treatment have highly developed cognitive capabilities that have served them well in their lives. Yes, their intellectual capacity may have been compromised by their condition, but the goal of treatment is to repair this damage and to correct cognitive distortions that have compromised them. Engaging with the patient on a rational level begins this process. In addition, engaging the patient in the realm of his or her intellect allows the treating professional to connect with the patient in a zone that is safe, familiar, and comfortable for the patient. As we've seen throughout this book, most elite patients are terrified of their emotions and of being vulnerable in relationships. While the ultimate goal of treatment is to enable the patient to begin operating on a deeper level of intimacy, it's counterproductive to the therapeutic alliance to expect an elite patient to advance to this stage in the first few days or even months of treatment. The Socratic method enables the patient and the professional to get to know each other and adjust to the discomfort of an intimate engagement.

Third, the Socratic method of inquiry focuses on positive evolution. It recognizes that the goal of treatment is not to stay stuck in damage but rather to move through these stages and into higher states of functioning and greater, more diversified levels of success in the world. To put patients back to status quo or to expect them to live the rest of their lives in contrition for the darkness of their past is a valueless and punitive proposition. Real value comes to these patients and their families by building on their resiliency and grit, personality characteristics that can be marshaled toward positive outcomes.

Finally, the Socratic method is designed to illuminate rather than shame. The goal of the Socratic engagement is not to contort patients into a place of humility through humiliation, but rather to help them understand the roles their mental health issues and personality presentations have played in their lives, their relationships, and their successes.

The "medicine" this technique provides is rendered ineffective if the delivery system through which it's delivered is suboptimal. Effectively utilizing a frame influenced by feminist theory and filled by the Socratic method of inquiry requires a working alliance with the patient that is based on a humanistic stance.

The conclusion I've reached through my research and clinical practice is not new. For decades, clinicians have known that success in treatment comes not from an expertise in delivering a technique, but rather from the integrity of the system delivering it. In clinical parlance, this delivery system is known as the therapeutic or working alliance the professional has established with the patient (Ardito and Rabellino 2011).

Carl Rogers, the celebrated father of what is known as client-centered psychotherapy, defined three conditions that are required for establishing a transformative working alliance with patients. According to Rogers, these ingredients are empathy, congruence, and unconditional positive regard (Rogers 1951).

Empathy is the ability to see the world through the patient's eyes. For most treatment professionals, individuals who were brought up in a middle-class value system, this can be difficult when they are working with powerful patients.

About a year ago, I helped a clinician I mentor, Kate, work through challenges she was having establishing a therapeutic alliance with an actress who was married to a successful tech entrepreneur. The husband had what's known in financial circles as a liquidity moment in which he sold one of his startups for more than $300 million. After the sale, he began acquiring trophy properties around the world. The patient was constantly traveling between these homes and going on extended exotic vacations. In one session, the client offhandedly mentioned to Kate that her Malibu house cost her $35,000 a month to maintain. Kate, a single mother who supported herself and two teenage boys with her hourly fees, had a reaction she was not proud of: "I actually gasped when I heard the number." When I asked what it brought up in her, Kate responded with the clarity of an exceptional clinician. "Fear of financial insecurity and, I guess, anger . . . resentment . . . rage? My people—my family and friends—we actually live in our houses and struggle to keep them up. Seeing her spend that much money on a house she uses maybe two months a year . . . Do you know how hard I have to work to make that much money? . . . Do you know how many nights I lie awake wondering how I will ever pay for my boys' college education?"

By processing her feelings around her client's expenditure, she was able to move through her relationship to money and focus on her patient's emotional experience. "Once I was able to get past my stressful relationship to money—how I viewed it as a scarce resource—I was able to see the house as another way the patient avoided committing to just about everything that causes her discomfort. She always had an escape—the Malibu house was a concrete manifestation of this trait. And guess what, she could afford it. She lives in a world of material abundance. It's a world that's foreign to me, but it's a world that's very real to her and people in her social class."

Kate's ability to process her reactions outside of the therapeutic dyad was integral to her success in working with her patient. Absent an awareness of her reaction—a reaction that was completely valid based on an economic schema she'd internalized throughout her developmental path—and a willingness to process it, she would have compromised the integrity of the therapeutic alliance she was building with her patient. Kate could have remained blind to her reaction and stuffed it away, but her client would have felt it. This is because, in addition to having exceptionally honed cognitive capacities, patients with elite power have an exceptionally sharpened capacity to read other people's reactions and motivations. This is especially true when they're searching for signals regarding their safety and the trustworthiness of their companions.

The second element of Rogers's client-centered psychotherapy is *construct of congruence*. This refers to a clinician's ability to model his or her humanness with the patient with boundaries and in a clinically strategic way. Congruence doesn't mean burdening the patient with the therapist's internal processes, but rather dovetailing it into the construct of empathy by allowing the patient to connect with the clinician on a plane of human feelings. To establish congruence, the clinician may share his or her interpretation of a patient's reality in a way that honors the patient's challenges as a collaborator rather than judging them as a superior.

For example, in the situation cited above, once Kate acknowledged and worked through her reactions to her patient's housing expenditures outside of their therapeutic relationship, she developed a strategy to talk about the house with her patient through a clinical rather than a financial lens. In this case, Kate used the Malibu house to open up a discussion of the patient's struggles with depression and feeling disconnected from the world. "Your Malibu house," Kate began, "it feels isolated to me. Do you have a community out there?" Through this intervention, Kate acknowledged a feeling that had been shared by the patient and openly discussed between them (depression). She took a stab at suggesting what being in the house could possibly feel like for the patient (isolated) and exhibited an authentic curiosity over the relationship between the two (do you have a support system out there?). Through this process, Kate was able to get on the same psychological wavelength as the patient and deepen their therapeutic connection.

From the patient's perspective, Kate's observation was felt as a *possibility* rather than heard as a *declaration*. Through this nonauthoritarian approach, the patient was seen as a human struggling with what from the outside looked like a rarefied and enviable position—rather than objectified and shamed as an entitled and unappreciative cliché.

Central to the effectiveness of Kate's intervention was her ability to bracket her judgments around the costs of the home and cultivate unconditional positive regard toward the patient's ownership of it. According to Rogers, *unconditional positive regard* is the ability of the therapist to accept the patient without approval, disapproval, or judgment (Rogers 1957). For example, Kate needed to acknowledge the patient's lifestyle as one piece of objective data in a larger psychotherapeutic equation. This required her to integrate the details of the Malibu home into a dynamic and potentially ambiguous whole while recognizing that she, Kate, didn't need to understand it or have it make sense in the context of her, Kate's, life. Kate came to see the Malibu house as something that gave the patient a beautiful respite from the world *and* was isolating. It was expensive, *and* the patient could afford it. Finally, the house didn't make financial sense to Kate—*and* it didn't need to.

From this state of clarity around disparate issues that could never be fully integrated or completely resolved, Kate could hold her patient in an expansive frame through which she could provide care for the patient who, with this treatment, was getting clarity and internalizing a resolution. For patients with elite power, the elasticity of this frame is critically important. Through it, they feel understood rather than judged, emboldened rather than infantilized, and permitted to be rather than demanded to become.

By assuming a humanistic stance, the clinician—an outsider in the patient's eyes—will begin to see the patient *as the patient sees herself* and appreciate the complexity of her struggles. From this standpoint, the clinician can formulate collaborative interventions that intellectually engage the patient while developing clinical intimacy with her. Through this process, the patient will slowly—very slowly, in fact—begin to internalize the therapist as someone smart and safe, a mentor who can guide him or her through the terror of personal transformation and reparative change. With this internalization, patients become less isolated and less suspicious of clinicians and their motives, and less compelled to run away from the discomfort inherent in effective treatment.

Effective treatment of powerful patients will entail challenges to *both the patient and the clinician*. As indicated in Kate's story, the process of establishing a reparative therapeutic alliance with this patient population is slow, often painfully slow. At times, it feels like the task of Sisyphus, laborious and futile.

Patients defined by their elite power are not inclined to cede it, which is one of the primary obstacles professionals face when attempting to connect with them. They're used to being the smartest, prettiest, wealthiest, most famous person in the room. This need to be the alpha female or male hinders their ability to engage in a collaborative process with a person they see as an outsider, do not trust, and are skilled at manipulating and controlling. Managing this obstacle and utilizing it to reach a reparative outcome with the patient takes patience, humility, and thick skin as the patient challenges your competency and integrity. As part of my work, I've had to answer to the following direct and indirect inquests:

- Are you smart enough?
- Are you interested in me for my money?
- Are you going to talk about me in your book or on TV?
- Are you interested in me for the status my presence brings to your program?
- Are you going to ask me for money, either for yourself or your clinic?
- Why are you doing this work?
- Are you a narcissist? (I've actually had several patients tell me I am a narcissist.)

- Can I seduce you?

- Can I intimidate you?

- Can I manipulate you?

- How are you different from the other clinicians and treatment centers I've been to?

- Why should I stay here?

- How do you justify the prices you're charging?

- What's your success rate?

These questions made me realize that I'd better be able to tolerate the inquisition and come up with honest answers to that which my patients have a right to know. If I hadn't, I would have lost patients and tarnished the treatment industry by proving that which they had suspected all along—that the world views them as objects to be exploited and that no one can be trusted with their pain.

•

Throughout this book, you've observed the challenges powerful patients present when they finally muster the courage to reach out for psychological care. In this process, I hope you've discovered points of connection that pierce the labels that divide human beings into polarities of *us* against *them*. The takeaway I hope you got from this work is the capacity to empathize with a group of people you've made assumptions about based on their external appearances and the messages you've been acculturated to believe about them by your family, your community, and even your religion. Our implicit biases are developed as a result of many factors and over long periods of time. We only begin to evolve these beliefs, as subconscious as they may be, through empathy and connection.

If you're a person who lives in one of the identities I've addressed in this book, I hope you feel seen and understood. If you're a professional who works with this distinct population, I hope that you will take a look at your motives and develop new skills to provide effective and culturally competent care to human beings who are looking to you for a reparative experience. Last, but certainly not least, if you're a person who feels that you'd be happier, more contented, and imbued with peace of mind by attaining a position of elite power, I hope you see that the fragility inherent in power often destroys the very things we believe it will provide.

Acknowledgments

The road to this book's publication has been long and circuitous. On it, I've been blessed with the support of human beings who assisted me in abandoning misdirected paths and others who supported me as I moved in a reparative direction. Those in the former include the late William Brown, John Brody, Robin Smith Hoke, and Rusty Schuermann, whom I had the privilege of working with at the law firm Kegler Brown Hill + Ritter in Columbus, Ohio. Those in the latter include the late Herb Hampshire; Jody George, MA; Joy Turek, PhD; Stephen Pritzer, PhD; and Dr. Dennis Jaffe, PhD. While training at the Caron Treatment Centers' New York City office, I had the good fortune to work with and be introduced to Pat Pollack, Wendy Caplan, Gjyste Camaj, Todd Whitmer, Michael Herbert, Lynn Garrett, Neil Lasher, and Heather Hayes. This book would have never happened without the steady and gracious encouragement and professional advice from Richard Socarides, Jo Ann Miller, Dina Parvaneh, Kathleen Sturgeon, Jill Jordon, Anita Devlin, Elizabeth Bernstein, Debbie Resnick, David Ebershoff, and Susie Smith Coughlin. I'd also like to acknowledge the unwavering support and encouragement I received from my colleagues in London—Samantha Quinlan, Caroline Curtis Dolby, Kathleen O'Hara, Michael Rowlands, and Adrianna

Irvine—as well as the entire clinical team at Urban Recovery led by the dynamic and visionary Denise Bertin-Epp. Last but not least, I'm incredibly grateful for my extraordinary editor at Hazelden Publishing, Vanessa Torrado, who believed in this work and gave it a voice.

References

Addis, M. E., and J. R. Mahalik. 2003. "Men, Masculinity, and the Contexts of Help Seeking." *American Psychologist* 58 (1): 5–14. http://dx.doi.org/10.1037/0003-066X.58.1.5.

Albert Ellis Institute. n.d. Accessed February 11, 2019. www.albertellis.org.

American Press Institute. 2015. "How Millennials Use and Control Social Media." March 16, 2015. https://www.americanpressinstitute.org /publications/reports/survey-research/millennials-social-media.

American Society of Addiction Medicine. 2011. "Definition of Addiction." April 12, 2011. https://www.asam.org/quality-practice/definition-of -addiction.

Ardito, R. B., and D. Rabellino. 2011. "Therapeutic Alliance and Outcome of Psychotherapy: Historical Excursus, Measurements, and Prospects for Research." *Frontiers in Psychology*. October 18, 2011. http://dx.doi .org/10.3389/fpsyg.2011.00270.

Ariona (@httpariona). 2018. Twitter. January 1, 2018. https://twitter.com /httpariona/status/948007041972367360?ref_src=twsrc%5Etfw%7 Ctwcamp%5Etweetembed%7Ctwterm%5E948007041972367360&r ef_url=http%3A%2F%2Fnymag.com%2Fselectall%2F2018%2F01 %2Flogan-paul-suicide-forest-video-youtube.html.

Atkins, D. C., K. A. Eldridge, D. H. Baucom, and A. Christensen. 2005. "Infidelity and Behavioral Couple Therapy: Optimism in the Face of Betrayal." *Journal of Consulting and Clinical Psychology* 73 (1): 144–50. http://dx.doi.org/10.1037/0022-006X.73.1.144.

Baker, A., and J. C. McKinley. 2018. "The Case Against Harvey Weinstein, Explained." *New York Times*. May 25, 2018. https://www.nytimes.com /2018/05/25/nyregion/weinstein-case-legal-explainer.html.

Beck, A. T., and A. M. Freeman. 1990. *Cognitive Therapy of Personality Disorders*. New York: Guilford Press.

Bernath, M. 2017. "How to Spot Switzerland's Truly Rich: An Insider's Guide." *Bloomberg.* March 19, 2017. https://www.bloomberg.com /news/articles/2017-03-20/an-insider-s-guide-to-spotting-the-truly -rich-in-switzerland.

Borrell-Carrió, F., A. L. Suchman, and R. M. Epstein. 2004. "The Biopsychosocial Model 25 Years Later: Principles, Practice, and Scientific Inquiry." *Annals of Family Medicine* 2 (6): 576–82. http://dx.doi.org/10.1370/afm.245.

Braun, S. 2017. "Leader Narcissism and Outcomes in Organizations: A Review at Multiple Levels of Analysis and Implications for Future Research." *Frontiers in Psychology.* May 19, 2017. http://dx.doi.org /10.3389/fpsyg.2017.00773.

Brown, B. 2010. *The Gifts of Imperfection: Let Go of Who You Think You're Supposed to Be and Embrace Who You Are.* Center City, MN: Hazelden Publishing.

Buffardi, L. E., and W. K. Campbell. 2008. "Narcissism and Social Net-working Web Sites." *Personality and Social Psychology Bulletin* 34 (10): 1303–14. https://doi.org/10.1177/0146167208320061.

Calfas, J. 2018. "A Ranking of the Richest Women of the Kardashian-Jenner Clan." *Money.* July 5, 2018. http://money.com/money/4950313 /kardashian-net-worth.

Celebrity Net Worth. n.d. "Rachel Uchitel Net Worth." Accessed February 11, 2019. http://www.celebritynetworth.com/richest-celebrities/rachel -uchitel-net-worth.

Center for Substance Abuse Treatment. 2005. "Groups and Substance Abuse Treatment." In *Substance Abuse Treatment: Group Therapy.* Treatment Improvement Protocol (TIP) Series, no. 41. Rockville, MD: Substance Abuse and Mental Health Services Administration. https:// www.ncbi.nlm.nih.gov/books/NBK64223.

Chamberlain, V. 2012. "Harvey Weinstein, the King of Hollywood—Again." *The Times.* March 3, 2012. https://www.thetimes.co.uk/article /harvey-weinstein-the-king-of-hollywood-again-g8hvrpzfsxp.

Chester, J. 2017. "'I Wanted to Turn My Divorce into a Positive': Gwyneth Paltrow FINALLY Explains Why She Used 'Dorky' Term 'Conscious Uncoupling' for Chris Martin Split." *DailyMail.com.* June 2, 2017. http:// www.dailymail.co.uk/tvshowbiz/article-4565666/Gwyneth-Paltrow -stands-conscious-uncoupling.html#ixzz4yz2tkizK.

Clance, P. R., and S. A. Imes. 1978. "The Imposter Phenomenon in High Achieving Women: Dynamics and Therapeutic Intervention." *Psychotherapy: Theory, Research and Practice* 15 (3): 241–7. http://dx.doi.org/10.1037/h0086006.

CNN. 1998. "Poll: Clinton's Approval Rating Up in Wake of Impeachment." December 20, 1998. http://www.cnn.com/ALLPOLITICS/stories /1998/12/20/impeachment.poll.

Cowen, A. 2015. "Are the Wealthy More Narcissistic?" University of California, Berkeley. March 31, 2015. http://matrix.berkeley.edu /research/are-wealthy-more-narcissistic.

Darling, M. 2016. "Why 5 Women Cheated on Their Husbands—and How to Avoid the Same Fate." *Men's Health.* June 7, 2016. https:// www.menshealth.com/sex-women/a19522350/why-women-cheat.

Dickler, J. 2018. "Five Money Mistakes That Can Destroy a Marriage." CNBC. July 11, 2018. https://www.cnbc.com/2018/07/10/five-money -mistakes-that-can-destroy-a-marriage.html.

Drum, K. 2016. "Pussygate Might Be the Final Straw for Donald Trump." *Mother Jones.* October 8, 2016. https://www.motherjones.com/kevin -drum/2016/10/pussygate-might-be-final-straw-donald-trump.

Duckworth, A., and J. J. Gross. 2014. "Self-Control and Grit: Related but Separable Determinants of Success." *Current Directions in Psychological Science* 23 (5): 319–25. http://dx.doi.org/10.1177/0963721414541462.

Duckworth, A., C. Peterson, M. Matthews, and D. Kelly. 2007. "Grit: Perseverance and Passion for Long-Term Goals." *Journal of Personality and Social Psychology* 92 (6): 1087–1101. http://dx.doi.org/10.1037 /0022-3514.92.6.1087.

Economist. 2003. "Pots of Promise." May 22, 2003. https://www.economist .com/special-report/2003/05/22/pots-of-promise.

Ellis, A. 1994. *Reason and Emotion in Psychotherapy: A Comprehensive Method of Treating Human Disturbances.* New York: Citadel Press.

———. 2001. *Overcoming Destructive Beliefs, Feelings, and Behaviors: New Directions for Rational Emotive Behavior Therapy.* New York: Prometheus Books.

Ellison, N. B., C. Steinfield, and C. Lampe. 2007. "The Benefits of Facebook 'Friends': Social Capital and College Students' Use of Online Social Network Sites." *Journal of Computer-Mediated Communication* 12 (4): 1143–68. https://doi.org/10.1111/j.1083-6101.2007.00367.x.

Etcoff, N. 2000. *Survival of the Prettiest: The Science of Beauty.* New York: Anchor.

Fitzgerald, F. S. 1945. "The Crack-Up." In *The Crack-Up,* edited by E. Wilson. New York: New Directions.

Fragale, A. R., J. R. Overbeck, and M. A. Neale. 2011. "Resources Versus Respect: Social Judgments Based on Targets' Power and Status Positions." *Journal of Experimental Social Psychology* 47 (4): 767–75. https://doi.org/10.1016/j.jesp.2011.03.006.

Frankl, V. 1959. *Man's Search for Meaning.* Boston: Beacon Press.

Gelles, D., J. B. Stewart, J. Silver-Greenberg, and K. Kelly. 2018. "Elon Musk Details 'Excruciating' Personal Toll of Tesla Turmoil." *New York Times.* August 16, 2018. https://www.nytimes.com/2018/08/16/business /elon-musk-interview-tesla.html.

Giacobbe, A. 2016. "Women Are Now Cheating as Much as Men, but with Fewer Consequences." *New York.* May 26, 2016. http://nymag.com /article/2016/05/women-are-now-cheating-as-much-as-men-but-with -fewer-consequences.html.

Godin, S. 2015. "Abandoning Perfection." *Seth's Blog* (blog). June 16, 2015. https://seths.blog/2015/06/abandoning-perfection.

Golbart, S., and J. DiFuria. 2012. "Sudden Wealth Syndrome." *The Daily Show with Jon Sterwart.* In interview with Jason Jones. September 26, 2012. http://www.cc.com/video-clips/yv18fb/the-daily-show-with -jon-stewart-sudden-wealth-syndrome.

Goodstein, L., and S. Otterman. 2018. "Catholic Priests Abused 1,000 Children in Pennsylvania, Report Says." *New York Times.* August 14, 2018. https://www.nytimes.com/2018/08/14/us/catholic-church -sex-abuse-pennsylvania.html.

Gordon, K. C., D. H. Baucom, and D. K. Snyder. 2004. "An Integrative Intervention for Promoting Recovery from Extramarital Affairs." *Journal of Marital and Family Therapy* 30 (2): 213–31. https://doi.org/10.1111 /j.1752-0606.2004.tb01235.x.

Gottman, J. M., and N. Silver. 2000. *The Seven Principles for Making Marriage Work.* New York: Harmony Books.

Gould, T. J. 2010. "Addiction and Cognition." *Addiction Science Clinical Practice* 5 (2): 4–14.

Haaken, J. 1990. "A Critical Analysis of the Co-dependence Construct." *Psychiatry* 53 (4): 396–406. https://doi.org/10.1080/00332747.1990 .11024522.

Hammond, C. 2014. *The Exhausted Woman's Handbook*. Maitland, FL: Xulon Press.

———. 2018. "The Narcissistic Cycle of Abuse." *Psych Central Professional: The Exhausted Woman* (blog). November 10, 2018. https://pro.psychcentral .com/exhausted-woman/2015/05/the-narcissistic-cycle-of-abuse.

Hands, M., and G. Dear. 1994. "Codependency: A Critical Review." *Drug and Alcohol Review* 13:437–45.

Hayes, C. 2018. "The Idea That the Moral Universe Inherently Bends Towards Justice Is Inspiring. It's Also Wrong." NBC *Think*. March 24, 2018. https://www.nbcnews.com/think/opinion/idea-moral-universe -inherently-bends-towards-justice-inspiring-it-s-ncna859661.

Hoffman, L., G. Bensinger, and M. Farrell. 2018. "Uber Proposals Value Company at $120 Billion in a Possible IPO." *Wall Street Journal*. October 16, 2018. https://www.wsj.com/articles/uber-proposals-value-company -at-120-billion-in-a-possible-ipo-1539690343?mod=searchresults &page=1&pos=1.

Hokemeyer, P. L. 2014. "Luxury Treatment: Guidelines for Culturally and Clinically Competent Care." Pro Talk. May 7, 2014. https://www .rehabs.com/pro-talk-articles/luxury-treatment-guidelines-for-culturally -and-clinically-competent-care.

Hopwood, C. J., L. C. Morey, J. C. Markowitz, A. Pinto, A. E. Skodol, J. G. Gunderson, M. C. Zanarini, M. T. Shea, S. Yen, T. H. McGlashan, E. B. Ansell, C. M. Grilo, and C. A. Sanislow. 2009. "The Construct Validity of Passive-Aggressive Personality Disorder." *Psychiatry* 72 (3): 256–67. http://dx.doi.org/10.1521/psyc.2009.72.3.256.

Horton, R., and C. Sedikides. 2009. "Narcissistic Responding to Ego Threat: When the Status of the Evaluator Matters." *Journal of Personality* 77 (5): 1493–1526. http://dx.doi.org/10.1111/j.1467-6494.2009.00590.x.

Hull, S. K., and K. Broquet. 2007. "How to Manage Difficult Patient Encounters." *Family Practice Management* 14 (6): 30–34. https:// www.aafp.org/fpm/2007/0600/p30.html.

In Touch Weekly. 2018. "Matt Lauer Is 'the Loneliest Man in the World' After Sexual Misconduct Scandal." May 4, 2018. https://www.intouchweekly .com/posts/matt-lauer-miserable-lonely-158336.

Jackson, B. 2008. "The Budget and Deficit Under Clinton." FactCheck.org. February 3, 2008. http://www.factcheck.org/2008/02/the-budget-and -deficit-under-clinton.

James, W. 1902. *The Varieties of Religious Experience: A Study in Human Nature.* Reprinted in 1961. New York: W. W. Norton.

Johnson, R. S. 2018. "Codependency and Codependent Relationships." BPDFamily. May 13, 2018. https://www.bpdfamily.com/content /codependency-codependent-relationships.

Jung, C. G. 1963. *Memories, Dreams, Reflections.* New York: Crown Publishing Group / Random House.

Kenton, W. 2018. "Ultra-High Net-Worth Individual (UHNWI)." Investopedia. July 16, 2018. https://www.investopedia.com/terms /u/ultra-high-net-worth-individuals-uhnwi.asp.

Kernberg, O. 1975. *Borderline Conditions and Pathological Narcissism.* New York: Jason Aronson.

Kerner, I. 2012. "Sex or Money: What Makes You Happier?" CNN. October 4, 2012. http://www.cnn.com/2012/10/04/health/kerner-sex-money /index.html.

Kerr-Dineen, L. 2016. "How Does Gisele Bundchen's Monster 2016 Salary Compare to NFL and NBA Players?" *USA Today* For The Win. August 31, 2016. https://ftw.usatoday.com/2016/08/how-much-does -gisele-bundchen-make-2016-salary-nfl-nba-forbes-tom-brady-pictures.

Khatchatourian, M. 2018. "Demi Lovato 'Awake' After Suspected Drug Overdose, Rep Says." *Variety.* July 24, 2018. https://variety.com/2018 /music/news/demi-lovato-heroin-overdose-1202883079.

Kirshner, L. A., A. Genack, and S. T. Hauser. 1978. "Effects of Gender on Short-Term Psychotherapy." *Psychotherapy: Theory, Research and Practice* 15 (2): 158–67. http://dx.doi.org/10.1037/h0085856.

Kleinman, Z. 2017. "Uber: The Scandals That Drove Travis Kalanick Out." BBC News. June 21, 2017. https://www.bbc.com/news/technology -40352868.

Kohut, H. 1966. "Forms and Transformations of Narcissism." *Journal of the American Psychoanalytic Association* 14 (2): 243–72. https://doi.org /10.1177/000306516601400201.

Konigsberg, E. 2008. "Challenges of $600-a-Session Patients." *New York Times.* July 7, 2008. http://www.nytimes.com/2008/07/07/nyregion /07therapists.html.

Kransy, J. 2012. "Infographic: Women Control the Money in America." *Business Insider.* February 17, 2012. https://www.businessinsider.com /infographic-women-control-the-money-in-america-2012-2.

Lee, C. 2004. "A Hard Look at Himself." *Los Angeles Times.* November 14, 2004. http://articles.latimes.com/2004/nov/14/entertainment /ca-cheadle14.

Litt, C. J. 1986. "Theories of Transitional Object Attachment: An Overview." *International Journal of Behavioral Development* 9 (3): 383–99. http:// dx.doi.org/10.1177/016502548600900308.

Lynch, J. 2017. "Meet the YouTube Millionaires: These Are the 10 Highest-Paid YouTube Stars of 2017." *Business Insider.* December 8, 2017. https://www.businessinsider.com/highest-paid-youtube-stars-2017-12.

MacMillen, H. 2015. "Demi Lovato Opens Up About the Mental Illness She Didn't Know She Had." Refinery29. May 28, 2015. https://www .refinery29.com/en-us/2015/05/88236/demi-lovato-opens-up -about-mental-disorder.

Marie Claire. 2016. "16 Celebrity Quotes on Suffering from Impostor Syndrome." November 11, 2016. http://www.marieclaire.co.uk /entertainment/celebrity-quotes-on-impostor-syndrome-434739.

Maté, G. 2010. *In the Realm of Hungry Ghosts: Close Encounters with Addiction.* Berkeley, CA: North Atlantic Books.

Mayo Clinic. n.d. "Narcissistic Personality Disorder." Accessed February 11, 2019. https://www.mayoclinic.org/diseases-conditions/narcissistic -personality-disorder/symptoms-causes/syc-20366662.

National Public Radio. 2016. "Tom Hanks Says Self-Doubt Is 'A High-Wire Act That We All Walk.'" April 26, 2016. https://www.npr.org/2016/04 /26/475573489/tom-hanks-says-self-doubt-is-a-high-wire-act-that -we-all-walk.

Nietzsche, Friedrich. 1966. *Beyond Good and Evil: Prelude to a Philosophy of the Future.* Translated by Walter Kaufman. New York: Random House.

O'Brien, S., N. Black, C. Devine, and D. Griffin. 2018. "CNN Investigation: 103 Uber Drivers Accused of Sexual Assault or Abuse." CNN Business. April 30, 2018. https://money.cnn.com/2018/04/30/technology/uber-driver-sexual-assault/index.html.

Persaud, R., and P. Bruggen. 2015. "The Lipstick Effect: How Boom or Bust Effects Beauty." *Psychology Today*. October 10, 2015. https://www.psychologytoday.com/us/blog/slightly-blighty/201510/the-lipstick-effect-how-boom-or-bust-effects-beauty.

Politi, D. 2016. "Trump Is OK With Calling Ivanka a 'Piece of Ass' and Other Horrible Things He Told Howard Stern." *Slate*. October 8, 2016. http://www.slate.com/blogs/the_slatest/2016/10/08/trump_to_howard_stern_you_can_call_ivanka_a_piece_of_ass.html.

Raconteur. 2015. "The Beauty Economy." September 27, 2015. https://www.raconteur.net/the-beauty-economy-2015.

Robehmed, N. 2018. "How 20-Year-Old Kylie Jenner Built a $900 Million Fortune in Less Than 3 Years." Forbes.com. July 11, 2018. https://www.forbes.com/sites/forbesdigitalcovers/2018/07/11/how-20-year-old-kylie-jenner-built-a-900-million-fortune-in-less-than-3-years/#7138e14faa62.

Rogers, C. 1951. *Client-Centered Therapy*. Boston: Houghton Mifflin.

———. 1957. "The Necessary and Sufficient Conditions of Therapeutic Personality Change." *Journal of Consulting and Clinical Psychology* 21 (2): 95–103. http://dx.doi.org/10.1037/h0045357.

Ronningstam, E. 2011. "Narcissistic Personality Disorder: A Clinical Perspective." *Journal of Psychiatric Practice* 17 (2): 89–99. http://dx.doi.org/10.1097/01.pra.0000396060.67150.40.

royals198569. 2013. "Stars Who Faded from A List Stars to B List or Became Washed Up." IMDb. August 19, 2013. https://www.imdb.com/list/ls056654246.

Russell, K. n.d. "23 Sheryl Sandberg Quotes That'll Motivate You to Do Just About Anything." The Muse. Accessed February 11, 2019. https://www.themuse.com/advice/23-sheryl-sandberg-quotes-thatll-motivate-you-to-do-just-about-anything.

Ryan, R. M., and E. L. Deci. 2000. "Self-Determination Theory and the Facilitation of Intrinsic Motivation, Social Development, and Well-Being." *American Psychologist* 55 (1): 68–78. http://dx.doi.org /10.1037/0003-066X.55.1.68.

Savitsky, S. 2017. "'View' Co-hosts Slam Critics of Hillary Clinton's Marriage but Trump-Melania Relationship Fair Game." Fox News. September 18, 2017. http://www.foxnews.com/entertainment/2017/09/13/view-co-hosts -slam-critics-hillary-clintons-marriage-but-trump-melania-relationship -fair-game.html.

Schonfeld, Z. 2013. "Wives Are Cheating 40% More Than They Used to, but Still 70% as Much as Men." *Atlantic.* July 2, 2013. https://www.the atlantic.com/national/archive/2013/07/wives-cheating-vs-men/313704.

Sischy, I. 1997. "Matt and Ben." *Interview* magazine (December): 118.

Smith, E. 2009. "Rachel Uchitel: The Night I Met Tiger Woods and My Life Spun Out of Control." *New York Post.* December 1, 2009. http:// nypost.com/2009/12/01/rachel-uchitel-the-night-i-met-tiger-woods -my-life-spun-out-of-control.

Statista. 2017. "Revenue of the Cosmetic/Beauty Industry in the United States from 2002 to 2016 (in Billion U.S. Dollars)." https://www .statista.com/statistics/243742/revenue-of-the-cosmetic-industry -in-the-us.

Steinmetz, D., and H. Tabenkin. 2001. "The 'Difficult Patient' as Perceived by Family Physicians." *Family Practice* 18 (5): 495–500. https:// doi.org/10.1093/fampra/18.5.495.

Stengel, G. 2014. "11 Reasons 2014 Will Be a Breakout Year for Women Entreprenuers." *Forbes.* January 8, 2014. https://www.forbes.com/sites /geristengel/2014/01/08/11-reasons-2014-will-be-a-break-out-year -for-women-entrepreneurs/#7b537d983f71.

Sun, F. n.d. "Are You in a Codependent Relationship?" WebMD. Accessed February 12, 2019. https://www.webmd.com/sex-relationships/features /signs-of-a-codependent-relationship#1.

Szalavitz, M. 2012. "Should States Let Families Force Addicts Into Rehab?" *Time.* October 3, 2012. http://healthland.time.com/2012/10/03 /should-states-let-families-force-adults-into-rehab.

———. 2013. "Wealthy Selfies: How Being Rich Increases Narcissism." *Time.* August 20, 2013. http://healthland.time.com/2013/08/20 /wealthy-selfies-how-being-rich-increases-narcissism.

Technavio. 2017. "Global Male Aesthetics Market 2017–2021." https://
www.technavio.com/report/global-health-and-wellness-global-male
-aesthetics-market-2017-2021?utm_source=T3&utm_medium
=BW&utm_campaign=Media.

Telling, G. 2018. "Matt Lauer Is Heading for a $100 Million Divorce:
What's at Stake?" People.com. May 16, 2018. https://people.com/tv
/matt-lauer-heading-100-million-divorce.

Twenge, J. M., S. Konrath, J. D. Foster, W. K. Campbell, and B. J. Bushman.
2008. "Egos Inflating Over Time: A Cross-Temporal Meta-Analysis of
the Narcissistic Personality Inventory." *Journal of Personality* 76 (4):
875–902. https://doi.org/10.1111/j.1467-6494.2008.00507.x.

University of California, Irvine. 2016. "UCI Study Links Selfies, Happiness."
UCI News. September 13, 2016. https://news.uci.edu/research
/uci-study-links-selfies-happiness.

Urbanoski, K. A. 2010. "Coerced Addiction Treatment: Client Perspectives
and the Implications of Their Neglect." *Harm Reduction Journal* 7 (13).
https://doi.org/10.1186/1477-7517-7-13.

Vessey, J. T., and K. I. Howard. 1993. "Who Seeks Psychotherapy?" *Psychotherapy* 30 (4): 546–53. http://dx.doi.org/10.1037/0033-3204.30.4.546.

Walker, L. E. A. 2019. *The Battered Woman Syndrome.* New York: Springer
Publishing Company.

Watson, P. J., T. Little, S. M. Sawrie, and M. D. Biderman. 1992. "Measures
of the Narcissistic Personality: Complexity of Relationships with Self-
Esteem and Empathy." *Journal of Personality Disorders* 6 (4): 434–49.
http://dx.doi.org/10.1521/pedi.1992.6.4.434.

Way, N., A. Ali, C. Gilligan, and P. Noguera, eds. 2018. *The Crisis of
Connection: Roots, Consequences, and Solutions.* New York: New York
University Press.

Werb, D., A. Kamarulzaman, M. C. Meacham, C. Rafful, B. Fisher,
S. Strathdee, and E. Wood. 2016. "The Effectiveness of Compulsory
Drug Treatment: A Systematic Review." *International Journal of
Drug Policy* 28:1–9. http://dx.doi.org/10.1016/j.drugpo.2015.12.005.

Winerman, L. 2005. "Helping Men to Help Themselves." *Monitor* 36 (7):
57. https://www.apa.org/monitor/jun05/helping.

Winnicott, D. 1958. *Through Pediatrics to Psycho-Analysis: Collected Papers.* London: Tavistock Publications. https://llk.media.mit.edu/courses /readings/Winnicott_ch1.pdf.

Yang, Y., and A. Raine. 2009. "Prefontal Structural and Functional Brain Imaging Findings in Antisocial, Violent, and Psychopathic Individuals: A Meta-Analysis." *Psychiatry Research* 174 (2): 81–88. http:// dx.doi.org/10.1016/j.pscychresns.2009.03.012.

Young, S. M., and D. Pinsky. 2006. "Narcissism and Celebrity." *Journal of Research in Personality* 40 (5): 463–71. http://dx.doi.org/10.1016 /j.jrp.2006.05.005.

About the Author

DR. PAUL L. HOKEMEYER is a clinical and consulting psychotherapist who works with individuals and families in the United States, the United Kingdom, the United Arab Emirates, and the European Union. A member of the American Association for Marriage and Family Therapy, he is licensed in New York and Colorado as a marriage and family therapist.

In addition to holding a PhD in psychology, Dr. Paul holds a doctorate in law and an MA in clinical psychology with a focus on family dynamics.

He regularly provides insight and commentary for CNN International, Al Jazeera, *Good Morning America*, FOX News, and *TODAY* and is frequently quoted as an expert by the *New York Times*, *Wall Street Journal*, *U.S. News & World Report*, MarketWatch, WebMD, *Daily Mail*, *Men's Health*, *Prevention*, *Women's Day*, Yahoo, and others.

Contribute to the #FragilePower dialogue by connecting with @drpaulnyc on social media and online at www.drhokemeyer.com.

About Hazelden Publishing

As part of the Hazelden Betty Ford Foundation, Hazelden Publishing offers both cutting-edge educational resources and inspirational books. Our print and digital works help guide individuals in treatment and recovery, and their loved ones. Professionals who work to prevent and treat addiction also turn to Hazelden Publishing for evidence-based curricula, digital content solutions, and videos for use in schools, treatment programs, correctional programs, and electronic health records systems. We also offer training for implementation of our curricula.

Through published and digital works, Hazelden Publishing extends the reach of healing and hope to individuals, families, and communities affected by addiction and related issues.

For more information about Hazelden publications,
please call **800-328-9000**
or visit us online at **hazelden.org/bookstore**.

OTHER TITLES THAT MAY INTEREST YOU

The Gifts of Imperfection

*Let Go of Who You Think You're Supposed to Be
and Embrace Who You Are*

BRENÉ BROWN, PhD, LMSW

With Brené Brown's game-changing *New York Times* best seller *The Gifts of Imperfection*, we find courage to overcome paralyzing fear and self-consciousness, strengthening our connection to the world.

Order No. 2545; also available as an ebook

Changing to Thrive

*Using the Stages of Change to Overcome the Top Threats
to Your Health and Happiness*

JAMES O. PROCHASKA, PhD, and JANICE M. PROCHASKA, PhD

In this groundbreaking book, the authors guide you through a six-stage process designed to help you assess your readiness to change and then tap the inner resources necessary to thrive physically, emotionally, and socially.

Order No. 4860; also available as an ebook

Codependent No More

How to Stop Controlling Others and Start Caring for Yourself

MELODY BEATTIE

With instructive life stories, personal reflections, exercises, and self-tests, *Codependent No More* is a simple, straightforward, readable map of the perplexing world of codependency.

Order No. 5014; also available as an ebook

Hazelden Publishing books are available at fine bookstores everywhere.
To order from Hazelden Publishing,
call **800-328-9000** or visit **hazelden.org/bookstore.**